MEDITATION TO HEALING FREEDOM THRU INFINITE LOVE

Bill Dunn Jr.

Quantum Discovery
A LITERARY AGENCY

Book copies may be ordered through booksellers or by contacting:
Quantum Discovery, a Literacy Agency & Facilitator of this book

Mailing Address:
admin@qdiscovery.org
501 W Broadway Suite 800, San Diego, CA 92101
Phone #: (888) 523-1025 Fax; 619-880-5355

Library of Congress Control Number: 2025909131

ISBN
978-1-957378-07-7 (Paperback)
978-1-957378-06-0 (eBook)
979-8-89641-071-3 (Hardcover)

DEDICATIONS

- To my two children with their immediate families whom I dearly love.
- To Fr. Leonard A. Coppenrath, who while serving at Incarnation Parish in Melrose, MA. during the late 1950's/ early 1960's, facilitated my interest in the possibility of becoming a Priest.
- To my lifelong friend 'Perry' who back in 1963-1964 enlivened me to examine the overall subject of spirituality from a worldwide perspective.
- To my current dear wife who suffered extremely during her childhood under the yoke of another; to anyone else as an adult or child who has suffered any kind of sustained hardship involving other people, the environment, or other factors, may this work on meditation provide the basis for healing, and may it lead to sustained peace on a personal as well as worldwide basis.
- To my daughter Nicole, whose invaluable assistance in reviewing the book and insightful suggestions as a publicist helped bring this project to life.
- And lastly to myself, for the patience and attentiveness devoted to spirituality in overcoming decades of doubt in a Higher Power, and resurgence of belief through the help of meditation.

TABLE OF CONTENTS

ACKNOWLEDGEMENTS

I want to acknowledge the many authors and thinkers with their thoughts mentioned, quoted, and referenced within this book. I am very grateful to the following authors for their writings reviewed or quoted in this work: Eben Alexander MD, Uell S. Anderson, Brother Andre Bessette, Fr. John Bettridge, Todd Burpo, Theolyn Cortens, Benjamin W. Decker, Neville Goddard, Betty Eadie, Eric Von Daniken, davidji, Wayne Dyer PhD, Betty Eadie, Victor Frankl, Saint Germain, David Hawkins MD, Esther Hicks, Alice Miller PhD, Anita Moorjani, Dr. Bruce Perry MD, Florence Scovell Shinn, David Simon, Matthew Sokolov, Worthy Stokes, Paramahansa Yogananda, and Maharishi Mahesh Yogi ™. For specific components and tools in establishing a successful meditation practice, the following authors are especially noted for their key ideas and contributions: Eben Alexander, davidji, Benjamin W. Decker, Wayne Dyer, Florence Scovell Shinn, Matthew Sokolov, and Worthy Stokes. But within this work the thoughts of all the above authors, as well as my own, form a mosaic of themes, ideas, and concepts, providing the tools (i.e., worldly and spiritual healing strategies) necessary to help people to transform healing from their past difficulties.

GOING FORWARD AND INTRODUCTION

While seated at the breakfast table in a small foyer by the kitchen in my home, I reflect on proceeding forward from the past twelve-year venture of writing and publishing my first book, "Love and the Infinite, My Memoirs", and then reorganizing, renaming, and republishing that book as, "Love and the Infinite, Healing from Childhood". My dear Daughter has encouraged me to move on and write a shorter 'sequel' work, specifically aimed at the adult public, stressing a guided meditation process with themes that utilize and build on prime healing principles and highlights from my first book. My vast lifetime experiences include the writing/rewriting of my first book, plus advances or refinements made in my meditation practice through writing a second book focusing on innovative, unique, and relatable meditation techniques. This includes a collage of reflective narrative meditations. My meditation practice in conjunction with these techniques has dramatically helped in resolving negative carryovers from earlier-in-life difficulties I endured. The techniques will certainly help others who have endured similar past fates.

Based upon the overall experience of writing and re-doing my past first work, the prime subject and theme that emerged and evolved during its preparation dealt with the concept of Infinite Love, which of course was intended and expressed in the first part of its title "Love and the Infinite". What ensued in the final stages of writing that work was the development of spiritually based meditations, with an emerging focus on Infinite Love itself as representing the heart and soul of the invisible 'Infinite Almighty', 'Universal One', 'God', or 'Great Spirit' at the center of a Universe of ultimate all-goodness. What ensued and emerged further from this was a focus on Infinite Love as representing the center from which healing could occur in this world. Just focusing on Infinite Love through meditation can be healing.

The present work herein, "Meditation to Healing Freedom thru Infinite Love", offers an expansion of highlights and themes from my past first work. The present book focuses on presenting the basis for selected meditation practices along with narrative meditations to facilitate the translation of awareness about Infinite Love, to directly offer healing possibilities for anyone who has undergone any kind of significant lifetime difficulty or tragedy that has left residual negative effects in their present lives. In the book, the author adds credence to the existence of Infinite Love in this life by offering concrete, dramatic examples of this Love that have occurred within his own lifetime experiences. Clinical proofs of the presence of God's Infinite Love occurring within the author's life along with its positive effects are presented in Ch.1, Theme 2, and Ch. 3, Theme 2. These themes relate to life-changing and transforming experiences, particularly in reestablishing for him the faith in a Higher Power and adding to or developing further his regular meditation practice.

The two themes above, plus key aspects of many of the other themes in Part I of the book, establish the basis for being an ideal Spiritual backdrop and platform for anyone in developing their successful healing meditation practice. This Spiritual platform/basis is best advanced via peoples' emphasis of positive thinking and feelings, which effectively counters the destructive effects of human ego, competition, and negative acts. Several other themes provide an in-depth analysis of Worldly-based Love in comparison to Infinite (Heavenly) Love. Another theme provides credence as to the actual existence of Infinite

Love and its goodness via various peoples' descriptions of Near-Death Experiences (NDE's) in which each encountered 'the Infinite Side'. Still other themes describe the vestiges of Infinite Love occurring within our lives here, e.g., (1) a perfect Spiritual 'Soul' existing in each of us, making us all 'equal'; (2) certain worldly-based happenings that have significant spillover influences from 'the Infinite Side'. Together, the themes counter all the challenges and difficulties we each endure in this human life by opening the next-Life doors of Infinitely borne Wisdom, Joys, and Love, and welcoming each of us inside with open, accepting arms of an all-Good and Loving 'God' or 'Creator'.

I am convinced that any kind of lifetime tragedy or sustained suffering can leave negative lifetime after-effects which can be best resolved through a regular practice of meditation. This practice calls on a quiet and reflective conscious connection with each person's eternal and perfect spiritual essence within themselves (identified as their 'Soul'), with the intent of healing any negative after-effects from past lifetime difficulties. Through the regular practice of guided meditation which focuses on meditation concepts and practices with healing themes, strategies, and meditations offered in the work, abatement of many of these negative lifetime after-effects can certainly occur. This will help any person who has suffered in the past to evolve into a much better overall mental, attitudinal, and physical health condition, rendering a much greater reality of peace, ease, joy, and freedom during the remainder of their lives.

MOVING FORWARD WITH THIS WORK

<u>Infinite Love</u>- It is truly incredible to reflect and think on the absolute magnitude of Infinite Love within that State (i.e., the 'Other Side'), that describing it in the human mind or language contexts is next to impossible. People who have truly experienced Near-Death Experiences (NDEs) know first-hand just how incredible this Love is: the total dimensionless euphoria, warmth, gloriousness, joy, happiness, and transcendent love without a giver and a receiver or having to 'earn' it, which can never be taken away. Infinite Love is way beyond any unconditional love within our worldly contexts, a love that is wider, deeper, and more voluminous than all the Universe of outer space, and/ or all the depth and width of the world's oceans combined. Just reflecting on this expanded Love from worldly perspectives and extending that reflection out in a present-time mode for several minutes is healing.

PART I

THE BACKGROUND IN CREATING MY MEDITATION PRACTICE

CHAPTER 1

DISCOVERING INFINITE LOVE

Theme 1- How 'Love and the Infinite' Was Born

The backdrop theme of my first book (re-edited and renamed) from its original title "Love and the Infinite, My Memoirs" to its subsequent title "Love and the Infinite, Healing from Childhood", basically explores the different dimensions of Love: (1) conditional love (if you do this or that for me I'll love you, but if you don't I won't), versus (2) unconditional love (I accept you for all that you are, no matter what you have endured, what you have, what you represent, or what you've done), versus (3) Infinite Love (a love that is immensely greater than any love in this life, that is limitless, boundless, untrammeled, and everlasting, which can never be taken away as worldly love can be). The loves of this life (conditional & unconditional) including romantic, depend upon a giver and a receiver, meaning that love can be given and then taken away in an instant, whereas Universal Infinite Love always was, is now, and always will be, and doesn't have to be 'earned' nor periodically 'taken away' like love in this life.

My first (re-edited/renamed) book focuses on the good and kind love called parental or maternal love that all of us are supposed to have upon our entry into this life as babies, infants, and children. But this sharply contrasts for many of us with the reality of love denied in our earliest years via abuse and mistreatment, causing physical and/ or emotional traumas with devastating after-effects that are often sustained throughout our childhood and adulthood years. The work delves into both worldly and spiritual healing solutions to adult damages resulting from childhood traumas suffered during a victim's early years. These solutions focus on the need to completely reprogram the quite complex to understand negative-oriented thought patterns that become inculcated in the developing child's mind from any kind of lasting or traumatic abuse, which often destructively follows these victims throughout their adult years.

Of course, we want to give all good credit to those of us who came from good parents, where we were treated by them throughout our childhood experience with all due respect, love, and appreciation as to just who we were back then. This means that despite being little and growing, we were treated as if we were fully grown adults with all due respect, and were not denigrated for being small, learning, and evolving, as we were moving toward achieving that evolved adult level as children. A happy child from a well-treated background radiates upon the world a happy, trustful, and productive attitude, which in turn radiates back to that person as a positive reward in feelings of usefulness and appreciation.

But for many others, this was not the case. Significant numbers of children go through a prolonged period of abusive experiences during their earliest years. This sets the tone for unhappiness, which carries over into adult life. As an adult, conflict, confusion, fear, angst, lack of peacefulness, rage, and even physical-mental health problems often overshadow those people who lacked fair parental or caretaker treatment during their childhood.

While being very young, we are prone to involuntarily develop behavioral patterns from memory that supposedly will best help us to survive and develop successfully into adulthood. The developmental components of evolution did <u>not</u> have abusiveness as useful or helpful in the human survival process. The reality is that early on in life (childhood) experiences occur when the imperfect human brain is rapidly developing toward its full capabilities. This creates an inculcation to the memory process, whereby repeated and dominant good or bad early life experiences become 'locked-in' or 'hard-wired' into each child's developing mind. This produces a tonality or impression of life (up or down), significantly impacting a particular person's thinking, feelings, and actions throughout their subsequent adult lifetime.

When children are repeatedly physically and/or mentally abused during childhood, these same persons during their adult lives will often attempt to 'get even' or 'make up' for the past abuse by projecting nasty, abusive, or violent thoughts or acts onto innocent others. This includes their wives and children, colleagues, acquaintances, citizens-at-large, or even themselves. Usually, these thoughts or acts are unconscious, autonomic, and unplanned. Three words typify the after-effects of child abuse: (1) <u>stigma</u>- abusive after-effects sticking (particularly mentally) with the person for a lifetime; (2) <u>insidiousness</u>- abusive after-effects sneaking up unexpectedly on the person; (3) <u>denial</u>- a victim often turns away from admitting about the past abusive realities for a lifetime.

Human evolution developed the process in the imperfect human brain from primal-based life over the last million or so years up to the very recent past to respond to an almost constant state threat to life survival. Responses to sustained fear-based trauma threats were particularly inculcated into child-rearing practices during primal times, which were often immediate, non-negotiable, and brutal, which over eons of time have been carried over into modern child-rearing practices. Although modern humankind has much fewer constant-state threats to life, primal responses to fear can be 're-awakened' as a result of modern-life repeated or sustained childhood traumas or abuse conditions. These primal-based responses often stay awake just below a person's conscious awareness long after the modern trauma threat has ended. These 'awake' responses resurface years later in the person's life as unconscious negative tendencies, urges, or reactions (e.g., PTSS) to ordinary life situations, as if they were still entrained with sustained threat conditions during their past abusive state.

The following summarizes principal <u>healing</u> strategies from past abuse in "Love and the Infinite, Healing from Childhood":

The overarching theme that pervades all the healing strategies focuses on the power of **<u>awareness</u>** (1) of our childhood past and how any resultant negativities from that may be impacting our adult life; (2) if past negativities are affecting our current adult lives, that our negative abusive past is gone and will not return; (3) of our surrounding environment and others around us that we are currently interacting with, that their 'strange' behaviors towards us could well reflect their past childhood difficulties; (4) to be open to <u>all</u> possibilities for healing negative effects in our adulthood from early-life adversities we suffered during childhood; (5) that a Higher Power exists within each of us as our 'Soul', which via conscious awareness can help us in our adult life to overcome carry-over negative residuals from early-in-life abuse or traumas.

<u>Strategy #1, Spirituality</u>- Having faith and belief that an all-good, perfect, and healing 'Higher Power', 'Infinite Source', or 'God' underlies the entire Universe, which is not necessarily associated with a particular faith, denomination, or set of established beliefs. The author is convinced that some sort of conscious awareness, faith, and belief in a 'Higher Power' is essential for facilitating complete healing and recovery of any carryovers from sustained mistreatment or hardship of any sort. While healing is possible without spirituality, it may not be complete. Through awareness and intention, each of us can tap into our inner sanctum of perfection and love within (i.e., our 'Soul') to help heal ourselves.

<u>Strategy #2, Our Inner Child Cries Out for Healing</u>- If we have come from an abusive childhood, our inner child cries out that it wants to be released and re-created into a happy child, without the constant worry and fear over the next set of suspicions, angry words, accusations, or punishments without justification that were often headed our way during childhood. As adults now, it is suggested that we should feel sorry for our inner child if it suffered so much debasement and mistreatment, at the same time regret that we lacked back at that time the adult maturity and awareness to help rescue it. We need to offer a complete apology now to our inner child for these unavoidable indiscretions which we really could not avoid due to having been so young and unaware of the complexities of why we were being mistreated. We need to reclaim the happiness that was denied by re-enlivening that long-lost child as one who was then and is now deserving of being treated as a tower of absolute love.

Strategy #3, Promoting a Positive State-of-Mind Now- 'I am' (or 'I AM') is the self-definition of 'Source' or the 'One', namely the identification with 'God' or the name of 'God'. The Law of the Universe is that 'like seeks (and/or seeds) the like.' Neville Goddard suggests that positive thinking, e.g., 'I am' healthy, 'I am' abundant, results in these things, and conversely negative thinking, 'I am' sick, or 'I am' poor brings on these[1]. All negative thoughts, acts, violence, war, and child abuse are predicated on negative thinking and fear; therefore, we all need to do our utmost to think all positive and dissuade all that is negative. Man is the principal creator of positive or negative thinking with its consequences, i.e., we can either create a heaven on earth or a hell on earth—it is purely our choice (via 'free will'). The author, Uell Andersen, claims that the conscious human mind (via ego) associates with physical bodily survival, which generates 'prompters' or negative feelings, e.g., lack, fear, unhappiness, guilt, doubt, and loneliness. These restrict us from the positive power of the Infinite, which is Love.[2] Instead we need to think positively.

Strategy #4, Awareness, Feelings, and Emotional Release from Our Past- From Dr. Alice Miller, Dr. Bruce Perry, Florence Shinn, and my work herein, each of us needs to become fully aware and conscious of our childhoods, and if there was repeated abuse, to become fully cognizant of how it may have negatively impacted our adult lives.

Awareness and self-expression of associated feelings from our childhoods are prime pathways for healing leftover residuals in adult life from past early-in-life difficulties. We must have the willingness to freely express and release these locked-up emotions. From Neville Goddard's works, human feelings are the doorway to the 'Soul' or that infinitesimal perfect piece of Love that lies within each of us.[3] Expression of feelings gets us the fastest there. Awareness of feelings with their pathway to our 'Soul' or Infinite part, as well as the actual release of those feelings via expression and emotional release, are prime pathways for assisting us to heal in adult life from past early-life sustained abuse or traumas.

Strategy #5, Imagination as Key in Healing from Past Childhood Abuse- Imagination is a spiritual sensation. Picture an image of a wish desired and give it full clarity and dimensions of reality by thinking and feeling mentally as if it were already available and here now. As for the past, e.g., child abuse with its aftereffects, these seem inalterable, but the past is connected to the present in that it still exists as time and affects the present, therefore it can be altered. Unrevised scenes from the past can be altered by imagining in the present what should have been in the past. Going back into the past and replaying scenes as to how they should have been during childhood, i.e., cuddling and closeness instead of meanness and abuse are revision, and revision results in repeal. In my case, I imagined a mother who, instead of distance, coldness, and strictness, cuddled me with unconditional warmth, love, and acceptance throughout my early childhood years.

Strategy #6, Reprogramming of the Human Mind Toward Healing- Early-in-life misfortunes often immobilize a person by having negative emotions 'locked within' their unconscious mind, preventing them from doing anything consciously (choice-wise) such as expressing or releasing these emotions to 'free themselves' from the mental prison they find themselves in. That is, the victim cannot consciously see the 'forest for the trees' until awareness of their past oppressions with their adult aftereffects emerges consciously and thereby awakens them. Once this happens, the former abuse victim must repeatedly make the convincing argument that the agony of the past is over with, no longer relevant, and will not return. No one else, i.e., a counselor, friend, or lover can do this for the victim. The ego-based feelings of 'poor me,' or 'pity me' because of the past abuse must be repeatedly quelled and replaced with the positive feeling of happiness that the 'new dawn of day' is currently here for the past victim's happier and brighter future.

Strategy #7, Finding True Love Opportunities Again- (1) Dr. Bruce Perry suggests that the former abuse victim develop a network of loving, trusting, and supporting individuals who can understand what the victim has gone through during their childhood years, and provide them with true love, understanding, and consolation for what they have endured.[4] (2) The author suggests that for those past victims who were denied true unconditional love in their earliest years, or who have lost love more recently in their adult lives, to enter whatever amenable 'social circles' that currently exist to actively seek and find new unconditional love opportunities to replace the love-denied or love-loss realities of the past.

Strategy #8, Education on Raising Children that Avoids Abuse- Global, national, and personal development strategies need to focus on public education dealing with the family, raising children properly without violence and abuse, and respecting the child as if it were a valuable member of the family and society-at-large. This can start with basic skill courses/modules on 'marriage and the family' type instruction in high schools, community colleges, and four-year colleges. This instruction would provide positive methodologies that young parents need to better gear them to raise their children in a non-abusive and non-threatening atmosphere, including proper discipline strategies that are non-abusive to utilize with growing children. These courses would also offer positive enlightening skills and knowledge about child development that a young parent needs to know. Education on non-abusive child rearing is needed for all future-to-be parents.

Strategy #9, Reviewing Significance of Near-Death Experiences- Folks that have experienced Near-Death Experiences (NDEs) by briefly encountering the 'Other Side' describe its incredible euphoric veil and cradle of Infinite Love and goodness. Each of the four NDE persons reviewed in, "Love and the Infinite, Healing from Childhood," and within my current work, "Meditation to Healing Freedom thru Infinite Love," had life-threatening health conditions that completely healed upon return to this life. Each was advised to return to this life, that this was the best place to be at this stage of their existence, that here the mind and bodily senses and feelings could provide an incredible dimension not available back in the Infinite State. Each learned that fear in this life and overcoming it was the highest priority leading to greater happiness in this life. One cannot have both fear and true love at the same time. None of us were born evil, bad, or violent; rather, we all came here in a perfect state. But, both human ego and rivalry in this life have eroded that in so many ways.

Strategy #10, Meditation- This is a process of bringing the mind off its daily routine of normal worldly dealings, into a mindset profile of reflection and quietude. The attempt is to awaken deeper spiritual levels via stillness of the body-mind through the routine practice of going within daily and accessing pure awareness, which refreshes and rekindles the mind and body. The process brings one from an individual to a Universal state, increasing one's capacity for peace, love, well-being, and happiness through silence, reading (or other visual/mental effects), sound, energy, sensory, yoga, or mantras. Practiced regularly, this process can truly promote healing for any person.

The overarching healing theme of awareness with the accompanying healing strategies just reviewed from my prior (renamed) book, "Love and the Infinite, Healing from Childhood", helps to set the stage in the present book, "Meditation to Healing Freedom thru Infinite Love", to identify Infinite Love, which is where the meditation journey with its healing capabilities begins. In this connection, Uell Andersen's only major lifetime book, "Three Magic Words", reveals near the end of his work the three magic words as 'You Are God', meaning that every person has this infinitesimal perfect piece of 'Infinite Love' or 'God' within themselves, colloquially known as their spiritual 'Soul'. To back this up, both Uell Andersen and Neville Goddard claim that the chief message of all Jesus's teachings is: 'the good news I bring you is that the Kingdom of Heaven is within each of us' (i.e., as our 'Soul'). Further teachings of Jesus indicate the 'Heaven within' as composed of nothing but 'perfect Infinite Goodness and (Infinite) Love'. Recognition and belief that 'perfect Infinite Goodness and Infinite Love' really make up our spiritual essence or 'Soul' is key to the beginning of finding healing in this life. The regular practice of meditation processes and techniques presented in Ch. 6, Theme 2 are key in connecting us with our perfect spiritual 'Soul' or 'Essence' existing in each of us. This links us directly with the 'One', our All-Loving 'Source' or 'God'. Through regular meditation practice and via our intent, this slowly but deliberately connects us directly to our healing.

Chapter 1, Discovering Infinite Love within the present Meditation book represents an introduction to the concept, meaning, and effects of Infinite Love in three parts. Theme 1- (covered just above) -- 'How Love and the Infinite Was Born', comes about as part of the title of my first book, "Love and the Infinite, Healing from Childhood". This represents a work that focuses on the tragedy of child abuse which has occurred historically throughout the world, and how various healing strategies (including worldly aspects of love as well as Infinite Love awareness) can be utilized to heal negative adult carryovers from this abuse. Theme 2- 'The Beginnings of the Author's Spiritual Reawakening', which occurred with the onset of awareness of Infinite Love from within himself (via 'Soul'), with additional examples presented as to how this Love might be experienced in worldly life. Theme 3- 'The Wonder at and Within the Falls', represents the author's experiences of annual visits to Niagara Falls where he interfaces with one of nature's renowned worldwide wonders, likely composed of spiritual Infinite Love energy of our 'Higher Power'. These three themes represent an excellent backdrop and lead-in to understanding Infinite Love as it is more fully explored in Chapter 2 of the present book on meditation practice and referred to often in the remainder of this work.

Theme 2- 'The Beginning of the Author's Spiritual Reawakening'

As revealed in the prior work "Love and the Infinite, Healing from Childhood" was my very sudden spiritual reawakening from dormancy of well over four decades of agnosticism. I explained that back in 2004, the love of my life was in a mental hospital in a suicidal condition, and with this and all the other life challenges that had occurred up until then, I cried out in mental anguish with an ultimate question: was there, in reality, any other ultimate purpose to life on this planet other than facing 'mundane' life challenges such as this? The following six paragraphs present the summation of my account which addressed this all-important question. This experience presented unmistakable evidence of providing me the opportunity of my life to feel the power of the Almighty (or 'God') to significantly bolster my faith in Him via His transformative healing influence of Infinite Love.

'I well remember reading near the beginning of Uell Andersen's work, "Three Magic Words", his comments about the challenges in many typical people's lives in which they endure difficult circumstances that are sometimes life-threatening. They desperately ask the essential question that so many people have asked throughout history: why are we here in this life and what is it all about? Many of these same persons never had nor developed ties with a 'God,' 'Creator', or 'Higher Source', or had somehow lost all belief or hope in any Divine reality.

I felt the same at that point: I had no God, no belief, and no hope. There had been once, decades before, a strong interest in entering the Catholic priesthood when I was in high school, but that interest rapidly faded early in my college years. I grew agnostic, close to atheism as my college career ensued. There was no objective, scientific proof to me that God or a Higher Power existed on any plane of which I was aware. Even my emotions and sharp intellect told me a resounding 'no.'

But, as I lay in my bed on a morning late in June 2004 with my wife seriously ill in the hospital, the ultimate question came to my mind: 'Is this all that there is to life; is there, or could there be anything else to living other than this'? I honestly felt miserable, to the point of not wanting to go on and live anymore. I had felt this way a few times before in my life, but this time my feelings were really in the pits. Because of this, a strengthening awareness developed that there <u>had</u> to be something else. My mind and emotions cried out that there was, and at that very instant I willed for some sort of signal from any Source or Higher Power for this assurance.

Suddenly, somewhere near my heart area under the left rib cage, I felt a distinct 'thud' or 'tap', then several seconds later felt another distinct 'tap', then seconds later another, then still another, and then others. At the same time, I felt a 'tingly' pins and needles feeling all over my body accompanied by a distinct tearing of the eyes, with an unanticipated feeling of incredible euphoria and pleasure throughout my whole body. It was truly a feeling of Nirvana. At that moment, I could not remember ever having felt anything like this before in my life! However, much later I recognized that I had experienced a similar euphoric event far back in 1987.

At this point in 2004, I clearly knew. I had moved from doubt, or maybe 'I hope to,' or 'I want to believe', to 'I do', or 'I am a believer'. The challenges I had been facing coupled with my wife's hospitalization forced the issue and changed profoundly serious doubt in my belief of a Higher Power into a certainty that it truly existed. The very distinct repeated thuds or taps that occurred near my heart area with accompanying feelings of extreme euphoria changed all doubt into acceptance that there truly was an Ultimate Source.

I have since developed a keen sense of intuition suggesting that every human being who has or will come into this world will have at least one similar opportunity during their lives to receive some sort of significant signal from the Almighty (our 'Source') of awareness in the reality of Its existence and power. I would suspect this occurs most frequently during or just following a crisis or extremely stressful situation that an individual becomes involved with. These are signals from the Infinite to 'awaken us spiritually'. Only those who really 'listen' to and 'harbor' these signals as to their real significance become consciously aware that these represent a starting point in their spiritual awakening and discovery pathway to their spiritual progression'.

Following that day some 21 years ago, I have developed other thoughts of real-life examples that have helped me and hopefully will help others to develop a better more definable, and provable visualization of the existence of our Source, or God, with Its incalculable Power, Perfection, and limitless Infinite Love.

- Have you ever held a rose in bloom and been amazed at its wonderfully aromatic scent (or smell), intricate color, and exquisite design and arrangement of its petals; this is a small example of perfection in our world and the Universe at large.
- Other wonders of nature besides the rose example: (a) an ice crystal with its perfectly flanked and geometrically arranged edges, angles, and points; (b) a diamond with its sparkling beauty and geometrically arranged edges and points, brilliantly shining from within due to outside light shining around, though, and within it; (c) waterfalls, such as Niagara Falls (Ch. 1, Theme 3); (d) other places of spectacular scenic beauty, such as Grand Canyon, Yosemite, Sequoya Park, or Lake Tahoe; (e) the birds of the air, cloud formations in the sky, colors of the rainbow, beauty of beaches, shorelines, oceans, rivers, the sky above, mountains, and natural landscape.
- Uell Andersen during the time of agnosticism in his college days slowly developed an awareness of the existence of an Infinite

Source (God). This occurred when the chaplain at his college suggested that the Infinite can be visualized and experienced right within this life each day by viewing and experiencing the 'perfections' or wonders of nature that surround us. These represent the 'face' of the Infinite or God. The chaplain also saw the face of God in all people and things surrounding him every day. Similarly, it has been noted that St. Francis of Assisi saw the perfection of God in the beauties of nature and the people surrounding him in his day.

- The magic that is generated from a mental focus on the present time while being engaged in a particularly pleasurable activity. While doing this activity, keeping focus as if there is no past, nor future, just <u>now</u> (with no time clock) enhances the pleasure of doing the activity.

- The thought of being loved unconditionally without reservation, no matter what is said or happens, or one's past or present mistakes, faults, sins, or wrongs. Now fathom the thought of Infinite Love on the Infinite Side as being in unimaginable dimensions and in every way greater than any worldly unconditional love.

- The thought that one (or I) can do no wrong, or error, nor do something that typically would be criticized in this life.

- The thought that one (or I) has nothing to <u>fear</u> from threats of other people, losing or running out of money, raising children, getting sick, getting old, or dying.

- The thought that one (or I) has no conflicts with people, rather having the best time with them without any worry.

- The thought of a 'Nirvana' feeling, like 'life' cannot get any better, (e.g., for me being on a beach by the ocean on a nice, warm summer day).

- The thoughts of Infinite Love as touching the 'Soul' of each person we are engaging with or loving, which amplifies the quality of the love in the relationship and increases faith in our Higher Power.

- The thought of a person having the feeling of absolute peace of mind.
- The thought that there is absolutely nothing to worry about, to be able to finally stop worrying and put all trust in our Higher Power or God, that thru God all would be worked out satisfactorily.
- The thought of entering eternal lasting Infinite Love in the next State at the end of this life. This means no negativity, judgment, or punishment in purgatory or hell because of 'errors', 'sins', or things left unaccomplished in this life.
- The thought of no health problems physically or mentally, i.e., that one (or I) has perfect health.

Theme 3- 'The Wonder at and Within the Falls'

This theme refers to the essence of healing messages revealed during a recent annual visit/retreat to Niagara Falls in Ontario. I happened to be spending reflective and meditative time at a Canadian side site overlooking the Falls by experiencing within myself a restful flow of healing spiritual energy from viewing and experiencing the roar of the falling waters. A gentleman passerby happened to interrupt my thoughts by politely asking me what I knew about the location of the border between Canada and the U.S. on the Niagara River at the Falls. Also, he wanted to become aware of any accounts of the geological history behind the formation and progression of the Falls. Since geography and glacial geology have been lifetime interests of mine, I commenced to enthusiastically explain answers to both of his questions. But after a few moments, he gently interrupted me with a different and startling statement: that coming to the Falls for him provided a sort of good feeling which he described as 'spiritual Soul consolation'. Being rather surprised, I suggested to him my 'read' of why multitudes come to the Falls each year is the tremendous peace they find in viewing and hearing the falling waters, that behind this feeling of peace is the Infinite Good Spirit ('Source', or 'God') which composes and resides within the Falls.

I further related to him the Niagara-area Native American Legend-Story, 'Maid of the Mist'. This accounts a young Native American woman who long ago deliberately chose to go over the Falls in a birch-bark canoe to her death over defiance of a wish by her tribal group, which formerly resided by the Falls, that she should marry an elderly chieftain from her group. Most visitors are unaware of the actual legend story. The legend story further reveals that following that event, her Infinitely Loving Spirit quietly and mysteriously resides within the falling waters of the Falls, affecting vast multitudes of visitors who experience and view the Falls with the euphoric feeling of tremendous peace and freedom. I further explained from my historical research that this legend story likely did occur some 1,000 years or so ago in the vicinity of the north side of the present Niagara Falls on the American side in New York.

Curiously, the gentleman went on to ask me what I thought about all the formalities and garb (as he called it) of the various major religions in the world with their various practices. To say the least, I was a bit stunned by this question, as he knew nothing about the book I was just completing, nor my keen interest in the whole topic related to his question. As we both stood at the overlook viewing the beauty and the sound of the roaring Falls, I explained my thinking. That is, the Infinite Loving Spirit (or God) was everywhere (e.g., even here within the Falls) and a part of everything surrounding us, not necessarily any part of Church doctrines, beliefs, traditions, or garb, which are all 'human-borne' in origin, produced for strictly human-cultural, organizational, or other purposes. It is suggested that the Infinite Loving Spirit is way beyond all human forms, devoid of anything cultural, controlling, or negative, as all these aspects are people's inventions for strictly human purposes within this life.

I went on to explain that it seemed to me that all these faith-based traditions were strictly human-created inventions or interpretations about 'God,' 'Source,' or 'Infinite Spirit', and not necessarily representative of the true nature of our 'Higher Power'. Perhaps the best pathway for opening one's door to the true spiritual light of the Infinite Loving Source begins with assumptions devoid of all prescribed teachings, beliefs, or practices such as those espoused by many of the major world religious organizations. This discussion returned to my new friend's original question on the 'formalities and garb' of various religious systems. It was suggested to him that while many practices and traditions of religious organizations that stress good intent bring one closer to 'God' or 'Infinite Spirit', it seemed to me that the Infinite Spirit could be best felt by precisely experiencing and viewing what was right in front of both of our eyes at this moment. This would result in enhancing the joy of experiencing the fantastic falling and roaring waters of the Falls, including imagining within those falling waters a total, accepting, everlasting Love that is <u>always</u> there, a Love that can never be taken away, like it is so often in this human life. At the same time, we could further imagine a healing and everlasting Infinite Love energy flowing from within the Falls to infuse healing in the body and mind of each viewer (like us two) who happened to be experiencing the Falls.

Subsequent reflection on this meeting event secured in my mind exactly why I have returned annually to this particularly inspiring and beautiful site for many decades. That is, continued healing from past early-life difficulties through inspiration by viewing the beauty of the Falls, and meditation over the recognition, presence, and benefit of the healing Infinite Love of Spirit residing within those falling waters.

CHAPTER 2

INFINITE LOVE

Chapter 2 consists of two parts: (1) <u>Chapter 2(A) Infinite Love Definition</u>; (2) <u>Chapter 2(B) Proof of Infinite Love</u>

CHAPTER 2(A)

INFINITE LOVE DEFINITION

Chapter 2A defines Infinite Love via Theme 1- Contrasting worldly types of conditional love and unconditional love with Heavenly Infinite Love. Theme 2- Describing the Infinite Love of Heaven by perceiving this Love through the vastness of the Universe of outer space. Theme 3- Contrasting the different energy states of Heaven versus worldly life. Theme 4- Identifying love and time differences between Heaven and this life.

Theme 1- 'Worldly Love Contrasts with Heavenly Infinite Love' (In-text: 'I' refers to anyone; 'I AM', the name of God who lies within each of us as 'Soul')

I go within myself to my spiritual core or essence (my 'Soul') where there is total silence and peace, away from the noise of the outside world with all its clamor. All of Divinity is there within me and starts within me. It connects and is 'One' with everything in the Universe. My spiritual core (or 'Soul') represents a part of myself that consists of tremendous everlasting beauty, perfection, power, warmth, and love. It has truly been 'me' for all eternity. My physical incarnate body represents only a shadow of my overall being, which is composed of both body and 'Soul'. My body is only temporary, but my 'Soul' is everlasting (eternal). My body through its senses, emotions, and ego experiences conditional love in this life, and only occasionally experiences unconditional love.

Conditional love is generally the rule in this physical life: 'If you do this or that for me, I will love you, but if you don't I will not'. This includes most aspects of romantic love. Our bodies and minds are programmed or 'hard-wired' into this reality, which is inculcated into all of us from the moment of our birth into this life. Unconditional love is a much less prevalent occurrence in this life: 'I will love you for what you are, no matter what you've done, what you've said, or how you've performed, no matter what your feelings are, how you look, what you possess materially, or what you represent'. This is the maximum dimension of unconditional love, coming anywhere close to Infinite Love, that our bodies, our senses, and minds are capable of perceiving or experiencing within this life. And this unconditional love would only represent an infinitesimal piece of Infinite Love. Unconditional love is an occurrence within this life that is intermittent, that comes and goes according to the human emotional and human will situation, but Infinite Love always was, currently is, and will ever be within the Infinite State. Infinite Love can make extremely rare and brief 'glimpse' occurrences within this life. In defining Infinite Love from our limited language context, a quote (repeated later) from one spiritual thinker and author will help to enlighten us as part of this theme:

> From Neville Goddard's work, "The Law and the Promise": 'The greatest thing that exists in the world is love, that the love of God or Infinite unconditional love has tremendous meaning. Nothing ever imagined by man could ever be compared to this love, which is the unconditional love of God. The most intimate relationship on earth is like living in separate cells compared with the magnitude of God's Infinite and vast love.'[5]

That Infinite Love surpasses all expectations and experiences of the best romantic or unconditional love in this life, which is better, deeper, clearer, longer lasting (eternal), and perfect is incredible to imagine and meditate upon. Nothing to buy to satisfy another, nothing to anticipate from another, nothing to judge or grudge one against another, no egos of one or another to hurt, and no brain to concoct reasons for loving or not loving. This is an Infinite Love that is thousands of times greater in magnitude than any unconditional love in this life. We can only perceive or feel exceedingly small vestiges of Infinite Love within this life's state because we live with time, but Infinite Love within the Infinite State <u>is</u> that Love and State, as this Love always was, is now, and always will be for all eternity. And Infinite Love there cannot <u>ever</u> be taken away once it has been given (unlike the typical takeaway situation in this life).

Picture in your mind the most elated moment you have ever experienced in your life in feeling the greatest happiness, positive feeling, ecstasy, joy, and Nirvana like you were 'on top of the world.' All of us very occasionally experience these brief (in worldly time) glimpses of Infinity, or Infinite Love within our worldly experiences here. Through our feelings, these glimpses of glory represent small, vestige pieces of Infinity, surrounded and subsumed here in this life by typical conditional and unconditional love, with expectations of a giver and a receiver through the human contexts of senses, emotions, egos, and time. We are principally in this life to experience the contrasts between conditional and unconditional love and bring these comparative memories with us upon return to the Infinite State. This will result in deepening our perception and pleasure of the whole dimension of Universal Infinite Love once we return there. Time does not exist in the Infinite State since everything happens there simultaneously.

A suggested way of perceiving Infinite Love within the timeless Infinite State is via a contrasting example, e.g., picture an extended (in time) this-life endeavor such as a 40-year work career, or decades of caring for a sick family member. Now imagine substituting for that time an extended Nirvana feeling of total acceptance, peace, and freely available Infinite Love without having to work for it, and along with these, total joy, clarity, happiness, ecstasy, and pleasure. As for your entity-being, things just cannot get any better. Imagine this absolute ecstasy lasting timewise for a whole 40-year work career or decades of family life. Now picture this bliss extending beyond time into eternity and lasting forever.

Reflecting on Infinite Love's timeless and dimensionless ecstasy, joy, and feeling of Nirvana, touches the Infinite part of each of us (i.e., our 'Soul'), increasing the power of faith in our 'Higher Power' or 'Source.'

Our human minds are the principal blocker and weapon hiding us from feeling the real romance of the Infinite Love of God, and once we can blot out our mind with all its effects, then true feelings of Infinite Love can begin to <u>flow</u> from our Source (God) via our 'Soul'. This will commence the road to true physical and mental healing. Let us take a few moments here to try consciously to block out of our mind all judging and grudging thoughts that the mind typically concocts in defending our ego (i.e., our physical survival and material betterment instincts), and seize these few moments to think the thoughts expressed within this theme on the nature and reality of Infinite Love. I AM Infinite Love, Infinite Perfection, Infinite Peace, Infinite Warmth, and Perfect Clarity throughout my being for the healing of all my hurts and woes. I AM both healed and freed via Infinite Love.

Theme 2- 'The Infinite Love of Heaven'

(Picture above from the Hubble Telescope)

The next time you are outdoors on a clear, starry night, look up at the 'heavens', (i.e., 'heavens' as an expressed 'colloquial' term when viewing the moon, planets, stars, and galaxies in the nightly sky), and simply imagine this present physical view before you as representing the Universe, Infinity, and Eternity. At the same time, view the picture above and imagine it as representing a 'piece' of the entire Universe, Infinity, and Eternity. Now just imagine that same Universe filled to the brim with the Creator's total Infinite Love, Goodness, and Healing. Imagine that Universe with its volumes of Infinite Healing Love being returned to you via your eyes and connecting with your Infinite Loving eternal 'Soul.' People who have been lucky enough to encounter a small piece of this Infinite Universe through space flight describe outer space as a strange void of darkness, at the same time brilliant light, with an indescribable, mysterious feeling and thrill of wonderment and euphoria of incredible dimensions, unlike anything experienced here in this life. Henry Vaughn, an English writer, once imagined and remarked about this void as representing the presence of a Creator for the entire Universe: 'There is some say, in God, a deep and dazzling darkness'.[6]

From Eben Alexander, M.D.'s description of his Near Death Experience (described later on), he describes this 'void' of space or 'heavens' comprised of darkness at the same time incredible light as being the home of the Infinite Spirit, Source, or God whom he identified as 'Om'.[7] While experiencing this void or home during his NDE, he experienced a radiated energy of incredible euphoria with Love, joy, warmth, acceptance, and compassion far greater in magnitude than anything of the sort that we could ever experience here in this physical life. And he felt that this 'Infinite Spirit,' 'Source', or 'Om' as he identified it as caring about, in a completely loving sense, each of us back in this life far more than we could ever fathom or imagine because 'Om' knows how very difficult life here can be.[note 7]

Look at the picture above and think of it as what you would see gazing up at space above you on a clear night—and just imagine—a void filled with darkness at the same time radiating an incredible and mysterious light. With this same void filled to the brim with incredible and completely accepting Infinite Love that is unlimited, never ends, which absolutely cannot be taken away like happens so often with love in this physical life. Now picture a Universe beyond this picture above, extended out far beyond its visible dimension, filled with non-stop Infinite Love that is boundless, limitless, timeless, and never ends, unlike typical 'love' in worldly life that is so frequently limited, narrowly defined, and often temporary. Also, this Infinite Love Universe is completely devoid of anything 'evil,' this being a product and concoction of the human physical-life state.

Now picture through imagination in your mind, a spirit (such as you, via your 'Soul') within the midst of this Universe-wide incredible Love consisting of dimensions far greater than all the possible colors in a rainbow, with your spirit fully embracing and embellishing this Infinite Love's total euphoric joy, warmth, reward, good feeling and acceptance without any reservation or doubt—and your spirit within this dimension drifting or flying at warp speed through space or the Universe, viewing on the way a rich diversity and tapestry of stars, celestial bodies, and worlds with 'spirit' beings in a far more advanced state than those back in this world—with your spirit expecting to find or locate an end, edge, or corner to this vast Universe of Love—but, no—your spirit just keeps moving on and on without end—yet this search or journey clearly does not disappoint nor get tiring like similar ventures back in this life, but instead creates an energy of euphoric joy, warmth, acceptance, and Love that just grows as your spirit hurtles effortlessly onward through this beautiful Universe—and, along with you on your journey are all the 'Soul' essences of folks you once knew of, loved, and enjoyed company with back in this life who are enjoying with you the euphoric joys of this wonderful adventure.

But, while your bodily being is still back in this physical life, picture capturing a piece of this Infinitely Loving, joyful, and euphoric adventure that you are imaginatively experiencing with your spirit 'friends' and transferring the love and euphoria from your journey back into your present physical body via your spirit or 'Soul', bringing complete peaceful joy and healing to both your body and mind. Through your imagination, picture this whole experience as completely ameliorating and healing all the hurt, anxiety, and negativity that is currently affecting you in your present physical life, particularly from significant love-loss experiences or other hardships of the past. Since the truth of 'Infinite Intelligence', 'Source of the Universe', or 'God' clearly does not know of or deal with these negative things, conscious touching of the imagined and wonderful Infinite Love 'void in space' journey with your spiritual essence or 'Soul' back in this life enervates the radiation of positive, healing energy that forever erases from your body and mind all the negative physical, emotional, and mental effects from your past or present life experiences. This begins to return your overall being to its original spiritual state before this life, which consisted of Infinite Love, joy, warmth, euphoria, acceptance, and bliss.

Once again, before leaving your upward view into the Infinite starry night, feel the Infinite Loving Spirit Energy (including that of your spirit friends) filling the vast, limitless Universe above you enter through the view of your eyes and directly touch your Infinite 'Soul', moving your physical body and mind toward the desired soothing of healing love, peace, and freedom.

Theme 3- 'Different Energy States of Heaven and Earth'

What I often perceive from the many writers, speakers, and experts about spirituality is their sense or attitude of 'knowing it all', in that many of these persons seem to portray and project the attitude that they have all the answers, that by following all their prescriptions and suggestions, one will eventually arrive at the gates of 'Nirvana'. This perception comes from similar attitudes apparent from chief spokespersons of the major worldwide religious organizations. My view is that other than Jesus of Nazareth, Buddha, Lao-Tzu, and select others, it seems that a vast majority of folks who have spoken out on spiritual subjects throughout human history have little right to the claim of 'knowing it all.'

What I want to clearly express here is that I do not possess a monopoly on knowing all the answers, as all my thoughts are only nuances, perceptions, and possibilities based upon experiences, interactions with people, readings, meditation, and thinking over past decades. It would seem to me that, save for Jesus and select others, the average person such as myself possesses few clues as to the complete truth regarding 'the Other Side' or the spiritual realm. It seems to me that the precise definition of the Infinite State remains mostly a mystery and that considerable surprises await all of us when we finally do arrive at those 'Pearly Gates' of everlasting life, i.e., the Infinite Love State, after this life.

From my readings and research, both the worldly and spiritual realms appear to be completely different energy systems or states. These two states seem to differ because of 'energy' or 'vibrations,' as opposed to being different physical places or worlds. At the beginning of this incarnate life at conception/birth, we lost all spiritual awareness from our prior perfect Infinite State existence. Within this worldly state, time is of the essence, but in the Infinite State time does not exist, and instead, everything there happens on a 'simultaneous' basis. The only spiritual component maintained from the former Infinite State existence is our infinitesimal spiritual essence or 'Soul,' which came as the spirit within our new bodily existence. This is our permanent connection with the Other Side or State. As each of us grows and matures in this life, we can connect with this 'spiritual' essence through our mind (intent) and awareness, our body and its functions of senses, and our emotions. But throughout human history, connecting with our spiritual core through our bodily functions has proven to be a challenging process. Additionally, very few of us save for Jesus and select others have had any clear perception of the totality of the spiritual essence within us, or what truly does lie in the Infinite State Side.

Likewise, due to being different energy state dimensions, few of us when we were in the Infinite State Side before coming here had cognizance really of what the realities would be in this worldly state, or what would happen to us physically within this state. Select authors on spirituality, including those who have experienced Near Death Experiences (NDEs) in this life by briefly experiencing the Infinite Side, claim that we excitedly and voluntarily chose while still in the Infinite State to embark on this physical life journey. This was based upon the inspiration that while being here, we would experience new dimensions of love through an incarnate body, mind, senses, and emotions. Part of the excitement to embark on life here may have been an awareness that we would enter into this state as a minute embryo within another human being and would develop from that into a separate, fully-grown, mature, aware, and physically loving (human) being.

But how we would specifically do that, what we would go through i.e., the suffering, joy, and just what each of us would accomplish within this life were not on our radar screens when we were back in the Infinite realm. It also seems that while we were still within that Infinite realm, we had little to no cognizance of concepts such as judgment,

27

punishment, hell, violence and killing, genocide, war, hurt (including childhood suffering), nor any of the other possible negative venues we would encounter within this realm. We found out about all these things after we came here by experiencing childhood and later adulthood, and we learned here how to deal with these things by discovering love via our various bodily faculties, i.e., the mind through awareness and learning, and the feelings through our senses, ego, and emotions. Due to the different two energy states of the Spirit life and this life, likely, we were not cognizant of the specifics of this future (forward) encounter, nor specific bodily faculties before leaving the Spiritual realm.

Before each of us embarked on this new life adventure while still in the Infinite State, we were cognizant that an eternal Infinite 'Soul,' essence or spiritual part would always accompany us throughout our new worldly state adventure. This accompaniment gave each of us the 'insulating protection' or assurance we needed to willingly embark on the journey of this life. I perceive that we were made somewhat aware that part of the experience here would be: (1) the loss of spiritual awareness at our life's beginning, and (2) the need and ability to somehow re-find this spiritual perfection and connection as we matured. These two aspects invariably played into producing the thrill of embarking on the adventure of this experience.

It appears that before embarking on this new experience, we received assurance that by coming into this life we would have love opportunities mirroring those we were leaving behind in the Infinite State. In other words, upon arrival via birth into this new state, each of us would maintain vast possibilities to give and receive love as experienced back in the Infinite State. We might have perceived before leaving the Infinite State that love's translation or actualization within this new state might be 'different' as compared to back in the Infinite State. If it is true that each of us arrives here with an equal capacity to love, this would completely <u>falsify</u> the typical reasoning we so often hear that evil preexists for a certain number of us upon entry into this world. That is, a certain number of us are born with natural or biologically based love-less, evil, or wicked intent.

My perception is that awareness and knowledge of contrasts between the two energy-state realms from either of the realm's standpoints are completely absent and that being in a particular energy state produces little or no perception of what exists or is going on in the other state. I lack the perception or insight as to the reason(s) for this except that each of these states operates based on quite different energy-vibration realms, which in and of themselves are hard or next to impossible to recognize or delineate from one another while being within either one of these states.

Theme 4- 'Identifying Love and Time Differences between Infinite and Worldly States'

The rule of thumb with 'love' in this human life is 'conditional love', but this is not the rule within the Infinite Love State. We specifically came here to experience, contrast, and feel less-than-perfect love so that when we return to the perfect, Infinite Love State at the end of this life, we will enter there with a <u>higher</u> awareness and energy state of appreciation for the overpowering vast, joy, and goodness of Infinite Love. This will place our eternally existing essence ('Soul') in an unimaginable depth of Infinite Love's gloriousness as the result of having had contrasting memories of less-than-perfect love from our experiences and challenges here in this life.

If we can comprehend the contrast of this life's imperfect love with Infinite Love's perfection, unlimited gloriousness along with its continuous, never-ending euphoria, and imaginatively extend that out in our worldly 'time' frame for several moments, this gives us a hint of Infinite Love's limitless dimensions within the Infinite State. Infinite Love within that State never ends, unlike here in this life where it is experienced in microscopic pieces (time and dimension-wise). In a nutshell, Infinite Love is 'God', or 'Source', or Our 'Higher Power', and no human mind or language capability can delineate the totality and extent of this multidimensional and multi-faceted Love, which ties the entire Universe together under an umbrella of a Unified 'One' vast and limitless Love.

One can contemplate vestiges of this Infinite Love while here in this life by viewing spectacular scenes in nature, such as the vastness of outer space on a clear night outdoors, the beauty of the ocean and waves at the seashore, or the power and roar of the Falls at Niagara, or the magnificent beauty of the Grand Canyon, Yosemite, or Lake Tahoe. Anyone can do this by imagining while physically viewing each of these scenes as filled to the brim with God's Infinite, unlimited, and everlasting love which can never be taken away, unlike love in this life which is so typically given and then easily taken away. And, one doesn't have to work for or earn this Infinite Love as they must for love in this life!

Time is only realistic within this worldly life, but does not exist in the Infinite State, which means that we should bring the emphasis of the past and the future into the present by strictly living and thinking in the 'now'. We can best practice emphasizing the present time mode (or now) by doing or imagining some activity best enjoyed, e.g., experiencing or imagining some beautiful scenic place like being at a beach by the ocean, by a lake, or a mountain overlook, and feeling the enjoyment of this in the present (without concern as the timeclock ticks). As the seconds or minutes tick by while continuing engagement in that activity, by continuing our thinking in the present-time sense, we will have increased pleasure and enjoyment in doing that activity. As we do this, there should be no concern about the past or the future.

Everything in the Infinite State happens simultaneously and eternally, or in our worldly time mode at the same time or instant. We here in the earthly state get closest to the simultaneous, eternal state by focusing on continuing a pleasurable activity in the present sense as actual time goes (or ticks) by. A conscious focus on continuing enjoyment of a particular activity in a 'present sense context' enervates eternal or simultaneous energy, which translates this same Infinite energy from our 'Soul' through our body and mind, creating elated, heightened feelings of pleasure and joy as we continue to engage in the activity. Even when we engage in mundane or boring tasks, focusing on the present sense context helps us to complete the task more readily and in a happier feeling mode.

CHAPTER 2(B)

PROOF OF INFINITE LOVE

Chapter 2B presents proofs of Infinite Love via <u>Theme 1</u>- Acquiring and building faith in a Higher Power composed of Infinite Love; <u>Theme 2</u>- Healing the afflicted by the efforts of both Jesus and Brother Andre (of Montreal) in having the afflicted recognize the 'perfection' or Infinite Love that existed within each of them (via 'Soul'); <u>Theme 3</u>- 'Near Death Experiences' (NDEs) whereby persons in this life briefly go to the 'Other Side' and envision our Higher Power and Infinite Love. <u>Theme 4</u>- 'Man as the arbiter of his fate', i.e., any member of mankind can act as an 'arbiter' or 'determiner' of their fate.

Theme 1- 'Acquiring and Building Faith'

This theme involves developing faith in a Higher Power, the organizer behind all existence in the Universe. This Higher Power does not exist as some sort of entity out in space somewhere but instead exists within each of us as our 'Soul' that is perfect at its core. This Higher Power also exists in everything throughout the Universe as a living Infinite Intelligence made up of perfection and Infinite Love. This perfection and Infinite Love represent key identifiers for initiating all physical and mental healing in this life. Belief in these is essential to begin this healing process. Faith is the way to achieve or manifest this belief. Faith is achieved through feelings, not the five human senses. Feelings are the doorway to the living Infinite Intelligence, or 'Soul', or perfection part within us.

In the work, "Three Magic Words", Uell Andersen describes his experience as a college student in the 1930s at Stanford University in California where he had discussions with his college chaplain about belief in a God or Higher Power. At that time, the young Uell stated that he was a non-believer in this Higher Power or God, that it was all a myth and mistake, and no proof could dissuade him from this opinion. His chaplain simply replied: 'Well Uell, I see the Creator (God) everywhere, within me, within you, and within people all around us; and I see the Creator in the brook outside the office here, with birds in the air, with animals, in the meadow across the way, in the trees outside the office, the landscape beyond, and at the seashore'.[8]

This is how St. Francis of Assisi perceived during his lifetime that God or the Infinite could be visualized directly through the beauty of nature, i.e., the landscape, flowers, vegetation and trees, animals, birds, and the environment. From this, his chaplain saw perfection and Infinite Love in all of creation, including both nature and humankind. I can say too that my faith has been increased through frequent visits to the seashore (or beach), annual visits to Niagara Falls, and occasional visits elsewhere to Yosemite Park, Lake Tahoe, the Grand Canyon, the Rocky Mountains in Colorado, or other spots of natural beauty.

From this point on, the young Andersen began to grow spiritually through assimilation of the meaning of his chaplain's statement, to begin recognition of faith through his feelings by increased perception and awareness of the significance and meaning of what his chaplain had said, that Infinite Intelligence or Infinite Perfection is manifested everywhere throughout the entire Universe. Faith begins through our basic feelings that there is something outside of ourselves, i.e., outside of our physical body with its five senses, ego, and all we go through just to survive, something beyond, far more powerful, far more long-lasting, and far more meaningful. [note 8] We should strive to feel and believe that it is true that this Infinite Intelligence with Its Infinite Love exists, as this cannot be proven through the five human senses.

Theme 2- 'Healing the Afflicted'

With the spiritual perfection of Jesus, his healing was done by revealing and identifying the spiritual perfection that existed within each afflicted person whom Jesus was attempting to help. He was attempting to help that person by inciting that the buried pains, hurts, and afflictions from the past within that person be forgotten by them, that the 'real you' within your person is perfect.[9] Turn to the spiritual self and perfection within and begin to regain your physical or mental health. The way to help heal a friend who has a physical health affliction: from the recognition of your spiritual perfection, reach out in meditation to the spiritual perfection within your friend and declare that they are healed of their affliction. Jesus, as well as Saint Brother Andre in Montreal, performed numerous miracles of helping and healing people during their lives. Jesus made multitudes of loaves of bread and fish from just a few pieces for vast multitudes of people to eat, and he also facilitated the healing of thousands of people at that time. Brother Andre, who promoted the construction of the Cathedral (Oratory) to St Joseph in Montreal, also participated in the healing of thousands of sick individuals there during the earlier part of the twentieth century.[10]

Both Jesus and Andre completely tuned into absolute faith that Infinite Intelligence and Power accomplished all this work. At the same time, they tuned in to the weaknesses and imperfections (i.e., colloquially known as 'sins') within each of the sick who they were attempting to treat and heal. Then these two people convinced these sick individuals that they should forget and forgive these personal imperfections by recognizing the Infinite Perfection that existed within each of them, then stand up tall and move on with their lives. One might assume that these weaknesses and imperfections represented negativity or past hurts in these peoples' lives, that both Jesus and Brother Andre were attempting to purge these.

These two individuals believing that the sick victims had faith and belief in the Infinite Loving and healing power within themselves (via their 'Soul'), coupled with convincing these same afflicted to forget/forgive their weaknesses and imperfections, may well have facilitated healing (i.e., created an actual healing process) in removing and curing the physical and/or mental maladies affecting these persons. Through unshakeable faith, the sick victims facilitated their healing.

Theme 3- 'Near Death Experiences (NDEs) as Proof of a Higher Power and Infinite Love'

According to people who have experienced Near Death Experiences (NDEs), natural wonders in this world are infinitesimal in comparison to the magnitude and constancy of Infinite wonders and joys we will encounter and enjoy in the next life. Many hundreds of persons have experienced NDEs in recent decades whereby their 'Spirit' or 'Soul' temporarily departed from the body due to a brief functional shutdown of many of their essential physical bodily functions, usually due to a severe illness or trauma. The separated (from the body) 'Spirit' or 'Soul' takes a temporary journey into the 'afterlife' of the Spirit World where it encounters certain experiences and realities. Often these are reported back through the person's mind, after their 'Spirit' returns to the (still) alive body, as a fantasia of incredibly beautiful and wonderful experiences and scenes accompanied by indescribable euphoria, bliss, and unending (Infinite) Love. Many of these same people return to this life in a 'cured' fashion from their pre-NDE life-threatening illnesses or traumas and live to relate their impressions of their journey into the 'afterlife.' If these experiences are regarded to be true, (i.e., to have occurred), they represent one of the best proofs of the actual existence of our 'Higher Power' with an associated wonderful 'afterlife,' Heaven, or Nirvana.

Anita Moorjani's full story is described in her recently published book, "Dying to be Me." She was raised in Hong Kong after her family relocated there from India. She had feared all sorts of things during her life, which evolved from her childhood fears of following what her parents (particularly her father) wanted according to the Hindu Faith which she had been brought up with. Her father had been particularly emphatic that she should follow all the traditions of that faith. This included whom and how she should marry (including both mates not meeting before the event). Later in adulthood, because of the frequent fears she had during childhood, she became obsessed with the fear of contracting cancer in her adult life, which became compounded when her best friend Soni developed it. Then, soon after that Anita was diagnosed with cancer. After coming back from a trip to India to attempt Ayurveda meditative healing, she deteriorated, and within 3 months became hospitalized with Stage 4B level Lymphoma and almost immediately went into a coma, and after more than 4 years of suffering she was barely alive.[11]

Suddenly, she experienced a most unusual occurrence of perceiving the departure from her physical body with all its long-term extreme pain from the cancer condition and going to the 'Other Side' as she later described. It felt like she had not gone anywhere, but rather had 'awakened' or 'reawakened'. Love, joy, ecstasy, and awe poured through her more than at any time during her physical life. All the pain and suffering from the 4 years of her illness were suddenly and completely gone. The love she now felt was complete, pure, unending (Infinite), non-discriminating, non-judgmental, and without any need to do anything to deserve it nor prove herself to earn it.[12]

She found out that the unconditional Infinite Love and acceptance on the Other Side was incredible, i.e., the oneness of pure essence with everything, without the aches, pains, and ego of a body. She realized that each of us has an inner state or essence (i.e., 'Soul') composed of perfection and Infinite Love, that once we become aware of it, we can translate this perfect love to have positive healing effects on our outside body. She learned that the fear she had from childhood had brought on the cancer condition.[13] During this experience, she met up with the spiritual essences of both her father and her best friend, Soni. Each had 'passed away' from this life earlier. Unlike being overbearing in

35

childhood, her father was totally loving and supportive now that all the layers upon layers of culture he had been trained in through perceptions of the five senses had all been removed. Both her father and friend Soni surrounded Anita with an unbelievable veil of unconditional Infinite Love. Before returning to this life, the essence of both her father and her friend Soni clearly advised her: 'Now that you know truly who you are, go back to worldly life and live your life fearlessly.'[14]

Another amazing thing Anita experienced through her NDE that should be mentioned as proof of a Higher Power, is the multi-dimensional joys felt there, including the absolute feeling of love, which was total, perfect, unconditional, or Infinite. She experienced and perceived these wonderful feelings on a level unprecedented as compared to the levels of pleasure and love felt in this life, without any need to 'work for' or 'earn love' like here.[15] Many of us in this life believe that we must work at being loved, but that means living in duality, meaning that there is a giver and receiver. Realizing that we <u>are</u> love transcends or goes beyond this. Within the Infinite State, the total meaning that 'each of us is love' will be the basis for the total joys we will each face and be embellished within that State.

In Anita's NDE state, she realized that the entire Universe is composed of unconditional Infinite Love and that every person is an expression of this. The Infinite consists of Universal life-force energy composed of love, which makes up each of us. She realized that she did not have to please nor serve someone else to be worthy of this love. This proved how hard she had judged herself and treated herself within her past physical life, and how she had punished herself over fear and worry of trying to satisfy others. She goes on to say that there is nothing to forgive for 'sins,' errors, or omissions committed in this life to fully experience the joys there.[16] The relief she felt from this responsibility was as magnificent a joy as any other absolute pleasurable feeling experienced there. In the NDE state, she saw herself as a beautiful child of the Universe, a beautiful 'Soul' and magnificence deserving of unconditional Infinite Love just because she existed. Her physical life had eroded all of that. When we know that we are made of love, we do not need to work at being loving towards others, but rather by loving ourselves through nurturing our 'Soul' and bodies, we become instruments of loving energy that touch everyone we encounter. ^{note 16}

The human-created names of the Infinite such as Source, God, Jesus, Krishna, Buddha, or whomever, represent labels that often lock us into a duality so that we view Infinite energy as separate from ourselves. But Universal energy, our pure state of consciousness, is limitless and formless, and we are all unified and connected to it as 'One.' Each of us has this magical life force going through every cell, which is not from some outside force in space somewhere, but rather from the inside, outside, and all around us. No matter what belief system we belong to, we are all intimately connected to this Universal energy or power, and we do not have to prove anything to access it. Anita's mind back in human life before was the limiting factor in comprehending this, but once she proceeded into the NDE and let her intellect and mind completely go, taking all the self-limiting beliefs with it, the floodgates of healing opened because her mind was absent to keep fighting against the true nature of the Universe.[17]

During her NDE she realized that all judgment, hatred, jealousy, grudges, and fear stem from people not realizing their true greatness, that is, their true perfection. Not realizing this keeps people feeling small and insignificant, which goes against the natural flow of life-force energy. Expressing ourselves as to who we truly represent shows our inner beauty, preventing judgment about what is right versus what is wrong which generates jealousy and competitiveness, making us act out negatively because we feel like we're not good enough.[18] The most significant aspect she learned from her NDE is that each of us should develop an awareness of our magnificence and have unconditional self-love, which will eliminate fear, leading to the healing of many of the ills that plague each of us here in this life.

During the NDE she was way beyond mind, in the sense of a pure state of being or pure consciousness or a state of oneness, the part of herself that was eternal, Infinite, and encompassing the whole. She was thereby able to contact who she was at the Infinite Level, way beyond what a human body could do with all its ego and emotions. It was not such things as positive beliefs that caused her to heal, but rather a state of pure awareness, creating a state of complete suspension of all previously held doctrines, dogmas, and beliefs, causing a 'resetting' of her body. Following the NDE, she realized that she is strongest by suspending all beliefs, disbeliefs, and previously held human notions, leaving herself open to all possibilities, i.e., uncertainties. Letting go and releasing all attachments to any belief or outcome was the leading point in her healing.[19]

She goes on to say that we chose to come into a physical bodily life to experience love, passion, and a full range of emotions not available to us in our former pure, Infinite Love 'Oneness' state. We are here to experience and advance this physical life and the people within it. We do not have to wait and die to experience Nirvana, as we can feel and experience our true wonderment and magnificence right here in this life. Humans in this life are so vulnerable and fearful due to all the ideas invented about God and the afterlife in human terms, but if people were to look at their experiences right now from the standpoint of their magnificence, then they would have nothing to fear.[20] The entire Universe is within each of us, or 'I am One with Universal Energy'. The ability to visualize her spiritual magnificence and to realize that she and the Universe are 'One,' that there isn't an external God separate from her, were other important factors in facilitating her total physical bodily healing. [note 20]

Betty Eadie describes in her book, "Embraced by the Light", that she encountered an NDE just after undergoing serious surgery, where she envisioned Jesus Christ as a great bright white light at the end of the travel of her 'Soul' through a long, dark tunnel.[21] What she experienced was total unconditional love and peace in His presence, instead of all the fear that she had for Him during her prior physical life. She found that her teachings in childhood had been completely different, based on fear, as opposed to what she learned during the NDE. She was told that we can increase our faith and heal illnesses by meditating on the fact that He (Jesus) is total love (i.e., Infinite Love), omniscient, all around, in and out, and throughout each of us.[22] The suggestion was also made for her to completely let go of the human ego.

If we are awed by the magnificence of strikingly beautiful rose flowers encountered in this life, these are extremely minor in comparison to the vast dimensions of beauty and perfection we will experience in the next Infinite Life. In her book, Betty describes how the flowers, vegetation, waters, and sky she experienced in the Infinite State had spectacular brilliance and colors, unlike anything she had ever encountered here in her prior life. Through the power of imagination (Neville), we can visualize and meditate on the vastness and beauty of that Infinite State of perfection and beauty and translate this down through imagination and feelings to manifest beauty and wonderment within our daily lives here.

Betty learned during her NDE that we were all part of the creation of the world in its beginning, including its conditions to support life. This includes the family into which each of us was born, that before this life in the Infinite State, we (as spirits) negotiated who we would partner with (parents and children) to encounter together the physical life here. But what the family would go through here with difficulties and successes, how they would relate to each other, or how the children would be treated were not yet on our radar screens back in the Infinite State before coming here. [note 22]

The talents given to us are primarily for us to love, grow, and help to benefit others by serving them. When we serve others, we grow. When we find someone difficult to love, it is because it reminds us of things inside ourselves that we dislike. All things are created by spiritual power, and each element has Infinite intelligence, spirit, and therefore joy. Positive and negative energies occur according to our free will and our thoughts. What we express verbally is extremely important in what we will bring about or produce for ourselves. All creation begins in mind, thought, or imagination, which can be either wonderful or terrible according to our thought. We should never fear the Lord, only love Him. Fear creates negativity, which moves us away from God. For the first time in her life, she realized that there was a God to love and not fear, a God who was warm, compassionate, and loving whom we could draw on as part of Heaven as well as this life. She saw that all healing comes from within, not from the outside.[23]

Concerning illnesses, we need to verbalize their remedies and have faith that Infinite Intelligence will work toward healing. Lack of healing is an indication of the need for spiritual growth which increases faith and belief. All worldly experiences help us to grow. The spiritual law regarding faith is that it increases as we use it through serving others. We are in this life to grow through experiences, and our progression of spirit and faith is always more than we think. We must gain the maximum knowledge about the spirit while in the flesh, as the more we know and become aware of spiritually, the more we progress towards a higher point in the next life. She claims that if we could see ourselves before each of us was born into this life, we would be amazed at our magnificence, glory, and power. Birth represents a putting to sleep of awareness of this former spiritual state, greatness, and power.[24]

A final thought from Betty's NDE is her indication that each of us progresses spiritually on an individual basis according to our life experiences. There are various levels or platforms of spiritual progression for people to utilize. There are a variety of spiritual resources and organizations that are appropriate to anyone's level of spiritual progression at a particular point in time. Most of us move along a line of spiritual progression, so resource and organizational support needs may frequently change. We should never criticize any person's spiritual level they are at, religion, or spiritual belief because each of these is appropriate for the progression stage or level that each of us is at a particular point in time.[25] From my further careful reading, her intent here is to fully respect any person's spiritual level, religion, or belief when it strictly focuses on good intent, thoughts, and acts, but not evil.

For myself, though raised Catholic with all the useful structure it provided at that time, I have since experimented with and gravitated toward a more non-denominational, transcendental, or universalist-oriented approach to spirituality, which seems at this stage to best provide the freedom and flexibility for my continued spiritual progression or growth. However, someone else might feel more comfortable promoting their spiritual progression under the umbrella of a particular faith or organization. Yet in this process, I still highly respect various aspects of the Catholic tradition in reverence to the Holy Family, various spokespersons, and saints, along with certain prayers and meditations, some of which are mentioned within this work as I feel that consideration of them by any former suffering person can assist in their overall healing from past life difficulties.

A third NDE involves the highly trained and experienced neurosurgeon, Eben Alexander, M.D., who wrote about his experiences in the book, "Proof of Heaven, a Neurosurgeon's Journey into the Afterlife." Before his NDE, the former belief in the existence of God or a Higher Power was extremely weak at best. In the past, he had thought that spiritual experiences (such as NDEs) described by others were generated by human brains under great stress.[26] In his early fifties age-wise, he contracted some sort of strange and rare spinal meningitis via an E. coli bacterium, which was completely resistant to antibiotics. He grew extremely sick, and lapsed into a prolonged 7-day coma, at which point his spirit journeyed outside of this world into a fantasia of incredible experiences, finally culminating in his meeting with whom he claimed was the Ultimate Divine Source and Creator of all the Universe, identified to him as 'OM'.[27]

In his book, he reveals that before this experience, during his life as a neurosurgeon, he was not able to reconcile his knowledge as a doctor with his belief in a God or Ultimate Source, a Heaven or an afterlife, or a spiritual part or 'Soul' within himself. But after this experience, he came back to life as a doctor who positively believed in an Infinite Source or Power, who also possessed a spiritual everlasting 'Soul' capable of incredible love, healing, and joy. Also, what was incredible following the return from his NDE was the complete healing of his body from an almost 100% certain death by an incurable bacterium that had attacked his central nervous system. This complete healing was like Anita Moorjani's total healing. In his case it was shown during his NDE that death of the body and brain does not mean the end of consciousness, rather existence continues in an Infinitely more glorious and fantastic way after we die. More importantly, he found out that this existence continues under the venue of a God or Source who is Infinitely Loving and caring about each of us within the totality of that Source's Infinite Love, which encompasses the entire Universe, including this human life.[28]

From his NDE, he learned that the human brain and our language blot out the whole dimension of God's unconditional love. The ego within this life represents a barrier to higher levels of experience, knowledge, and awareness of our spiritual dimension of magnificence. He found that there are countless worlds in the Universe, most at a much higher level than here with only traces of evil as compared to our world. Alternately there is greater evil in our world, in fact sometimes overwhelming, yet even here the good outweighs the bad. He found out that evil exists here because of the offering of human-related free will, which is the essential concept and process for beings here such as us to grow toward the Divine.[29]

During his NDE trip, he was taken on a journey by the beautiful image of a woman on the wings of a butterfly. The image he found out much later on was the spirit of a very kind, long-lost sister (whom he had never met in life) from his original birth family, who had died a few years before his meeting up with his birth parents.[30] Her image suddenly appeared along his side as a beautiful girl with high cheekbones, deep blue eyes, and tresses of golden-brown hair on the sides of her face. She had been dressed in a simple outfit that had super bright colors and was alive like the rest of the surroundings there. He described his experience and impressions alongside her:

> 'She looked at me with a look that if you saw it for a few moments, would make your whole life up to that point worth living, no matter what had happened in it so far. It was not a romantic look. It was not a look of friendship. It was a look that was somehow beyond all of these, beyond all the different types of love we have down here on earth. It was something higher, holding all those other kinds of love within itself while at the same time being more genuine, and pure than all of them.'[31]

We should digress a moment to similar thoughts on Infinite Love as expressed by Neville Goddard, which was discussed earlier. In his essay narrative, 'The Law and the Promise', in the "Neville Reader" he states that:

> 'The greatest thing that exists in the world is love, that the love of God or Infinite unconditional love, (agape love as St. Paul calls it), is a mere phrase that has tremendous meaning. Nothing ever imagined by man could ever be compared to this love, that is the unconditional love of God. The most intimate relationship on earth is like living in separate cells compared with the magnitude of God's Infinite and vast love.'[32]

'Conditional' or false love, or even true unconditional love that we typically experience in this life are infinitesimal and insignificant in comparison to the fantastic Infinite Love that both Eben and Neville describe as the reality of what we will experience in the Infinite Love State.

During Eben's encounter with the beautiful lady on the wings of a butterfly, she expressed to him a spiritual message, not in language, but in spiritual thought: (1) 'you are loved and cherished dearly forever'; (2) 'you have nothing to fear'; (3) 'you can do no wrong'; (4) in summation, 'you are loved and accepted totally without any reservation'.[33] With this, no selfishness, jealousness, or judgment was possible, rather only complete acceptance and unconditional Infinite Love. No human words or actions can adequately describe this sort of love. This message gave him tremendous relief as if these were the rules and the basis of everything that he was supposed to have been following in his own life but had not up to then.[34]

During his trip, he experienced the 'Core' or ultimate home of the Higher Power ('OM' as he called it). He described 'OM' as omniscient, omnipotent, and all-loving. This place, or home of the Infinite, consisted of an Infinite black darkness at the same time incredibly bright light, or as Henry Vaughn, an English writer once said, 'there is, some say in God, a deep and dazzling darkness'.[35] Eben further described it as a place or state where the pleasurable feeling and acceptance of Infinite unconditional love was incomparable to anything back on this side. Also, 'OM' possesses qualities of love, acceptance, warmth, compassion, irony, and pathos not only like humans are capable of but incredibly greater, more genuine, and believable, which sympathizes with our human situation in this life much more than we could ever imagine as this Infinite power knows how difficult and painful our life here can be.[36]

An interesting sidelight insight given from the writings of the three authors above, who each encountered NDEs on the Other Side and then returned to life on this side, was that once they returned here, each was convinced that this side was the best place to be at this point of their existence. This would indicate that despite all the wonderful things they learned and encountered on the Infinite Side, present life within this life's realm was the most desirable thing to be experiencing at this point, as each was thrilled to have made the decision (via free choice) to return to this life instead of remaining in the Infinite State.

What was learned while they were each in the Infinite State was that the perfection and Infinite Love making up the entirety of that state could be experienced in bits and pieces within this physical state through conscious awareness, the senses, and emotions. Also learned there was that manifesting unconditional love or worldly romantic love here in this life is something fantastic that cannot be replicated within the Infinite State because of the human body, feeling, and emotional aspects applied to love here. Each realized they had unfinished 'business' back within this realm consisting of educating people here about the existence of great beauty and Love in the Infinite realm, how Infinite Love can be replicated and experienced here, the 'oneness' of everything in the Universe, and how awareness of these things can help lead to healing of health and other afflictions within this life.

The principal thing that all three NDE authors discuss in their books is what they perceive from the Other Side relative to the chief negative component that everyone suffers from here in this life, namely <u>fear</u>, and the need to understand and overcome it. Overcoming fear seemed to be the highest priority suggestion learned on the Other Side to be applied back in this realm, leading to the creation of an atmosphere of joy and peace in this life. Each of these three individuals who encountered their NDE learned from the Other Side that fear generates most of the negative side effects that occur in this world. These include ego behavior, competition, violence, hatred, racism, misogyny, oppression, crime, physical and mental illnesses, and other mistreatments of people. The prime message that all three perceived from their experience on the Other Side was that once we can overcome all aspects of fear, then we can enjoy many aspects of this life more fully, including being more loving towards others and having fun in this life.

Incredible as it sounds, each of these individuals experienced what it felt like to have a total absence of fear while they were in the other realm. Each indicated that fearlessness was a product of Infinite, Unconditional Love and that this Love could be received and felt effortlessly on the Other Side without having to 'earn it' or 'work for it' as we might expect here with love in this life. In the other realm, there is nothing to achieve or to forgive, rather it is to feel absolute unconditional (Infinite) Love, which according to them is the greatest feeling in the entire Universe. The total lack of fear accompanied by Infinite Love was unlike anything they had ever experienced back in this life. Although Infinite Love is not as easily achieved back in this physical life, a practical application of it which was perceived and learned by the authors experiencing NDEs in the Infinite realm was the idea that we should be manifesting fearlessness to the maximum extent possible within our lives here.

The NDEs just reviewed have significantly strengthened my faith in the existence of a Higher Power. The mere fact that a huge unconditional Infinite Loving force lies quietly behind this physical world was definitely revealed from the accounts and descriptions of these respective NDE authors. From these accounts and the numerous other related readings that I have encountered over many years, it is clear to me that a huge loving force is close at hand, which is an integral part within each of us, and not outside somewhere in space or in some distant location or separate state of being as many of the organized religions teach.

From these NDEs, the clear fact is demonstrated that each of us in our physical existence and presence here is composed of a much more magnificent and powerful part than just our physical bodies, consisting of a spiritual essence or 'Soul' which is all-powerful, Infinitely Loving, and eternally existing. These accounts reveal that there is something quite special to live for, to eventually look forward to in the next life, which through emotions, awareness, imagination, and meditation can be tapped into while we are here in this life. We do not have to wait to die and go to the next life to experience the realities of Infinite Love's healing power, but instead, through imagination and meditation can experience it here in this life.

Upon completion of the narrative story on these three NDEs, I wanted to add a fourth true NDE story, namely that of a small boy's astounding NDE trip to Nirvana or Heaven and his return to life here with his family in the Midwest. His story was told in the book entitled, "Heaven is for Real," by Todd Burpo, his father, who is presently the Pastor of Crossroads Wesleyan Church in Imperial, Nebraska. Todd lives there with his wife Sonja and three children. In 2003, his four-year-old son

Colton developed an undetected Appendicitis, which ruptured into a Burst Appendix that was not clinically diagnosed for several days until after he had lapsed into unconsciousness and near death at the Great Plains Regional Medical Center in North Platte, Nebraska.[37]

During this hospitalization, he had an NDE whereby he left his body and had an enlightened encounter with Heaven, where he met Jesus and sat on his lap. During this NDE, Colton was completely aware of what his parents were doing and saying at the hospital. Later, they were amazed at what he revealed on this score, plus other factors related to his NDE. When he was asked after the NDE, he estimated that his unconscious time out-of-body was 3 minutes, yet the experience seemed to him to last much longer. [n. 37]

Jesus taught Colton many things, including the existence of Infinite, Unconditional Love in Heaven, and that people back in worldly life could most easily get to Heaven by becoming more sympathetic toward children through appreciating, and loving them at the young stage of their lives. After he returned to this life and recovered from all the aftermath ill-effects generated from his Burst Appendix, he slowly over several years began to reveal to his parents what he had learned and encountered in the afterlife.

Some examples of the things that he learned include: (1) emphasis in many sayings and thoughts by Jesus: 'Let the little children come to me', or 'unless you act like or sympathize with a child, you cannot enter Heaven'; (2) that people in Heaven have wings, with a light (halo) over their heads; (3) rainbows with very diverse colors existing in Heaven, and Jesus clearly depicting all children as precious rainbows; (4) Colton meeting up with various relatives in his family whom he had never met or known in his life, e.g., (a) 'Pop' the father of Sonja, his mother, who was a very unusual, kind-loving guy, who took an immediate liking to Colton, whom Colton remembered well upon return to his bodily state, (b) Colton's sister he never met in physical life because she had died unborn following two months of his mother's pregnancy; (5) Colton's meeting with 'John the Baptist', a cousin of Jesus; (6) in Heaven, no one looked old, rather they all looked young as if they were in their 20s when they were in this life.[38]

When Colton returned to this life, after being shown by his father hundreds of possible images of Jesus, he definitively identified him from a beautiful painting created by a girl named Akiane, from a family in the Midwest devoid of religious adherences (see Subs. 7(D), Medit. 10). This girl at an incredibly early age began to have ethereal Divine encounters and insights, which from her skills at poetry and painting were translated into remarkable and beautiful works of art depicting Jesus and other heavenly figures and scenes. From the painting, Colton clearly and immediately recognized Jesus as completely true to form from whom he had seen and met with in the Infinite State, that he was a very nice masculine-looking man with beautiful eyes. [note 38]

This NDE was truly a remarkable experience and certainly complements the other three NDE accounts reviewed earlier in this theme. Particularly pertinent in all four NDE accounts (including Colton's) was an almost immediate and complete healing that occurred upon return to this life for each person who encountered the NDE. At the beginning of their NDE, each of the four had severe life-threatening health conditions, on the verge of actual death by accounts from treating physicians and nurses at the specific health treatment facility where each was. But after each returned from their NDE, their dire health conditions rapidly and completely recovered within a couple of weeks.

After returning to this life, each of the four NDE accounts reported a love experience in the Infinite State of unparalleled dimensions and magnitude, with euphoric feelings of unprecedented pleasure and joy, incredibly greater as compared to anything they had ever experienced back here before their NDE. It was a Love that each did not want to part with, even though each was either convinced or told that they should return to this life. But to each, the indication was provided that, through their memory, at least pieces of the wonderful (Infinite)

Love they had experienced in the 'afterlife' could be envisioned and remembered back within their remaining lives here.

Theme 4- 'Man as Arbiter of His Fate'

'I AM' (or 'I am') is the self-definition and foundation of the absolute definition of God (Neville). 'I AM' (or 'I am') is the statement declaring and defining Infinite Mind or Infinite Intelligence. Also, 'I AM' (or 'I am') represents the identifier of God who lies within each person's spiritual essence or 'Soul'. 'Let the weak say, I am strong' (Joel 3:10). Do not say things like 'I am weak, sick, feel bad, or tired', etc., but rather say 'I am strong, healthy, loved, or well rested'. The 'I am' concept of oneself becomes projected as an effect in any person's conscious world. The 'I am whatever' sends a signal to the subconscious mind, which is impersonal and unchanging, and this returns to the conscious world of that person as physical reality. The great discovery of cause reveals that good or bad, man is the arbiter of his fate, in that his concept of himself determines the world he will live in, and that his actual thoughts will create his actual living conditions. To consistently believe and say 'I am healthy' brings good health; contrarily, 'I am unhealthy or not well' produces poor health or health problems. 'I am strong,' 'I am abundant', and 'I am loved', produces those positive things.[39]

Consciousness is the only reality that conceives itself to whatever is desired and said, which frees destructiveness from outside forces in life to affect and dictate one's consequences. The conscious mind is selective and represents ego (physical survival), and the subconscious mind is non-selective and impersonal (unchanging). The womb of creation is the subconscious or Universal Mind of God, which receives signals from the conscious mind and sets about to create that reality back into the life of the individual who originated the idea. Feelings are the doorway to the 'Soul' or subconscious and are the principal communication medium to it. Subconscious (the Infinite or God) impressions determine the conditions of the world since they never fail to express what is impressed upon it and set about to produce in the outer world the exact likeness of that feeling, down to the smallest amount of detail. note 39

Wayne Dyer, a noted author, was diagnosed with Leukemia disease a few years back, and he described the process by which he was completely healed in his book, "Wishes Fulfilled Mastering the Art of Manifestation". He had to heal any (and all) relationship conflicts with unconditional love given to all those involved in the conflict, at the same time to resolve any long-held conflicts and beliefs about himself.[40] He claims that creation is the result of subconscious impressions, which is the power of manifesting physical reality from thought. He goes on to say:

> 'This is how I choose to deal with my diagnosis of Leukemia, I choose to feel good, i.e., to feel God, and to offer unconditional love to everyone, including those who played a major part in any or all conflict dramas that once defined my life. I go by how I feel, and the truth is, I am well, I am strong, and yes, I am God, and I am resolving any (and all) conflicts with massive doses of God's unconditional love. This is what I choose to imprint on my subconscious mind, and this subconscious mind accepts as true what I feel as true'.[41]

As a reinforcement to Wayne's concept of desiring to feel good is his very recent public interview with Esther Hicks, which was written and published by the two in the book, "Co-Creating at its Best, a Conversation between Master Teachers." Esther has developed the capacity to tap into a collective consciousness within the Infinite Side known as 'Abraham.' The key concept of this consciousness is that each person has the capability of reaching their high-frequency alignment with the Source (or God) by getting into a positive energy vibration by (first) thinking good and (then) feeling good. This creates a law of attraction response to these high-energy good feelings by bringing into one's life the things that the person desires through those good feelings. [42] The principal concept and process revealed here are for a person to correlate how they feel with what they are thinking, which explains the reason why one feels the way they do. One can change the way one feels by changing the thoughts that one is thinking, e.g., by having positive thoughts, one creates positive feelings.

Everyone has access to that energy of well-being and vibrations of least resistance from the Source for healing without the need for help from or respect for another person such as a counselor or a 'guru' type leader. However, a particular person of intense respect for the victim can act as a facilitator-median to help soften the negative feelings, resistance, or hatred the victim has toward someone else who was formerly abusive or cruel towards them. This would soothe any negative vibration or hatred the victim has, thus allowing healing to flow from Source, or God, to the victim.[43] Through the victim's focused concentration on the person of respect, the former fear toward the cruel or abusive person is allayed or vanquished, allowing healing energy from the 'Source' to flow to the victim more easily and freely. [note 43]

CHAPTER 3

INFINITE LOVE WITHIN; BUILDING 'SOUL' POWER

Theme 1- 'Infinite Love Within and Positive Thinking' (In the text: 'I am', the name of God, who lies within each of us as our 'Soul')

This theme follows the story of my spiritual reawakening in June 2004 when I experienced repeated 'taps' near my heart area, tearing in the eyes, and euphoric feelings throughout the body, reflecting for the first time in many decades a clear realization of the existence of a Higher Power (Ch. 1, Theme 2). No, I did not have a Near Death Experience (an NDE) with its dramatic spiritual reawakening like Anita Moorjani and others discussed just above, yet there was enough of a positive signal from within me to give solid proof of the existence of an Infinite Spirit or a Higher Power, far greater than I was. This represented a definite sign of the existence of an Infinite Source or Power in the Universe, a very real and pragmatic signal from feelings that truly came from <u>within</u> me.

The repeated 'taps' I felt near my heart area under the left-side rib cage came from within me (a 'Source', or 'God' from within my actual being), and not from the outside, i.e., a God out in space or somewhere else. This was truly strange and new to me. A God or Higher Power coming from within is the central message and essence of the experts and writers that will be discussed within this theme. Many organized religions, at least those in the Western world, emphasize a creator or God that exists outside the incarnate body and physical world out in space somewhere, with the person's 'Soul' or invisible Infinite Part lying dormant within their body until death.

Many Eastern religions and philosophies, including some Western writers such as those discussed in this chapter and theme, reveal a Creator or Higher Power that exists within each person as a spiritual core or 'Soul' entity. This entity can become active and thriving during this human life to positively help and benefit a person's incarnate body if through conscious intent the person believes that this 'Soul' exists and wishes it to help. In the same vein, this internal Spirit is perfect, representing the Infinite or 'God' or our 'Higher Power,' within each of us and is part of a Unified core consisting of all animate (i.e., living) and inanimate (i.e., non-living) things that exist in the entire Universe. All these things make up the totality of existence and are Unified or combined as 'One' and are composed of Universal Infinite Love.

Despite extensive study of Catholicism during my upbringing, the distinct physical signals that occurred from within me back in June 2004 began my quest of pursuing Spirit from the context of the Eastern world. This Eastern context espouses that the 'Soul' or Infinite invisible part of each of us is potentially active and alive, and not dormant until death as taught in the Catholic and many Protestant Faiths, and that this Infinite essence can manifest significant creative power within this human life. Additionally, this potential spiritual power, if you call it that, can either be for good or bad (evil) intent depending on the imaginative human intent (i.e., through free will) of each respective individual. This explains the origin of evil, suffering, and bad things that happen to us humans in this life.

With my re-discovery and revelation on the existence of God, including an Infinite 'Soul' part within each of us, I would like to highlight and review the thoughts of four contemporary authors on our 'Higher Power' and our Infinite 'Soul' part, in association with all-goodness and positive-based thinking. This will reinforce and add credence to my current thinking on these two aspects. These four authors include Uell S. Andersen, Neville Goddard, Wayne Dyer, and Florence Shinn.

Uell S. Andersen- He claims that the prime principal and positive message from all of Jesus's teachings is that: 'the good news I bring you is that the kingdom of Heaven is within each of us and is composed of nothing but Infinite Unconditional Love and goodness'. Uell's thinking is that all thoughts on evil and negativity come through mankind's imagination and his thinking, as God is not aware of the existence of these things. He asks: how could an all-good intending architect and maker of the entire Universe seek to destroy itself by allowing underlying evil to exist, persist, and compete within its Kingdom?

He adds that since people are brought into this world with free will capability, they are left to invent their own situations, including the events and happenings related to evil and suffering. The conscious human mind associated with all thinking related to the physical body and its survival (ego) generates what Uell calls 'prompters', which are negative feelings that are then linked in memory from the conscious mind to the subconscious mind. He defines the subconscious mind as the Universal Subconscious Mind or God. The 'prompters' are negative feelings such as lack, limitation, unhappiness, guilt, fear, remorse, doubt, loneliness, and other negative feelings which restrict and prevent us from the proper use of the great power of the Infinite, which is Love.[44]

A person's conscious mind conceives these negative feelings and projects their images into one's subconscious mind, and these come back to revisit the conscious mind with creations of actuality. The Law of the Universe is that like seeks and renders the like: negative or 'prompter' thoughts and feelings will render the same negative realities in real life. On the other hand, positive thoughts projected from the conscious mind to the subconscious, e.g., I am healthy, will render positive realities in life, namely, good health.[45] Uell goes on to say that the willingness to think purely positive thoughts is the basis for all human-related goals, accomplishments, and successes. The suggestion is made 'think with conviction', that whatever I want I already <u>have</u>, not that 'I wish to have it', because admitting that I do not have it suggests and is a failure. This thinking goes on to say: know the Universal subconscious mind or God for its Infinite power and learn to use this power to fill our lives with good and abundance.

In discussing the life of Jesus, Uell relates the fact that He (Jesus) had a very highly developed consciousness through awareness of the spiritual perfection in every living thing. Healing someone's malady or disease was best carried out through Jesus by revealing to the afflicted person the perfection that existed within themselves (i.e., their 'Soul'). Prior awareness of a buried painful memory within the afflicted person's mind had produced the person's physical or mental malady. Jesus' banishing a person's sins was inciting that the buried pains, hurts, and afflictions in their lives should be forgotten by that person, that this would generate healing from within the person.[46]

Put another way, what Jesus was saying was that 'the real you is good and perfect', to let go of ego, competition, bad feelings, and/or misfortunes, and turn to the perfect inner self (or 'Soul') within you and recognize its spiritual perfection, thereby regaining your physical health. The key to all of Andersen's thinking is that there is a key to unlocking oneself from their ego and its results, (e.g., destructive competition). This key is to believe unshakably that you are God, the secret of the Universe, that the God-consciousness within you (i.e., your own 'Soul') is immortal in that it was never born, nor does it die. Further the 'Soul' is eternal and made up of all-Infinite Goodness, and these beliefs will give you great treasures and the fortunes of goodness in this life.

Neville Goddard- 'I am' (or 'I AM') is the self-definition of 'Source' or 'One', the foundation of everything that exists, namely the identification with or the name of God, which is the permanent awareness of being and the center of consciousness.[47] 'I am' is ever the same, despite man's forgetfulness of who, what, and where 'I am' represents. An author somewhat earlier, Saint Germain, really coins this whole concept which he claimed was something that originated with Moses many eons ago with his calling of 'I am' as the true name of God. [note 47]

The great discovery of reality reveals that, positively or negatively, man is the arbiter of his fate, in that his concept of himself is what determines the world in which he lives. Use of the statement 'I am healthy' brings good health, and conversely, the statement 'I am not healthy' brings poor health. Neville claims that the Universe delivers whatever you claim yourself to be. 'Let the weak say, I am strong' (Joel 3:10). From this, the fact that 'I am weak' is rearranged by the statement 'I am strong'. The statement 'I am strong', or 'I am healthy' renders just that; on the other hand, 'I am sick', 'I am weak', or 'I am tired' will render the reality of those things in life. It is the 'I am' concept in and of itself that determines the form and substance of the actual reality manifestation. 'I am strong', 'I am loved', 'I am healthy', etc., establish those positive things in the world in which you live, i.e., you can create your world by your direct and strong 'I am' statement according to both Saint Germain and Neville.[48]

Consciousness is the only reality conceiving itself to whatever is desired, which can potentially free a person from negativity and oppression during their lives. Since 'I am' is the Infinite Unconscious Mind, Infinite Intelligence, or God, the 'I am' concept of oneself becomes projected as an effect in that person's conscious objective world. Neville divides the mind into conscious and subconscious: the conscious being personal and selective (ego), and the subconscious being impersonal and non-selective.

The conscious mind generates ideas and then, through feelings, sends them to the subconscious, impressing the idea on the subconscious from which all creation affecting humans comes. The subconscious which is the Universal Mind (or God) accepts the idea from the conscious mind and then sets about to recreate that idea reality back into the life of the person who originated the idea. The mechanism or 'womb' of creation is hidden within the subconscious, the Universal Mind, or God.[49] The subconscious contemplates a feeling as a fact existing within itself, and based on this assumption, proceeds to give expression to it. An idea goes through feelings, good or bad, to the subconscious Universal mind, and because of this, it must begin to be expressed as a physical reality in this life.

The body is an emotional filter that bears unmistakable marks of prevalent emotions. What you feel you are is dominant and can easily violate the perception of any of the 5 senses. Feeling the reality of the state sought and living and acting on that conviction is the way of all miracles. Subconscious impressions, defined as the Infinite or God, determine the conditions of the world since they never fail to express what is impressed on it and immediately set out to produce in the outer objective world the exact likeness of that feeling, and details that exactness down to the smallest level.[50]

To impress the subconscious with a desirable state, one must assume the feeling that would be theirs as if they had already received their wish. Rather, if you dwell on difficulties, barriers, or problems that might railroad getting the wish, then the subconscious processes these as reality in your outer world instead of giving you the wish. The subconscious never changes an idea, it simply always gives that idea form. To feel a state of impossibility or hopelessness renders failure in your outer world. [note 50]

Dr. Wayne Dyer- In one of his more recent books, "Wishes Fulfilled Mastering the Art of Manifestation," he often reiterates ideas and principles from the past writings of Saint Germain, Uell Andersen, and Neville Goddard. He discusses Saint Germain's principal work, "I Am Discourses," about the power one possesses as the result of identifying and expressing oneself. This means the moment a person states 'I am' (or 'I AM'), it sets into motion the Infinite Intelligence, Infinite Source, or God, to produce the form of whatever the subject the person's mind or intent is saying.[51] For example, an individual saying 'I am healthy' sets our Infinite Source into motion towards that stated reality, and the move towards positive health comes from within that person. The 'I am' represents the fathomless mind of God, or as Wayne reiterates, the name of God. This awareness according to Wayne's research was realized by Moses more than 3,200 years ago and was also clearly manifested in Jesus's actions during his public life. [note 51]

The 'I am' healthy statement reflects one's attunement with the simple truth that positive health comes from within oneself, from one's spiritual 'Soul' or core, and not necessarily from the outside, i.e., from counseling, doctors, medications, or a God in a distant location or out in space somewhere. Wayne reiterates what Neville claims in his work, "The Power of Awareness", that the typical statement made by people that 'I am not healthy', or 'I want to be healthy', or 'I will be healthy' rather than 'I am healthy', brings from our Infinite Source through the Universal Subconscious Mind the disposition of continuing to program unhealthiness for that person.[52]

In other words, simply 'I am not healthy', or 'I hope to be healthy', or 'I will be healthy', will, unfortunately, continue to program unhealthiness instead of improved health. Rather, a person saying 'I am healthy' spurns positive healing forces from the Infinite to bring about positive or perfect health, despite what any of the five senses might indicate at a point in time. Wayne very strongly reiterates what Saint Germain states in his "I Am Discourses", that a desirable statement to say is:

> 'I am the miracle-working presence in everything I require to have done'; and 'Your highest Self fearlessly proclaims I am God; I am the Almighty Governing Presence of my life and my world, and I am the health, well-being, and harmony self-sustained, which carries me through everything that confronts me'.[53]

Florence Scovel Shinn- She begins by saying in her book, 'The Magic Path of Intuition', that if a person has asked for the availability of any good thing, to act in the present (time) sense as if they have already received it. Prayer is communicating to God, and intuition is God communicating back to a person.[54] The subconscious mind of man is power without direction, in that whatever is impressed on it from the conscious mind (good or bad) is carried out in the smallest detail. For instance, she emphasizes that the game of life is that whatever you say or do to others comes right back to visit you via subconscious power. She talks about a deeper than the subconscious mind, namely, a super-conscious mind (i.e., via one's 'Soul'), which is perfection or God or the realm of intuition.[55]

Ms. Shinn suggests sanctioning every seeming failure instead with the opposite, namely, success. The world of adverse appearances and negative thoughts about oneself, (or the 'poor me' concept), is the fog most people live in. Never say 'I am broke' because this impresses on the subconscious a picture of emptiness. Rather say 'I am abundant', or 'I am immune to all hurts and frustrations', or 'the power within me is perfect peace and prose'. What you see in your inner mind via internal impression from the outside, you meet sooner or later in the external world.[56]

Our early training for the most part is largely negative. Our caretakers when we were young were often fearful of failure, unhappiness, or survival for us, and this was projected in numerous ways upon us as negative fashion and expression. Often when good things happen, the same caretakers express 'that it is too good to be true', or 'don't expect it to happen again'.[57] This negativity when expressed is absorbed into the non-rational subconscious, and it is very carefully carried out in that the good thing likely will not happen again. Rather express happy and orderly surroundings by enthusiastically saying: 'something that seems too good to be true, but is true, and can happen again'. note 57

A negative idea continually dwelled upon will create a similar thought form in the subconscious, manifesting a negative outcome in one's pathway in life. What you fear you attract. Rather, act fearlessly and say: 'The lions in my pathway will not impede my progress', or 'Today is the day of amazing prosperity', or 'I see myself bathed in the dazzling bright light of the Spirit, which dissolves everything not Divinely planned'.[58] Realistically, our bodies are composed of spirituality, which is incorruptible, indestructible, eternal, timeless, tireless, birthless, and deathless.

The best process to dispose of doubts and fears is to fully affirm the positive feeling of life clearly in the present time-mode by saying such things as, 'the tide has turned, for God has the right of way'. Or by showing active faith that there is a Divine plan in one's life, e.g., 'let the Divine design of my life flash into my conscious mind a perfect plan'.[59] Faith is knowing and trusting that God, or Infinite Intelligence, can follow one's intuition by allowing for the receiving of blessings asked for regardless of adverse appearances that the senses might indicate. Through fearless faith, mountains can be removed from one's subconscious, thereby making adverse realities disappear in the external.[60] In other words, trust in God and positive outcomes and the seemingly impossible will come to pass.

Theme 2- 'The Author's Discovery of Infinite Love'

Prenote to this Theme: The following relates to a prior innocuously forgotten 1987 experience that opened the doors to my spiritual resurrection and connection, but I did not realize that then. This connection was re-initiated over concerns with the poor relationship I had with my father in his late years, and the similarities of this with those of the world-renowned author Wayne Dyer (discussed in my first book). This analogy further reveals how healing transpired for each of us with our fathers. Wayne's story is related to his book "My Greatest Teacher" (summarized pp 62-3). Also, for significance in my present book, this theme traces the beginnings of my meditation practice in the mid-1980s by learning Transcendental Meditation TM (p 115-116). Then, years later, on a summer day in 2006 at Singing Beach, Manchester-by-the-Sea, MA, the theme relates to an intensive ethereal experience that occurred for me which involved the use of TM. (pp 64-8).

Earlier in Ch. 1, Theme 2, I described in detail my spiritual experience in 2004 of re-discovering both faith and belief in the existence of a Higher Power. At that time, positive signals were experienced from within me which gave solid proof of the existence of an Infinite Spirit or a Higher Power, far greater than myself.

Pre-dating the spiritual 2004 experience (Ch. 1, Theme 2), there was an earlier dramatic experience encountered in 1987 during a brief stop-over visit to Fiji, as part of a three-week trip tour to the Southwest Pacific area sponsored by Father John Bettridge to visit his homeland in Australia. As opposed to the later 2004 experience, I did not equate this 1987 experience to any personal spirituality aspect, faith, or belief in a 'Higher Power', nor to any awareness of 'Infinite Love'. As it would turn out, this experience in 1987 would represent my first real ethereal spiritual encounter acknowledging the existence and presence of a 'Higher Power' along with associated Infinite Love, but clearly, these spiritual aspects were not recognized by me as such back then. The following thirteen paragraphs recount my 1987 euphoric experience in association with the relationship with my father, its tie-in with Dr. Wayne Dyer's work "My Greatest Teacher", a later dramatic 2006 ethereal experience, with several later-on follow-up ethereal experiences:

'My father's health had been deteriorating somewhat just before the Southwest Pacific trip-tour in 1987. One morning while on a brief stay in Fiji, (on our way to Australia), I was walking along the most beautiful coral rock-lined beach that you could ever imagine or want to see, with the sun shining so bright and warm, the ocean looking so blue with wonderfully warm water, palm tree leaves swaying in the gentle winds, and all sorts of tropical birds abounding. While walking, I started to develop very strange euphoric feelings of great joy and pleasure, not only in response to the wonderful tropical environment that surrounded me that day but also the fact that I was halfway around the world and far enough away from my father to not be burdened by his constant hounding criticism about every 'turn' I had taken in my life. It felt so wonderful and relieved that after 43 years, I was far enough away as to not be bothered by him. Also, for some weird reason that day it seemed like he had somehow already 'passed' away. Now I realize these feelings were due to being so distant geographically from him that day. I felt so free and released from him! I had never felt this way about being so free from anything else in my life up until then. It felt so incredible!

My father and I did not have a joyous relationship, particularly after my mother had passed away some ten years before in 1977. Therefore, I thought at that time the euphoric, joyful feelings were mainly due to the thoughts of relief from him being so far away, and secondly due to the beautiful Fiji coastline environment. However, I did not think these feelings had anything to do with the presence of an 'Infinite Spirit', 'Infinite Power', or related 'Infinite Love'. Yet in a very strange way that day, I was beginning to wonder about identification with some sort of energy or source of power giving me these wonderful euphoric feelings, something way beyond me, but I could not in any clear way understand nor identify just what this energy or source was. I simply assumed it was because of being far away from my dad and enjoying the wonderful Fiji tropical environment. But I was to discover quite a bit later (in 2004 and particularly in 2006) just what this energy or source was, that our Higher 'Source' or 'Power' along with its Infinite Love was present and at the seat of my euphoria that day in 1987!

In this connection, I recollect the book, "My Greatest Teacher," written by Dr. Wayne Dyer and Lynn Lauber, and published in 2012, about the fictional story of a college Anthropology professor who had a father he never met, whom he had hated all his life for having abandoned the birth family when he was born. Subsequently, the aftereffects of this tragedy took a great toll on this professor's marriage and relationship with his young son. But later in his life, after decades of efforts in trying to locate and confront his father, the professor unexpectedly found him at a burial gravesite in rural California and absolved at this point that he must confront and overcome his unhealed wounds and move on with his life. From the professor's studies of older Brazilian native cultures, he recounted a Matis chieftain's story/metaphor: 'that a snakebite doesn't kill, but what can is a snake's lethal venom, unless the bite victim learns to release/extricate it from their system or assimilate/change it from being toxic into a medicine'. From this, the chieftain applied a primitive, yet highly evolved notion that we can look at the most damaging and painful sufferings in our lives and turn these into our greatest teachers, or gifts to help heal ourselves. The professor applied this metaphor to his situation by surrendering all past regret and hatred towards his father, <u>abruptly</u> replacing these with intentions of total forgiveness and love for his father, opening the door to psychic, physical, and spiritual healing for himself.

The book turns out to mirror Wayne Dyer's childhood and lifetime story of abandonment by his father from the natal family before his birth, and his lifetime of hatred and regret for his father over this. Ultimately, he found and confronted his father (in spirit) at a gravesite in rural Mississippi, and at that very instant had a sudden and abrupt surrender from hatred and remorse to total absolution and love for his father. In Wayne's case, he applied the Matis chieftain's metaphor/ story of 'the lethal venom from a victim's snakebite being assimilated/ changed from toxicity into medicine' to his situational dilemma with his father by abruptly changing his greatest personal lifetime tragedy of abandonment into his greatest lifetime teacher. This caused him to make an abrupt and complete change of heart by surrendering all past hatred and regret over his father's past abandonment into total love and forgiveness for him. This represents an example of a most exceptional lifetime change that anyone can make within their lifetime.

Although the stories with each of our fathers differ, certain aspects of Wayne's former feelings about his father once mirrored mine about my father, particularly with my dad's oppressive attitude, feelings, and treatment toward me during the latter part of his life. Yet after years of egregious consternation over my father along with lessons learned from Wayne's book, "My Greatest Teacher", I have finally been able to offer my dad complete absolution and unconditional love and have sensed feelings of Love return to me from his departed Spirit (Subsection D, Medit. 5, pp 177-8). I think this radical/abrupt change of heart resulting in complete Love towards both our fathers came from Infinite Love energy of 'Spirit' of our 'Higher Power'.

It was 19 years following the wonderful 1987 Fiji experience described above, and 2 years after my re-awakening 'Higher Power' experience in 2004, that in 2006 on a nice sunny warm day at Singing Beach in Manchester-by-the-Sea, MA*, I experienced a memorable ethereal encounter during a meditation**. This encounter was so revealing and powerful in clearly demonstrating, through my body and mind, that both the power of our Infinite 'Source' along with Its associated positive and elated energies had been present and combined as 'One' within me. This occurred following the start of a meditation mid-to-late one afternoon after being present on the beach for several hours that day. It should be noted that physically being present on any ocean beach for several hours completely relaxes me, providing both peace and freedom.

At the start of the meditation that day, I outstretched both arms in front of me at an approximately 90-degree angle between each arm and began to move both arms and hands in slow circular motions, each arm and hand in opposite directions, at the same time raising them both very slowly upward as if imaginatively reaching toward 'Heaven'. I continued these motions for approximately 45 seconds and then stopped, but continued to imagine a slow, upward, at the same time circular motion of both arms and hands for an additional minute or so. This arm and hand motion was not a regular part of any meditation routine of mine up to that time, rather the idea to do it just 'came on to me' as the meditation ensued that day.

As the meditation continued, a most wonderful 'feeling' completely enveloped me with a fantastic euphoric 'Loving' pleasure that seemed would last forever, which clearly came from within or inside me, not the outside from another source or 'place'. This was not like any typical love or loving feelings I had ever felt before in this life. And the feelings that day in 2006 felt far different than the prior 1987 and 2004 experiences, perhaps because I now more clearly sensed and realized from the outset that these were part of a 'Source' or 'God'. The love feelings on that day, though hard to describe, seemed so incredibly greater than the two prior euphoric experiences or any other prior love with people. As the intense euphoric feelings suddenly developed, an aspect of extreme clarity came through at the same time. This clarity can best be described as what seemed to envelop me was an impenetrable veil of total acceptance and purpose like there was absolutely nothing to feel sorry for, worry about, or be disappointed with anything I had done thus far in my life. That was truly incredible: no human blaming, no gaming right or wrong, no questioning or judgment, no negativity, nor punishment for mistakes or things left undone in my life, just totally accepting and unrelenting Love.

A 'tingly pins-and-needles feeling' that came on all over my body along with intense euphoric pleasure was somewhat like the 1987 and June 2004 experiences, the difference being that on this day in 2006, these feelings were so much greater in intensity, pleasure, and clarity. I felt the presence and definition of a Love coming through that was so incredibly huge, accepting, and assuring as if this Love could and would <u>never</u> leave me. This was so incredibly strange and new to me. And still bigger, it produced within me the feeling of freedom from any possible criticism or condemnation over anything I had done or encountered in my life, including all my father's prior hounding criticisms of me. It was a far greater feeling of freedom than that felt on the beach in Fiji in 1987. The feelings of pleasure and freedom were unbelievable, and memories of these remain with me to this very day. It is noted that up to the time of this writing, and even afterward as I attempt to find a publisher for this book, I haven't revealed details about this ethereal episode to anyone, (not even my present wife), as the incredibly pleasurable memories of this euphoric day have completely obviated any need for disclosing it to anyone.

As the experience ensued that day, I had initially suspected and feared having suffered some sort of minor stroke, heart attack, or another physical malady, but was immediately assured by a strange and subtle feeling, 'definitely not'. At the same time, all the beach surroundings around me (the water, sand, birds, sky, and people) became so transparent and intensely pleasurable to view, with gently bright and sharp colors. With the familiar beach and its background still around me, I was aware of not being in a new place or location. Rather, there had somehow been an awakening or re-awakening into a radically new and pleasant energy state or dimension of some sort while <u>still</u> being physically present at the same favorite beach location that I had frequently visited all my life. Perhaps, I was experiencing the reality of a small piece of Nirvana or Heaven. Also, an especially 'heightened' sense of positive feelings was experienced on this euphoric day, unlike any other in my life. I profoundly realized and recognized this 'energy' through my feelings as representing a 'Higher Power', 'Source', or 'God', which evolved as an identity and source representing Infinite Love.

I had just recovered from a virus cold, yet still had some residual bodily aches and pains along with nasal congestion. All of that quickly vanished during this experience and remained as such until well after I arrived home that night. Also, highly elated feelings continued throughout my drive home and remained as such for some time afterward, e.g., it seemed like the drive time home that day took only 25 minutes or so instead of the usual 1.5 hours. Upon awakening the next day, I began to emotionally return to a more usual 'life' mode as it was before the episode. This included a somewhat 'down' or 'depressed' feeling state with the realization that I had left that perfectly wonderful and euphoric experience and re-entered the more 'usual' normal worldly life state. But subsequent memories and reflections on the wonders of what had happened that day certainly heightened my confidence that a much

'Higher Order' or 'Source' had truly been present there. A further signal came to me (I think from 'within') that this experience represented a 'smidgen' of the joys that all of us would one day encounter at the end of our lives.

Over the next few years following that wonderful summer day in 2006, several additional episodes with heightened euphoric feelings occurred in conjunction with meditation at the same Singing Beach location. These happened in conjunction with meditation and imagining a slow raising of each arm and hand skyward in circular, opposite-direction rotation, which seemed to initiate each euphoric episode. These episodes had similar characteristics to the 2006 episode, with the accompaniment of distinct euphoria and pleasure, though with less intensity than the 2006 encounter. Yet, these ethereal episodes generated much greater satisfying euphoria and pleasure as compared with the more normal pleasure that one might expect with just being on any beach in the summertime. The onset of heightened euphoria and pleasure from these episodes would always occur after being on the beach for at least several hours. Also, these episodes would just 'come on' as my overall emotional mood and feelings became more 'relaxed'.

The lesser intensity and effect from these follow-up euphoric episodes after the 2006 experience were perhaps triggered by the differing spiritual concentration or my emotional mood during these events, or perhaps contrast memories of the dramatic 2006 experience with these subsequent events. Following each episode, the bodily and mental effects were like the 2006 event. That is, an absence of any physical discomfort or pain for several hours or more, along with lingering joy, euphoria, and pleasure lasting for the remainder of that day. The following day, a letdown occurred with the onset of sadness, coupled with an inability to concentrate or function very well at much of anything activity-wise. This would last only for that day, and then the following day I would return to a more ordinary feeling and activity level. I had left an elated state feelings-wise and re-entered the reality of the real-life world'.

*Meditation 7(D), (5), pp 177-8 describes Singing Beach, as a happy place of family childhood history remembered. ** see <u>Special Note</u> on Transcendental Meditation (TM) pp 115-116.

<u>Theme 3- 'Worldly Love Meets Infinite Love'</u>

I had just completed my second reading of Uell Andersen's work, "Three Magic Words", and particularly recollected from his chapter on 'Love', the discussion on the essence and origins of love and how it manifests itself within this human life. He stated that love governs all, that man is in constant search of it in this life, that through it there is a spiritual unity to all life, and that unconditional (Infinite) Love exists near our physical heart area as 'Soul' within each of us. Perfect love is within each of us, complete and absolute, and it cries out from the very depth of our being for expression. But because of ego, pride, competition, and negativity, we often block this love out.[61] This only hurts mankind, for love moves through the entire Universe, expressing itself through every person and every living and non-living thing, including every person, animal, insect, tree, flower, animal, rock, and raindrop. Unconditional (Infinite) Love exists within the core or essence of each person. The perfect seed of success and happiness lies within each of us, and there is a channel within each of us whereby that seed of love can become perfectly expressed.

But in human terms, it is so difficult to open this channel of love expression because of our egos, self-centeredness, competitiveness, and fear of failure—all the 'negative prompters' in the subconscious mind consisting of buried memories of love that were withheld or denied in our past, which make us pull away from present opportunities to love. But if we can only allow true love to manifest, it heals the body, comforts the loneliness, lightens the darkened paths, redeems evil and fears, and brings prosperity and positive meaning to life. [note 61]

Within that same chapter on love, Uell discusses sexuality. In the relationship between a man and a woman, the love-sexual act represents a complete physical, psychic, and spiritual union or fusion of one being for another. This is the <u>chief</u> supreme outlet of love between one another in this human life. He claims that the end goal of the sexual act is not producing children as many of the religions teach, but rather it is for the expression of love and satisfaction through fusion. Uell claims that this activity represents an outlet of love that is good, great, joyful, and beautiful, and is a distinct expression and representation of God's Infinite Love. The prophets of shame, fear, hate, and evil have made their inroads when they have inculcated into our thinking that all sexual closeness is for usufruct purposes only, i.e., producing children, and that pleasure and enjoyment from it is wrong and sinful.[62]

One might next think that these same proponents of evil, shame, and fear would also promote the idea that the first euphoric, joyful, and ecstatic feelings of one for another at the beginning of typical relationships are simply gluttonous greed for sexual pleasure and enjoyment. Further, these first euphoric and joyful feelings have little to do with promoting any sort of lasting relationship or have anything to do with spiritual meshing with an Infinite Source (or God). I would seriously beg to differ on both these points. Rather, I think that these initial, highly positive, and relative feelings towards each other may very well be the result of spiritual Infinite connections, energies, or signals between each person (via their 'Soul') combined with their physical attractiveness, shared feelings, and other bodily manifestations. We are all integrated both bodily and spiritually within the context of this life. All five of the authors (including myself) reviewed in Ch. 3, Theme 1 herein would agree wholeheartedly on this point.

Application of aspects of love as discussed by Uell Andersen, including the fusion of body with spirit through the normal sexual act of love, would be of prime importance to consider as an activity that would enhance a continuance of euphoria and joy that occurs at the initial part of most relationships. A healthy attitude toward sexuality, and the ability through feelings to express it, is certainly an important part of the equation of activities that a couple can share to best promote the continuance of initial euphoria and joy in relationships. Tantamount to this is the clear realization that the sharing of sexual expression is a perfectly healthy and normal bodily activity that is part of the good, the Infinite, and the eternal, and is not part of evil, shame, and fear.

It was not the intent at the outset of researching and writing this present work to bring up the topic of sex between couples. But the logical extension became clear to me after thinking about initial excitement between couples and fusing this with Uell Andersen's ideas of healthy sexual expression between couples. Beyond this healthy expression, how the application of his concept of 'negative prompters' applied to a person who has endured any sustained lifetime traumas or mistreatment (especially early on in life) might result in damage to that person later in their abilities to express and share in loving feelings with another or others. Any sexual mistreatment during a person's life can have particularly serious repercussions.

But, for that matter, any kind of sustained mistreatment in a person's life can have definite follow-up negative impacts on a person's ability to respond in fully expressing and sharing close-loving related feelings with another person. This could even have the effect of blunting emotions governing initial spontaneity and excitement with others at the beginning of relationships. These effects can be life-long lasting. I highly suspect that of all those folks who have suffered from sustained lifetime traumas or love-denied/love-loss experiences, many of these have had serious follow-up hindrances to fully enjoying and sharing in sexually related emotional experiences with another person.

With all that said, my first choice in a healing strategy for any person who has undergone any past traumatic love-denied or love-loss experience is finding or discovering new, true-love relationships. The past love-denied or love-loss victim should make the effort to enter whatever amenable social circles to meet other new people. This will take considerable effort and may require help from currently existing 'friendly' contacts that this person has. The goal would involve finding and sharing love unconditionally with another person or persons within the present time context. This should be associated with strong faith and belief through feelings that this new love is genuine and represents a real and true substitute for the mistrust generated by any past sustained love-denied or love-loss experiences in the person's life.

Any woes from past love-denied or love-loss experiences would be greatly relieved through complete faith and belief in the healing ability of our Infinite Love of Source, or God. The healing could take place by the conscious act of sharing true unconditional love thoughts and acts with others now, connecting (via conscious intent) with Source's, or God's, Infinite Love between each love participant's perfect and eternal 'Soul' essence. Tantamount in this process is conscious awareness and belief by the past love-denied or love-loss victim that the positive energy vibrations of Infinite Love connecting (via 'Soul') between folks who are sharing the newly found love will result, or better still have already resulted in healing for the victim.

In this regard, my second choice in a healing strategy would be reawakening, releasing, and recharging the long blocked-off emotions and feelings for any victim of past traumatic lifetime love-denied or love-loss experiences. This would begin the process for a person to regain their ability to have feelings that could more easily lead to sharing tenderness and pleasure with another, which would be important for successful sharing in a close personal relationship. For any past traumatized person, this healing strategy would be aided by (1) Counseling and/or therapy with an individual who would sympathize with whatever negativity their client has endured, be patient and understanding (i.e., non-blaming), which would help their client to successfully establish new, supporting, and loving friendships with others. (2) Writing and re-reading a diary that recounts highlights of the past traumas or difficulties, along with the person's feelings both then and now. (3) Consciously reminding themselves that the past difficulties are over and won't return, that now is the right time for correcting the past by thinking and acting more positively and lovingly, e.g., new relationships that share the love back and forth with others. (4) Establishing a spiritual 'awareness' dimension.

This spiritual 'awareness' dimension for healing is best stated from my intuition of healing as expressed by Florence Scovel Shinn in her book, "The Magic Path of Intuition":

'Let the bright white dazzling light of Infinite Intelligence shine from within each of us (i.e., our 'Soul'), casting out forever from our lives all doubts, fears, and negative memories from the past, filling our total body and mind with Source's (God's) Infinite Love, light, warmth, peace, happiness, guidance, and healing'.[63]

Theme 4- 'Self-Love Begins the Process of Healing' (In the text: 'I AM', as the name of God, who lies within each of us as our 'Soul')

The best doorway for reaching the Infinite well within, (i.e., our 'Soul'), is through love and appreciation of our physical self, our beautiful body and mind, our positive abilities, our work, along with our hobbies and other special interests in this life. To view the reflection of our eyes from a mirror and just rest there for a moment is one possible pathway to feeling and connecting with our spiritual perfection within. Once we can convince ourselves of our positive self-worth for being alive by eliminating any guilt feelings from past difficulties in our life, then we can more readily reach and tap into this inner well of spiritual perfection within. Self-love begins the process of healing, which is amplified by reaching within.

It seems to me that connection with the Spirit within cannot be found through or dictated by any religious organization, person, or other prescriptive systems, but instead must occur by each person's conscious connection through their awareness and intent with 'Source' or 'God' within themselves. This conscious connection needs to be expressed with the heightened emotional energy of mental joy and happiness in anticipation of God's Infinite Love and perfection flowing from within each of us via our 'Soul'. This contact should be done with ease, in a relaxed manner (not forced), and is best done through the regular practice of meditation (Ch. 6, Themes 1 and 2, and Part II, Ch. 7, The 100 Narrative Meditations).

Each of us has an inner essence or well within us made up of perfection and Infinite Love. Once we become aware of it and attempt to tap into it via regular meditation and have faith in its Infinite Power to help us to heal, then we can visualize and imagine this ('Soul') energy within us as beginning the healing of our physical body and mind. I AM Infinite Love, Power, Perfection, Clarity, Warmth, and Peace throughout my entire being, which coalesces with my solid faith and belief in healing any negative after-effects of anyone (including myself) from past lifetime love-denied or love-loss experiences.

Theme 5- 'Ultimate Healing Strategy via Perfection that Lies Within' (in text: 'I AM', as the name of God that lies within each of us as 'Soul')

Recognition and belief in the perfection that lies within each of us, (i.e., our 'Soul'), is the keystone for the initiation of all healing, which will eliminate the effects of all past Negative Prompters, i.e., negative feelings such as lack, limitation, unhappiness, guilt, fear, remorse, doubt, loneliness (U. Andersen).

Uell Andersen's only major lifetime book, "Three Magic Words," reveals near the end of his work the actual three magic words as, 'You Are God', meaning that our 'Source' or God exists within each of us as our spiritual essence or 'Soul', which is the vital part of our whole being (composed of body, mind, and 'Soul'). God, or our 'Source', does not lie out in space somewhere distant from us.

Two additional magic words coming from the ancients (Moses, et al.) representing the formal self-definition or name of God, or 'Source', as 'I AM' (or 'I am'), which has the implied, defined meaning of God within each of us as our spiritual essence or our 'Soul'.

Note that the 'I AM', and 'You are God' are similar and can be combined, in that 'I AM', the name of 'God' or our 'Source' has the presence within us as our 'Soul'. This is like 'You are God', meaning 'God' existing within each of us as our 'Soul', part of our whole being composed of body, mind, and 'Soul'. Therefore, for this Theme 5, we can combine these two as: 'I AM'.

Three additional magic words that define the Infinite within each of us: 'Infinite Love and Power'.

Two additional magic words that define the Infinite within each of us: 'Infinite Warmth'.

Three other magic words that define our Infinite Source: 'Infinite Perfection and Clarity'.

Three additional magic words that define God or our Source: 'Infinite Power and Peace'.

Three additional magic words: 'throughout my Being', defined as both our incarnate body and mind, and Infinite 'Soul'.

Taking Andersen's concept 'You Are God' along with Moses's 'I AM', and combining the two as 'I AM', and combining this with the five other word groups: 'Infinite Love and Power'; 'Infinite Warmth'; 'Infinite Perfection and Clarity'; 'Infinite Peace'; and 'throughout my Being', gives us: 'I AM Infinite Love, Power, Warmth, Perfection, Clarity, and Peace throughout my Being', providing the beginnings of a very powerful tool for whatever we may want to ask from our Infinite Source, such as perfect health and wellness, healing from any illnesses, healing from any negative residual carry-over effects from earlier lifetime difficulties, finding a new loving relationship, finding a new job, or for any other good wish.

Whenever there is a life problem that is challenging or bothering me, I immediately withdraw internally to my inner self for thought, reflection, and meditation on the power of these magic words: 'I AM Infinite Love, Power, Warmth, Perfection, Clarity, and Peace throughout my Being'. I reflect on these words along with the particular wish or problem to be resolved, e.g., (a) resolution of some illness, ache, or pain; or (b) peace of mind after a difficult issue has arisen at work, home, or in my life. I repeat these magic words several times with whatever wish I desire or problem I want to be resolved and let them permeate my mind and inner self ('Soul') via meditation. And very slowly (for the Lord takes 'His' time) I become less worrisome and fearful, as if something magical coming from our Infinite 'Source' is helping me to obtain the wish or resolve the conflict or illness, which makes the challenge much smaller and more manageable.

If my problem involves another individual either because the person is ill or there is a conflict with them, I meditate and imagine with total love and healing, or forgiveness toward the person. I meditate: 'I AM Infinite Love, Power, Warmth, Perfection, Clarity, and Peace throughout my Being, conjoining with 'I AM Infinite Love, Power, Warmth, Perfection, Clarity, and Peace of my 'ill friend', or 'person of conflict', conjoining with 'the Infinite Love of the Unified 'One' or 'God' in the Universe'. This begins the move toward the healing of my friend, or conflict resolution with a particular person. Via meditation with this statement coupled with strong faith and belief, in time the desire, illness, or negativity generating the challenge gradually lessens and becomes much more manageable.

CHAPTER 4

REMOVING NEGATIVITY/ EVIL/EGO VIA THE INFINITE

Theme 1- 'The Origins of Negativity'

I have always been intrigued by this topic. Understanding it in human terms can get to the heart and soul of understanding almost all human suffering and tragedies, as well as the emotional after-effect hurt stemming from these traumatic events. The discussion and examination of the background of negativism, threat, and fear may also cast some clues on the roots of much human violence throughout history, including the mistreatment of children as well as adults. The fact that humans have intelligence that can be broadcast via language (voice) and non-verbal communication (via body language), and the fact that human survival means that the young from the very beginning infant stage must be taught the skill sets necessary for survival when they grow up and go out on their own, sets the stage for positive or negative support building modes in teaching these survival skills.

This would also apply to adult relationships with dealings in 'normal' everyday social, educational, and life-maintenance activities. It seems that most people very easily slide into the commonly used teaching or law-abiding methodology, namely the <u>threat</u> mode, 'if you don't do it this way, the result might be this bad or terrible thing happening'. When people speak about the survival game and the skill sets necessary to survive, it somehow seems easier to speak in terms of the negative or threatening consequences of not following certain procedures or rules to accomplish whatever task is requested or is necessary. This is in direct opposition to a more positive approach to accomplishing the specific task.

Have you ever noticed (as I'm sure you have) the negative-sounding drama, as well as the cataclysmic slant with much of the news on radio, television, in newspapers, and the internet? Disasters, murders, robberies, sexually pervasive attacks, dramas, as well as all sorts of fantasized disaster-related cataclysmic stories in the news and movies easily pervade and dominate these media. Negative, drama-related, and fantastic happenings seem to make the news and draw attention, as well as generate sales and profits via advertising. Positive happenings in the news are not as commonly discussed and are perceived by producers as well as audiences to have low ratings, to be low money makers, or to be somehow boring.

Our whole modern culture and society (i.e., products of history) are constructed with a slant toward dramas and excitement in the entertainment field, often portrayed via negative happenings like violence, crime, and catastrophes. Positive-sounding and informative educational programs are perceived to be not as exciting, and the 'ratings' easily prove that. The threat and fear that 'bad things' are happening or might happen are the order of the day, e.g., 'if you don't do this or that certain thing, you could be arrested, go to court, be fined, sued, prosecuted, or even sent to jail'.

Our educational system and culture, as well as many of those throughout the world, seem to follow the same negative slant, threat, excitement, or drama-sounding format. It is simply easier habit-wise to say something negatively or excitedly with the threat of fear than to say it positively. For example, to threaten someone with negativity or drama-based fear, versus trying to convince someone to do something good and useful by building on good works that help other people. Negative-sounding 'bites' seem to draw attention quicker and more readily than positively pitched projects, objectives, or goals. Perhaps this is because threats (fear-based) to survival are real, and almost any issue can be slanted by the culture or media as a threat, setting the stage for establishing a negative tonality rather than a more positive approach in responding to a particular crisis.

Humans beginning eons ago found out that they got more immediate human arousal and attention by putting something like a roadblock to survival and its consequences in a negative, threatening mode rather than in a more positive mode or framework. That is, it seemed easier to get on an immediate track 'to get things done' with negative-sounding threat statements. In primitive times going back hundreds of thousands of years, human survival very often depended upon an immediate response, which naturally seemed most readily addressed with threatening and negatively stated prescriptions. This was interpreted through experience by early humans as the fastest and most expedient way to get its survival-based needs most quickly attended to. It was perceived that threat forced action, whereas non-threat left the door open for human in-action or to countervail. The threat of death was the most extreme enticer to force or produce life-saving strategies and actions. Throughout history, most human cultures inculcated within their social structures the threat and fear syndrome as the best survival methodology to actually 'get things done'.

This thinking became easily infused into child-rearing methods over eons of time. Historically, these applications were pervasive throughout a vast majority of world cultures in that it was most readily determined that parents or caretakers give negative threats to the child on how to properly accomplish tasks, rather than use non-threatening methods to accomplish the same tasks. Since what occurred in the child's life became the mirror for its adult life, all negative emphases in childhood virtually became the modes in the adulthood behaviors of these same people. These negative prescriptions were inculcated throughout almost all world cultures over time. As a result, negative tonality in life was passed down through multitudes of generations: from parent to child, to grandchild, to great-grandchild, etc.

Before leaving this theme, mention should be made of emphasis in many of the world religions in promoting negativity instead of a more positive approach. It has been my observation from Catholicism and many Protestant faiths in their clear emphasis on mankind's penchant to commit 'sin' or 'evil acts' as opposed to emphasizing doing positive or good acts. These faiths, as well as others in the world, offer the threat mode for an ultimate at-death fate, e.g., a cleansing purgatory process, or worse still damnation to a permanent 'hellfire' for those who have led sinful lives. The fear generated from a lifetime of worry over 'salvation' (i.e., to a Heaven or Nirvana), or 'not' (i.e., to 'purgatory' or 'eternal hellfire') is sure to cast a negative pall of gloom on the psychologies and lives of many of the world's people, increasing their negativism.

Many prayers in these faiths seem to overshadow the emphasis on doing good deeds with an emphasis on sin, its constant threat to mankind, and the need to exculpate it. At the same time, these faiths seem to portray the overall thought that 'we are in this life to suffer' which explains many of the hardships and difficulties in life that go on in our world, instead of emphasizing from the pulpit the goal for the reality of a better lifetime of joy, happiness, and bliss. Once again, threat and fear are the prime 'modus operand' to bring notice and obedience to church precepts or rules, or societal needs. This perhaps reflects a throwback to man's past primitive state of constant threats to survival with associated fear and the need to utilize mechanisms to actually 'get things done as fast as possible' to best ensure survival for humanity.

Theme 2- 'Tuning into Removing Evil and Ego via the Spiritual Unity of Infinite Love'

All five of the contemporary authors and thinkers (including myself) discussed in Ch 3, Theme 1, 'Infinite Love Within and Positive Thinking', have at the root of each of their philosophies the stated and likely reality which is quoted directly from Uell Andersen's work, 'Three Magic Words':

'At the first discussion of evil, let us sensibly get rid of both the devil and hell. Make up your own mind that the intelligence behind the Universe does not destroy itself! The pain-ridden ideas of evil and hellfire as a place for punishment for sin are man's morbid ideas.'[64]

Uell's thinking is that all thoughts on evil and negativity come through man's imagination and his thinking, as God is not aware of the existence of these negative things. He adds that since people are brought into this world with free will capability, they are left to invent their own conditions including the events and happenings of evil and suffering. He goes on to say that the willingness to think purely positive thoughts is the basis for all human-related goals, accomplishments, and successes. [note 64] The suggestion is made, 'think with conviction, that whatever I want I already have, not I wish to have it, because admitting that I don't have it suggests and is a failure'. This thinking goes on to say: know the Universal Subconscious Mind, or God, for its Infinite Power, and learn to use this Power to fill our lives with good abundance. [n. 64]

From Universal mind and unity back in the Infinite State under the Unified 'One' with Infinite Love, purity, and clarity, we come into this life all different and separate within a physical body. And throughout our incarnate life existence here we reach out to receive and give, to commune and love, only to return at the end of this life to Infinite Love and Unity. Love governs all and is the supreme law of life. Above all other things we seek love, and from that is derived the prime basis for all positive healing. On the other hand, all our hurts, i.e., negative 'prompters', are produced when our reaching for or giving love is rejected.[65] Negation of love produces the greatest prompter of all, namely fear, which generates hatred, leading to evil. But love overcomes all and dissolves all fear, hate, and evil. True love is recognizing the spiritual unity of all life. Once a person realizes that we are all part of the 'One', there can be no hatred. Positive health comes from positive thinking and mental peace; and mental confusion, negative thinking, conflict, and stress cause the onset of many illnesses, diseases, and poor health among people.[66]

Uell discusses the human ego, born with each human to best promote the physical survival of that individual. The effects of that ego result in conflicts of fear, hate, futility, bitterness, and negative thinking that move us away from perfection. These negative effects go into the Universal Subconscious Mind, which is then returned to the body with all sorts of physical bodily diseases. He claims that at least 80% of all these bodily diseases are mental in origin, formed by the conscious mind through our ego, which projects negativity from 'prompters' into the Universal Subconscious Mind, with these being returned into the physical world as sickness and disease.[67] He claims that the vast majority of people fall victim to disease through negative coping feelings that establish themselves through ego to deal with buried, painful memories of love that were formerly denied or lost. People need to replace these negative coping feelings with positive thinking and feeling, true love, and mental peace, along with doing good and useful thoughts and acts.

Wayne Dyer discusses the concept of ego in depth. He calls ego (or edging God out) a false sense of self. The ego is something that emerges with us after birth and expands thereafter through parents or caretakers and our culture. Ego trains and nags us through childhood to do our best, to compete, i.e., to get the best grades in school, to dress up the best, to be the best and win in sports, to win the highest honors scholastically and otherwise. And later on in adult life for us to be the most distinguished, earn the most money, have the best job, have the fanciest house on the block, and the most expensive car, etc.[68]

This emphasis represents the total opposite of staying in Spirit which we all consisted of before coming into this life. Spirit suggests and reminds us that we all share the same life force with everyone and everything in existence. Human culture and ego do just the opposite: we are all created differently from everyone else, therefore, we must compete to defeat others and accumulate what they possess as ours, or else we will feel negative or defeated. In other words, the ego says that we are in this life to defeat everyone else, we are what we acquire, and if we have or want little, then we are of very little value. Also, ego claims that we are what other people think of us, and if our reputation is tarnished at all we are even of less value. note 68

We are all indoctrinated with these values from day one in this life: from parents or caretakers, family, church, school, culture, friends, adversaries, our work, and the media. We are all nagged to 'fit in' or 'to compete' to accomplish everyone's dream of big status with tremendous earnings, wealth, and possessions. I have personally encountered certain groups of people from my life experiences whose whole focus in life seems to center around amassing big status, money, and material possessions, in that the quality of human relationships centers around competition over obtaining the maximum of 'things'.

Wayne recommends that the ego must be attacked, destroyed, and silenced. [69] Ego denies our original Spiritual perfection, which is what we were before this life, so it must be denied and replaced with the reality (contrary to the 5 senses) that we are Infinitely and eternally made of (Infinite) Love. Ego is not real, but our Infinity and perfection are. In dealing with the conflicts and trouble caused by ego, Wayne's suggestion is:

> 'I look for a way to be like God and stay loving, caring, forgiving, and peaceful within myself, suspending my need to be right, and knowing that in the next moment, it will all be gone, which is true of everything that's being played out in this illusory world.'[70]

When it seems like ego has convinced someone that Spirit or Infinite Love is absent, he suggests that the person continually remind themselves that there is no place in the Universe devoid of Spirit, that everything and every one is composed of Spirit either before, during, or after becoming manifest in physical form. [note 69]

Theme 3- 'Origins of Satan, Judgment at Life's End, and Hell' (In-text: 'I AM', the name of God that lies within each of us as 'Soul')

What if the meaning of this theme's title, depicting the dark side of God's Infinite Universe which many of us have been led to believe exists from Western religious training, can be exactly likened to man's imaginative creation of the dark side in the popular movie series, 'Star Wars'? Within our own real story of Christianity, the power of a 'Good side', 'Divine Intelligence', or 'Infinite Loving God' ruling throughout the Universe has been layered with a tradition of an opposite evil side in the same Universe consisting of 'Negativity', 'Evil', 'Satan', and 'Judgment' at life's end for many to a 'Purgatory' or worse still damnation to an eternal 'Hell'. What if the story of the 'Evil Empire', 'Darth Vader', and the 'Dark Side' in the popular Star Wars Series is precisely analogous to the 'Evil Side', 'Satan', and 'Judgment Day' from our Christian religious tradition? In other words, both the Dark Side in the Darth Vader Star Wars Series and our Christian tradition of the Evil Side and Satan are merely fictitious concoctions and inventions of human imagination.

We have already discussed Uell Andersen's contention from his work, "Three Magic Words," that the Divine Spirit, Infinite Intelligence, or God, together with Its associated Infinite Spirit does not know of things such as Satan, Hell, or evil. He further asks how an all-good Infinite Spirit could ever create or allow evil that would threaten to destroy itself. Uell goes on by implying that these words about evil with their associated meanings have been simply invented by humankind in this worldly state. The other authors discussed herein, including Neville Goddard, Wayne Dyer, Florence Shinn, and Anita Moorjani would lean in the direction of confirming Uell's contention that all negativity with its associated epithets such as 'Satan', associated 'Evil', and 'Judgment at life's end' have been created via free will by humankind.

My prior work, "Love and the Infinite, Healing from Childhood", focused on 'difficult' childhoods that many people have suffered from historically, with these very often having occurred due to some sort of caretaker abuse or mistreatment. I ponder at this point to ask: how much effect does the discussion over the past few thousand years on the existence of 'Satan', 'Judgment' at life's end, and eternal 'Hell' for many, had on how certain world cultures relate to child-raising related teachings and practices? Do threat-related teachings on the existence of evil, 'Satan', and 'Hell' create underlying feelings of threat, fear, and negativism, leading to an atmosphere of dominance and oppression in the ordinary undertaking of dealing with and raising children? What if all these evil, 'Satan', 'Hell', and 'Judgment Day' related teachings are creations of mankind's imagination to create threat, power, and control over human behavior, particularly in dealing with the raising of children?

What if the teachings about 'Hell' and 'Satan' with threats of 'eternal damnation' in the afterlife are false, that instead what lies ahead for each and all of us is admittance into an Infinite Spiritual State consisting of 'open welcoming arms', Infinite Love, acceptance, and bliss? What if this is the truth? If so, how would this affect our everyday sense of feelings? Would changing the woeful doom of negativity from threats of damnation in the afterlife to more hopeful realities of bliss at life's end change the entire dynamics of human behavior toward power and authority, particularly in dealing with children? Would this have other positive offshoot spinoffs or ramifications as to how we as adults behave towards other adults in this life, i.e., how we treat each other during adulthood?

It is quite true that the words of negativity, evil, and badness, along with what is taught and said with words and concepts about Satan and Hell, really do exist. But these negative insignias or epitaphs more than likely have been created by free will choices of humans within this life, not by 'Infinite Intelligence', 'Source', or 'God', nor are these a part of that Infinite Spirit's Infinite Loving Universe. We (mankind) can willingly through free will create either a 'hell' or a 'heaven' on earth. It is strictly our choice that presents and manifests evil, including the words that describe it, yet just as easily and alternatively, we can <u>choose</u> to promote the positive and good, with noble words and deeds within this life.

What this implies is that there may well be no such judgment or punishment awaiting many of us on the 'Other Side' such as a special 'Judgment Day' or an eternal 'Hellfire' led by 'Satan.' Instead, what could await us is total acceptance, understanding, compassion, euphoria, and bliss from an Infinitely Loving 'Source' or 'Intelligence' whose love for us is far greater in magnitude than we could ever imagine or understand. What if this is true? And if it is true, what does this do to the fires of threat, fear, and negativity that we humans constantly infuse into our culture and teachings which result in so many negative and threatening consequences throughout our daily lives here?

I reflect on a 'supposed' saying by Jesus recorded in the Scriptures to the effect that 'it would be easier for a camel to go through the eye of a needle than for a rich man to enter into the Kingdom of God', implying that it would be difficult, particularly for someone wealthy, to enter thru those Pearly Gates into Heaven. To add to this there is an offshoot, yet popularly taught iteration of the same parable in Christian tradition implying that the road to Heaven for all (i.e., rich, middle class, and poor) is indeed difficult, in that only a select few who live excellent human lives will eventually make it through that narrow 'needle's eye' into the eternal Heavenly State.

From this, I ask: how much does all this doleful tradition and teaching intensify fear, doubt, competition, greed, distrust, and negativism in peoples' common everyday lives? What if these supposed teachings (of <u>other</u> authors in the guise of Jesus) are deliberate misrepresentations or concoctions made up to scare people into obeying Church authority, the Commandments, or other 'teachings'; or to instill fear, discipline, and control over children; or exert authority, power, or control over adult people at-large?

If it be true, and people were made aware that only perfect (Infinite) Love, compassion, understanding, and bliss faced all of us at the end of our physical life instead of fear over judgment with threats of eternal hellfire, might this make folks think and behave with more kindness, compassion, and love towards each other? Might this create a more peaceful, loving life for all of us here? Might it also cast a better and more positive light on attitudes, behaviors, and outcomes in best raising our children? In other words, what would the overall effect be of: 'no negative judgment at our life's end', 'heaven instead of purgatory or hell', and 'entry into a Nirvana State of acceptance and Infinite Love'? What if this is true?

For me, I know what it does: a gradual relief and release from the mental prison of underlying negative feelings, suspicions, and distrust I have always had over a whole lot of 'prescriptive' religious teachings with their effects on us in this life. For I know how fear, negative thinking, and non-love get generated, (i.e., directly from mankind), and can understand that. With this realization, as the days pass, I distinctly feel less fear and stress by feeling better, relieved, and prepared to know that the all-good is <u>not</u> too far away and that it embraces and envelopes me even while still being in this life. Knowing this, I find myself feeling a growing release and freedom. Each time I re-read this I feel a growing reassurance, along with feeling better psychologically, knowing that the only 'judgment' reality facing me (and each of us) at death will be the open arms of a gentle, accepting, and Infinitely Loving 'Spirit', 'Source', or 'God' with reassurance that we are each <u>fully</u> worthy of being in 'His' hands. This should make me (as it should all of us) feel more confident with all that we have yet to endure going forward in this life.

CHAPTER 5

COMMON HUMAN ACTIVITY CONNECTS WITH INFINITE LOVE ENERGY

Theme 1- 'Initial Spontaneity and Excitement at the Beginning of New Love Relationships'

I awoke from a sleep one recent morning with some inspirational thoughts about our 'spiritual cores', 'essences', or 'Souls'. It seems evident that at birth we all had lost contact with our spiritual core or essence, and throughout many people's conscious lives it remains largely hidden or lost. From the time of our birth, or even before in the human fetus stage, each of us was wrapped up in the struggle for the physical survival of our bodily existence. Cognizance of any kind of spiritual core inside of us during those early days of our lives was not identified to us nor remembered. We somehow came into this world completely detached from all awareness of our pure 'essence', 'Soul', or spiritual part. Because of this, it does not appear that any of us were given real clues or opportunities on how to directly reconnect consciously with this hidden spiritual part except (as we grew up) through certain religious organizations, their practices, and traditions. These religious systems were supposed to help us reconnect with our spiritual part, and often they did somewhat. But, with Western religious traditions in particular, the precept of the 'Soul' or spiritual essence within us as being potentially vital, active, and helpful to us during this life has been very much downplayed throughout history.

My awakening inspiration, after focusing on our birth situation and loss of spiritual awareness, turned toward concern over the common and good goals in loving relationships between males and females, and what typically happens at the beginning of most relationships. What this means is the initial aura that most folks have with excitement, positive emotions/feelings, elation and joy, euphoria, and in many instances sexual attraction. But as time marches on in typical relationships, many of these initial positive and exciting emotions fade or get 'clouded over' with all the typical pressures of human egos and responsibilities of social and economic life. These things include marriage and raising a family, family-related health issues, getting an education, amassing money, jobs, careers, owning houses and cars, and paying bills and taxes, (i.e., all the mundane human factors). My thoughts focused on the fact that somehow the initial euphoria, excitement, spark, and positive energy in relationships need to be further fostered and continued. Typical responsibilities of ordinary human life do not appear to foster the continuance of this initial excitement and elation of love. And it is clear from social statistics that many long-term relationships, including marriages, do not last.

I think that this initial 'spontaneity' or excitement often experienced at the beginning of love relationships is somehow a meshing or meeting of energy between each partner's spiritual essence, or 'Soul', which somehow relates or connects with energies from the Infinite 'Source' Side. This 'spontaneity' could represent a throwback of energy, vibrations, or memories from within each person's 'Soul' (in the relationship) from their past, i.e., perhaps their Infinite State of existence before being born into this life. Remember, that our 'Soul' or spiritual essence has always accompanied (or has always been) us. Have you ever noticed how babies (infants) seem so enthusiastic about freely exploring, sensing, and touching their new surrounding environment? Being brand new here, they carry a direct, recent touch and connection from encounters or energies from their very recent Infinite past. This same sort of enthusiasm and exploration seems very apparent in so many new intimate human relationships.

In this connection, it might be speculated that the <u>source</u> of the euphoria, excitement, positive emotions, elation, and joy at the beginning of many love relationships could well be the result of Infinite Love energy harbored within each person's 'Soul' in the new relationship. The coalescence of this Infinite Love energy between each member's 'Soul' in the new relationship could well explain the offshoot of highly elated physical-related excitement and bodily joys.

If this initial 'psychic clicking' of excitement could somehow be maintained, relationships would fare much better in the long run. Since humans do have a powerful reserve of intuitive awareness of other people, and our spiritual components could well create a high sense of awareness and excitement when people first meet, the opportunity exists for nurturing and extending these beyond the initial excitement into the longer-term relationship. This would represent tying the couple together as a two-person spiritual architecture that would endure and last. Since our world through the normal course of human events and obligations does not lend itself well to nurturing this spiritual aspect, we need to foster the continuance of any initial spontaneity (energy) for each couple through awareness, love, spiritual prayer, meditation, and participation in activities that both enjoy. One thought that I have had on enhancing the quality of spiritual sharing for couples is for each person in the relationship to develop a greater awareness for sensitivity and tenderness towards the other's emotions, and to mutually share thoughts on these in a gentle, easy, understanding, loving, non-competitive, and non-egotistical manner.

I have often reflected in my own life that there are certain activities that I have enjoyed doing from the earliest times of my childhood to the present day. For instance, being by/experiencing water (lake or ocean), tropical vegetation and flowers, warm temperatures, exploring new places, shining flashlights in vast dark spaces, having cats as pets, tending to flowers, plants, and veggie gardens. These joyfully enhanced interests and activities could somehow have their origin and linkages to euphoric encounters or energies experienced in my prior Infinite State existence. It is well remembered at the start of both of my long-term relationships which eventually ended up in marriage, of combining certain of my favorite interests with those of my partner and enjoying doing either or both of our favorite activities together. But then, with the emergence of typical families and pragmatic lifetime responsibilities along with their inherent social expectations, continuing to do these things as a couple pretty much faded in the wind.

I wonder what would happen to the durability of relationships if the emotions of elated 'first love' euphoric feelings from shared energy via each partner's 'Soul' could be extended beyond the start of the relationship by nurturing a joint sharing of favorite activities, tender emotions, and prayer or meditation. Perhaps conscious awareness of this along with intending the creation of an Infinite connection between each partner (via the 'Soul' of each) represents an important first step. Importantly, this would be applying what authors Neville Goddard, Wayne Dyer, and Uell Andersen discuss in connecting to the energy of 'the God within' each person. Going beyond this would be the intent of each partner to combine their energies as 'One' for the couple through this joint sharing and enjoyment of activities, emotions, and spiritual prayer or meditation*. This would have the flavor of <u>combining</u> the spiritual essences and bodily related qualities of both, which I see as intensifying the reality and enjoyment of

---

* Spiritual sharing can occur when two people together (as a couple) conduct their meditation using the 'Japa' technique at a nice outdoor spot, or elsewhere (see lower p 140 & p 141).

real true unconditional love in the relationship, in conjunction with allowing each partner to develop increasingly closer ties with our Infinite Source.

Theme 2- 'Other Infinite-Side Spillover Influences Affecting Human Activities'

My prior work, "Love and the Infinite, Healing from Childhood," revealed the reality of imaginative love scenario encounters I had experienced over many decades, with the reasoning that these were the result of maternal love (i.e., closeness and cuddling) denied during my very earliest years. This lack of closeness likely occurred because my mother suffered both mentally and physically during and after her pregnancy with me. It should be pointed out from my past readings in the child psychology field, that many men who suffered under the yoke of a mother who withheld maternal closeness and love from them during their earliest years have typically had great difficulties with staying in long-term man-to-woman relationships.

Other recent insights of mine present a far different possible picture, which along with lack of maternal love early on in life may play an additional role in my case, as well as contribute to the widespread sociological problem of people desiring multiple partners on an intimate basis at the same time. Many new-age spiritual thinkers and writers have talked about the Infinite State being Unified as 'One' (I call it the 'Ultimate Singularity'), where everything in the Universe exists as equal and Unified under an umbrella of 'One'. This contrasts with the worldly state where everything in this life is separated into right versus wrong, white vs. black, good vs. bad, male vs. female, equal vs. unequal, married vs. unmarried, etc. Most love in this worldly state, including romance, is conditional in that you must earn it, i.e., 'if you do this or that for me, I'll love you, but if you don't, I will not'. But all Love in the Infinite State is unconditional and Infinite and consists of total acceptance, equality, and joy without any conditions, (e.g., you do not have to work at 'earning' it) and is absent of any evil. Also, all beings and Love in the Infinite State are unified as 'One' and not separated into various categories or compartments like here in this life.

One rather interesting and intriguing sidelight insight with this is that the sharp differentiation and competition between males and females which so often occurs with many types of relationships in this life, particularly with close one-on-one relationships, is likely completely absent within the Infinite State since there we are all defined as equal and Unified under the Infinite Umbrella of 'One'.

We came into a state in this life whereby love is very different than it was back in the Infinite State. Here we must 'work to earn love', thereby maintaining that love largely occurs on a 'give-and-take' conditional basis, plus the fact that romantic love with male-female or one-on-one relationships is tied up with all sorts of conditional rules and expectations. These rules and expectations are supposed to create and maintain civil/social order in controlling physical and sexual activities between people, maintain a stable environment for raising children, and follow prescripts taught by various religious and cultural traditions. All these prescriptions, restrictions, and limitations very likely do not exist in the Infinite State.

I feel that when we were in the Infinite State Side before our life here, we all had great flexibility in freely meshing our friendships there, which embraced and shared perfect Infinite Love along with associated involvements between spiritual friends within that energy state of existence. This free sharing of Love was far greater in magnitude and dimension in comparison with any sort of love sharing (including romantic love) that people typically experience in this life. Of course, it must be assumed that (Infinite) Love within the Infinite State is completely devoid of any sexual love or other bodily-physical contact aspects since there is no body or physical existence on the Infinite Side.

It could be speculated that when we arrived here within this worldly state, we each carried vestige memory imprints within our spiritual essence (or 'Soul') of the huge dimension of flexibility we once possessed with friendships on the Infinite Side. Mirroring freely flowing activities with a multitude of unconditional Infinite love-sharing spiritual partners and encounters on the Infinite Side, these vestige memory imprints may translate for many of us as unconsciously generated urges to have multi-friendships or partners here. This would include possible intimacy with people in addition to the one-on-one 'for life' relationships that most of us are tied to with worldly rules for marriages or long-term relationships. In other words, our human-cultural emphasis on being tied to one-on-one (e.g., male-to-female, or even same-sex) lifelong romantic relationships perhaps (or likely) goes against the 'grain' of the realities on the Infinite Side. That Side offers a very fluid, dynamic, and flexible 'meshing' of Infinitely Loving beings engaging in ethereal related experiences, energies, or events with each other within a spiritually Loving 'Unified One' energy state of existence.

What crosses my mind is that vestige memories from our prior Infinite State existence may play a role in the onset of depressive thoughts or even neuroses, particularly with certain people who have suffered past love-denied or love-loss situations earlier in their lives here. These people face the monumental task of re-creating true unconditional love that has somehow been denied to them earlier on in their lives here. This is 'tickled' somewhat by vestige, unconscious memory imprints (via their 'Soul') of fantastic, euphoric, and joyful Infinite Love ethereal experiences with spiritual friends back in their previous Infinite State of existence. Remember that our 'Soul' within us now existed back then in the Infinite State as wholly us.

It is as if our Infinite part, namely our eternally existing spiritual essence ('Soul'), acts as an energy receiver, recorder, and transmitter, (e.g., like a 'Wi-Fi', or Memory Chip), to receive, store, and send vestige memory images or energy vibrations that reflect parts of our prior Infinite State existence. These images or energy vibrations then get transmitted and translated via our powers of mental awareness and perception into our minds, affecting resultant actions in our present physical state. It seems that we are <u>not</u> consciously aware that this is happening, since these residual 'effects' are the result of vestige imprint memories or energies retained from a completely different energy dimension, namely our Infinite past.

In this connection, pleasant, positive, or productive activities that people typically engage in within this life such as enjoyment of nature, artworks, music, and movies; collecting, buying, or selling things; or producing artworks, music, or writings may represent Infinite-side related energy signals or memories. These signals/memories transfer via their 'Souls' into their minds, for people to conduct in this life positively related activities that render relaxation, enjoyment, or creations of various sorts. These signals may represent vestige memory imprints (within the 'Soul') of energies or encounters from our Infinite Side past. Or perhaps Neville's idea of human imagination plays in here, which would tap into the Infinite Divine and return to any of us as energies that create thoughts to pursue certain good, relaxing, enjoyable, or useful activities in this life.

If a past trauma victim has had difficulties in successfully creating true love opportunities in this life, this coupled with 'ticking' vestige memory imprints (via 'Soul') from their prior Infinite State existence of Infinite Love and joy could create frustration or conflict in that person's mind. This could set into motion negative energy vibrations leading to alienation, depression, or even worse (e.g., suicidal) thoughts. In the same vein, I wonder if the factor of experiencing repeated and severe trauma very early on in a person's life (i.e., during infancy) might have particularly damaging follow-up consequences for that person. This is because the tiny infant has so recently emerged from its prior Infinite Loving State existence into a bodily state (via birth) with an opposite situation of extreme trauma and suffering. These extreme opposite contrasts between each state clashing so closely together may very well be overwhelming for that small infant. As a result, damaging consequences such as bipolar illness, other mental illnesses, or other serious maladies could often follow that infant and develop in their later childhood or adulthood lives.

I have a serious hunch that spillover vestige memory imprints (via 'Soul') from our Infinite State past can unconsciously affect our daily lives much more than we consciously realize. For instance, I have observed the popular 'pop' music recording culture in America over the past 80- 90 years which has produced many artist recordings that focus on love relationships between men and women. These recordings portray imaginative themes of near-perfect, harmonious love scenarios, which often attempt within the music lyrics to overshadow or smokescreen typical troubled situations in many actual human-love relationships.

It does strike home to me that a lot of these music lyrics, which in and of themselves stir deep emotions, may be simulated via vestige memory imprints (energy vibrations) stored within the music composer's spiritual essence (or 'Soul'). Somehow, these reflect possible past Infinite energies and/or encounters from their prior Infinite State existence. These Infinite memory energy vibrations then get transmitted from their 'Soul' into the composer's mind, facilitating ideas for the creation of their music and accompanying themes. In the same vein, it seems that certain forms of music stir deep, euphoric emotions in many music listeners. These deep feelings could well indicate vestige 'connections' within their 'Soul' of memories/related energies from their prior Infinite State existence. Euphoric feelings experienced at a highly elevated level from the music could well be an indicator of vestiges of Infinite Love energy existing within this life (via 'Soul').

Similarly, our Infinite memory receiver and recorder (i.e., our 'Soul') may very well harbor vestige memories that affect our everyday lives in this physical life from the standpoint of the perfection that each of us was embellished with back on the Infinite Side. Conflict in our minds likely comes when these past vestige memories of perfection directly clash with the stark reality of <u>imperfections</u> that we all constantly face in this physical life. All of us spend so much time and effort in this physical life attempting to correct, change, or 'perfect' these imperfections as much as possible, which generates tremendous frustration for many of us. This is because perfecting or correcting these 'this-worldly' imperfections proves to be such a difficult task at best.

This would be another significant contributor to generating so much negativism or a negative attitude for people in this life, (a factor to add to Ch. 4, Theme 1). Our awareness of the conflict generated by imprinting Infinite memories of perfection contrasting with stark realities of imperfections in this life would be important in thwarting or reducing the intense frustration over the 'drive to be perfect' in this life, which so often consumes many people's lives. This 'drive to be perfect' includes attendant negative effects such as over-competition, ego-greed, dominance over others, bad habits, restlessness, and general unhappiness, all of which create so much misery in our social relationships, work, and everyday living situations.

So, any 'tickling' of vestige memory imprint energies (via our 'Soul') from our prior Infinite State existence can have an immediate positive or negative mental and/or emotional effect for any of us within this life. This would be contingent on our circumstances when this 'tickling' of Infinite memory occurs, particularly our feelings and state of mind (positive or negative) within this life at a certain point in time. That is exactly why stress is placed on our creating <u>positive</u> thinking and feeling concepts suggested by the authors in Ch. 3, Theme 1, as well as throughout other parts of this work. In other words, it is so important to be on the positive side in all our conscious thinking and feeling as much as humanly possible.

Theme 3- 'Personality Spillover Influences and Other Interests from Our Infinite Past'

During my life, I have often reflected on a phenomenon frequently observed whereby the offspring of children in a family of the same parentage typically display notable dissimilarities in personalities, motivations, interests, and occupations during their lives. Some geneticists would claim that instead, each child from the same parents should be distinctly more similar than dissimilar. But this isn't the case.

Our human behaviors are made up of a complex of past and present effects on each of us, which consist of (1) culture; (2) personality; (3) archetype; (4) parental or caretaker upbringing; (5) spirituality. Personality can be defined as a particular individual's 'persona' or imprint of uniqueness, delineated by body-mind individualities consisting of both genetic and familial-biological background which includes behavioral makeup, with a possible spiritual connection to one's prior Infinite State of existence. At this point, I strongly feel that one's connection with the prior Infinite Side is probably quite important in establishing individual personality differences. It seems that many of these traits follow from our Infinite past and represent a consciousness that has been carried forth here from that State of existence. Of course, influences from a particular person's cultural history, social background, archetype, parents or caretakers, and other peoples' interactions that affect them during their upbringing and development can also play key roles in personality development in this life.

Experiences from childhood can strongly influence our emotional balance, (i.e., either positive or negative feelings and emotions), often setting the tone for conscious and subconscious thinking during adulthood, subsequently affecting the actions and experiences of each adult person. Underneath these layers of feelings, emotions, and consequent experiences are special interests, motivations, and enthusiasms that demonstrate distinct differences between individuals. Geneticists might once again claim that these can be explained by anatomical-biological differences between individuals, which are all part of the evolutionary cycle of life equation that ensures diversity within the human species to best ensure its survival. Alternatively, I view this individuation of unique special interests, motivations, and enthusiasms as possibly influenced by vestige memory imprints within our ('Soul') of energy dimensions from the past, namely imprint memories from our prior Infinite State of existence.

Some would claim that our total physical existence consists of a series of multi-human lives, where each of us has been reincarnated many times through different bodily lives, which could explain the 'carry-over' of many of our unique special individual interests. Leaning instead more towards the belief in a one-physical life cycle reality for most people, I feel that often these unique traits came, via each of our spiritual essences (or Soul), in association with energies and encounters we experienced back in the prior Infinite State. We carry vestige Infinite memories of these energies/encounters from our Infinite past into this life (via our 'Soul'). For instance, my favorite activity of being by an ocean beach during summertime might have distinct energy-vibration similarities with associated energy encounters back in the prior Infinite State. That is, some kind of dimension of water and surroundings back there, but in a different, non-physical energy-related context, with an associated elevated energy 'feeling' of euphoria and pleasure like that experienced here when physically being present at an 'ocean and beach'.

What seems key is identifying similar 'energies' from their comparison in both states, rather than identifying and comparing specific places or activities in both states. For example, a special 'resonance' might occur when feelings and emotional energies from physical beach-going here somehow meet, mesh, or coalesce with similar highly joyful and euphoric energies that were experienced back in the Infinite Side. Our Infinite Spirit or 'Soul' picks up and identifies this coalescence from Infinite memory within (our 'Soul') and resonates/radiates a special sort of 'euphoric high' feelings through our mind and body when we engage in a particular activity (like beach-going) in this life. We developed and carried vestige memories of certain energies with us from our Infinite past into this life (via our 'Soul'), and when we engage in an activity here that enlivens or has similar energies, a special flavor of pleasurable 'euphoric high' bodily and mental feelings occur. It could be that this 'coalescence' of energies from both states leading to highly euphoric feelings in this life represents a key indicator of the presence of Infinite Love.

To carry this discussion further, a favorite and common activity for many people relates to exploration of all sorts, including traveling to or exploring new places, and developing new ideas. Developing new ideas includes inventing new, novel, or different things, e.g., products, technologies, gadgets, communications, and media, which include the writing of books with new and novel approaches, or creating music, artwork, or handicrafts—all 'exploratory' and/or 'creative' type activities. Perhaps, my work herein would fit into this framework as well. This common exploratory or creative interest and drive that a lot of folks demonstrate in this life could very well represent creative throwback 'energy' replications of similar type energies encountered back in their prior Infinite State of existence. In other words, many of us in our prior Infinite State existence encountered energy dimensions of an exploratory or creative context, with vestige memory imprints of these (via our 'Soul') providing the springboard for producing similar energy vibrations through certain activities in this life. This results in accomplishing certain exploratory, creative, or inventive activities, which create euphoric feelings of satisfaction and pleasure.

Have you ever noticed how babies and very young children like to explore, driving the adults around them crazy, by touching or trying to handle everything in reach and putting 'hand to mouth' with all sorts of objects/substances, all in a seeming maze of curiosity and wonderment of their new world surroundings? In raising two children of my own, I have witnessed this same phenomenon first-hand with stunning amazement and have pondered the incredible thought that perhaps many of these seemingly free desires of exploring all sorts of things early on in their lives represent carryovers of memories. These memories represent images carried within their 'Soul' depicting exploratory experiences or energies encountered back in their very recent past Infinite Side existence.

Another activity or interest of note that stands out, which could have particularly close ties with activities or related energies from the Infinite Side, would be the various spiritual type activities that many people engage in here. This would include memberships in religious, church, or other organizations with associated worship, prayer, or meditative activities, along with raising funds, giving alms, or conducting activities and programs to help the poor and unfortunate. The intent and participation in these activities with their associated emotional energies could very well coalesce with vestige memories (via 'Soul') of similar spiritual energies encountered back on the Infinite Side. Part of the 'persona' or 'personality' of a person to be devotionally religious and/or spiritually engaging in this life could certainly have close ties with certain spiritually related energy dimensions encountered back in their prior Infinite State existence.

Because of possible contextual tie-ins between spiritual interests and energies with both states, we should reconsider author Betty Eadie's suggestion learned from her NDE (Ch. 2(B) Theme 3). Namely, that at any point in time, we should never criticize anyone's religious leaning, faith, orientation, organization, or developmental 'level' that is suggestive of a Loving and Good Higher Power, since this is suggestive of anyone's intent to have close ties with Infinite Loving Spirit.

Lastly, my recent thoughts reflect on the 'Magic of Christmastime' as representing an annual event that radiates dramatic, clear signals of highly euphoric, positive, and loving human spirit which offers unconditional love along with brief visages of Infinite Love. Over many decades, I have observed that during this happy holiday season, so many people set aside other people's misgivings and indiscretions through forgiveness, kindness, and expressions of love. To me, this closeness of good spirit and cheer is brought about by the annual presence of the spiritual influences of both Jesus and Santa to bring love, good tidings, cheer, and worldly hope to so many of the world's people. Love feelings and acts between people radiate special euphoric highs, joys, and pleasures, which represent the intent of the 'Almighty', or 'God' for mankind to embellish in loving activities. These could certainly be indicative of vestige signs of Infinite love-based wonders in this life, and a 'smidgen' of the joys we will enjoy in the next life.

CHAPTER 6

―――――――――――⟋⟍―――――――――――

MEDITATION PRACTICE AND HEALING

Theme 1- 'Preparation to Meditation for All People-Equality' (In the text: 'I AM' or 'I am' as the name of God who is within each of us as our 'Soul')

Prenote to Theme: 'Equality of all people who have ever lived' is the cornerstone of the author's view of where meditation should both start and lead. What opens the door to true healing for people is clear recognition through consciousness and belief in the equality of each person's body, mind, and 'Soul' with everyone else who has ever lived, which are all merged with all things in existence in the Universe under an umbrella of a Unified Infinite, All-Loving 'One' (or God). Belief in bodily spiritual equality for each of us as an integral part of this Infinite, All-Loving 'One' (or God) represents a 'golden' key for opening the door to healing remnants of earlier lifetime challenges that still haunt many of us now in our mind memories. The healing arriving through that door comes with a person touching the Infinite via certain meditation practices or techniques (see Ch. 6, Theme 2).

To get each of us ready for meditation, let us imagine that we are part of a group of people who know each other, (e.g., perhaps a counseling growth group that meets periodically), in an amenable room, sitting comfortably in chairs, preparing for a group spiritual exercise. I would ask each of us to imagine raising a hand to our heads as if we were preparing to take off a dress hat, baseball cap, or whatever other hat that we might envision to be on our heads. While doing this, imagine for a moment that this hat represents for each of us an ego-type representation that we carry in our ego-suitcase of life that identifies our character with other folks whom we regularly interact or have contact with, in whatever activity we may be sharing with them. As we imaginatively remove that hat from our heads, we are symbolizing to ourselves and each other that we are coming into this spiritual exercise as 'equal' partners. We were all born with spiritual equality via each person's 'Soul', meaning being equally capable of loving and being loved. Although each of our lives after our birth may not have continued in that spirit of equality, since we are engaging in a spiritual meditation involving the Infinite, let us imagine that for this time we are symbolizing a return to that equality state.

Now, let us take off that hat, the one that best describes, represents, and symbolizes our ego state: that is, being a doctor, teacher, professor, psychiatrist, lawyer, boss, parent, head of a family or organization, guru, leader of a project or group, or whomever/whatever that ego identification might represent. Let us imagine for the moment that we are all together in this room and are all equal in the sense of being equally capable of loving each other, by both giving and receiving back that love as we would define it in an unconditional sense. In this connection, each of us needs to imagine that we are all equally capable of unabated empathy and compassion toward each and all the others in our group.

We want to feel equal in being able to reach within our own 'Soul', and with intention, willingly share the Infinite Love and compassion from within It with the Infinite Love and compassion existing within the 'Soul' of each member of our group. Conjoining these truly represents Infinite Love of 'Our Source' or 'God' under His umbrella of the Unified 'One' in the Universe. Manifesting strong belief and faith through our feelings in this fact of equality, that we are all equally capable of both loving and being loved unconditionally without any question or reservation, positively calls on strengthening our faith and connection with 'Our Source', God, or Infinite Intelligence. This sets the stage for embarking on the meditation process to best create true healing possibilities from all our past and present hurts.

As a 'sidebar' to the discussion of equality with its spiritual connections think for a moment of our Country and its great philosophical foundation under our Constitution with its mainstay of 'equality' for all people, no matter the race, sex, religion, persuasion, or character of each person. Think of the great 'I Have a Dream' speech by Martin Luther King delivered on that great day in August 1963, focusing on the freedom of all peoples from oppression. When I reread his speech, though the message was intended to reflect racial equality, especially for black people, I can also sense a strong spiritual message that speaks of equality and freedom for all people, no matter their race, circumstances, age, background, or whatever oppressions or challenges they might have faced in their lives. Doesn't this great speech consist of, in great part, the Infinite speaking and connecting Its Divine Intuition and Universal, Unified Intention of Infinite Love and Equality for all of us humans in our world, opening the door for all sorts of human healing? I think and believe so!

Reflecting on the rationale that creates racism in general, I see skin color or cultural differences as superficial in comparison to the effects of early-in-life childhood environmental and learning encounters from both the family and the wider group that influences each child. From my earlier work, Dr. Bruce Perry's suggestion expressed that adult attitudes and behaviors often mirror those learned and experienced in childhood, which get inculcated into the developing child's mind as memories of patterns of behavior and opinions that follow that same person throughout their adulthood.[71] Being raised in a particular environment and culture (e.g., Black, White, Asian, or whatever other) locks into the developing child's mind certain dominant behaviors and expectations of that culture.

Later in adulthood, experiencing new people and cultures proves to be foreign and new. These new experiences will often be difficult or uncomfortable for that person because of the imprints carried over within the memory templates of their mind from their own 'usual' culture that they were exposed to and became familiar with earlier in their lives. Most cultural and supporting educational systems 'lock-in' thought and behavior patterns favoring the culture that the person was brought up with, when in fact these systems should more freely and regularly promote contact, familiarity, respect, and love for other races, cultures, and groups from the very earliest childhood age.

Writing and thinking about the concept of equality from both a worldly and Infinite sense has resulted in my becoming more aware of a 'key' crucial insight that is directly applicable to both the central and overall purpose of writing both my prior work on child abuse and present work on meditation, which concerns Infinite Love and healing. From all my numerous readings and experiences over many years, it has become increasingly clear to me that at birth we came into this world equally capable of both loving and being loved, and when we die, we will all return to that same dual loving state. But within this life, equality in giving and receiving love somehow largely erodes because of lifetime imperfect experiences with love in conjunction with the negative influences of people's dominating and competing egos, with their often-resultant destructive effects on the sharing of true love acts between people.

We came into this life to experience these imperfections and to learn through adaptations of the human mind, senses, emotions, and imagination how to adjust and adapt to these life challenges. We accomplish this by recognizing love denials and losses affecting us, and through awareness and behavioral changes to institute actions that achieve or regain experiences associated with creating new and better (unconditional) love opportunities. But, at the end of this life, we will all return to the Infinite State of total Infinite Love and perfection. This life is only an infinitesimal piece of our total eternal existence.

We also came here to experience through our senses and emotions the difference or contrast between equality and inequality, unconditional and conditional love, and what these mean from human bodily and ego standpoints. We will carry the knowledge and meaning of these experiences and feelings with us into eternity. Many recent spiritual thinkers and writers often refer to the Infinite, or God, by using the Universal term 'One', meaning that everything in the Universe is Unified and composed of God. We are all part of that Unified 'One' state now and will remain as such throughout eternity. I for one feel that the concept of 'equality' of all people represents one the best examples in this life of what the term 'One' really means from the Infinite Side standpoint. This means that everything in both the worldly and Infinite States is merged and equal under an umbrella of the Unified 'One', namely the Infinite Love of the All-Good 'God', which comprises the entire Universe.

Within each of our spiritual essences (or Souls), Infinite Love and equality have been always maintained despite all the worldly circumstances of inequality and ego that may have affected our bodily existence. Our spiritual essence watched us while we were growing up and when we became adults, as many of us endured suffering at the hands of people and/or the environment that surrounded us. We were not being treated 'as equals' for so many reasons as mentioned in my earlier work and within this work. But each of our Infinite parts, or Souls, was present as a witness to all that was happening, at the same time being 'equal' with all other 'Souls' that have ever existed through all eternity. And each of our Souls maintained that equality (under 'One') despite the ego whims and sufferings imposed by the people around us, or the difficult environments that our physical bodies and minds had to endure. These hardships may have negatively affected our bodies and minds, but not our Infinite Loving parts (or 'Souls') which have existed as perfection and equal to all other Souls throughout eternity, including this life. The key reason why we are here in this life is to learn this, i.e., our Soul's perfection, equality (with all other 'Souls'), and indestructibility, and once we learn this, we move closer to embracing our All-Loving 'God' or 'Higher Power', along with Its Infinite Love and healing.

In the present-time mode, now that we are adults and have a clear focus on 'the track record' of what has happened to us during our lives thus far, we can choose by our thinking and feelings to take back our right to be equal in both body and mind. But each of our Souls has always remained equal under the 'One' throughout all our life difficulties and traumas of the past, are presently equal and will remain as such through all eternity. Recognizing the clear fact of merging bodily and spiritual equality for each and all of us represents a 'golden' key for opening the door to help heal the remnants of those earlier lifetime challenges that still haunt many of us now through our mind memories. What opens the door to true healing for a person is clear recognition through consciousness and belief in the equality of each person's body, mind, and 'Soul' with everyone else who has ever existed, which are all merged with everything in the Universe under an umbrella of a Unified Infinite, All-Loving 'One' (or God). Namely that:

- I AM equal in combined body, mind, and 'Soul' with everyone else who has ever been created and am merged with everything in the Universe under an umbrella of the Unified Infinite, All-Loving 'One' (or God).
- I AM Infinite Love, Power, Warmth, Perfection, Clarity, Peace, and Equality throughout my Being (repeat as needed). This transfers the energy of truth on the equality of combined body, mind, and 'Soul' with everyone else who has ever existed, in removing all inequality that one's mind might still harbor, imagine, or feel from all their past lifetime difficulties.

- This truth translates lost feelings of inequality into newly found feelings of acceptance and freedom due to total equality within and about oneself, as is true with every other person who has ever lived.

- This equality transforms (moves toward and results in) my healing. I AM ALL that I AM, and I AM equal to every other person who has ever lived, as in the same instant I AM merged, equal, and Unified with everything in the Universe under an umbrella of all-goodness of the 'One' or 'God'.

- 'I AM the Light' which coalesces with 'I AM the Light of all other people' who have ever lived.

Theme 2- 'The Science of Meditation Practice'

Prenote to Theme- This theme presents an overview of important meditation practices, and techniques, with their effects that the author has become familiar with in his practice. It also recounts how this practice has evolved over forty years. Significant healing has occurred for the author from the recent regular daily utilization of certain unique meditation techniques. Critical here with his practice is developing a closeness to God i.e., by making conscious contact with Him during meditation by blocking as many 'worldly' thoughts as possible from coming into his (or any person's mind). And for each of us, thousands of thoughts float through our minds each day. Priority meditation techniques used by this book's author to help block out incessant mind thoughts include (1) Transcendental Meditation (TM), pp 115-116 herein; (2) 'Getting in the Gap' and 'Japa' Technique and Medication (Wayne Dyer), pp 117-122, (3) Preparatory to Meditation: Exercises to Consider, pp 122-5; and specifically # 4- 'Using 'Japa' to Refresh', pp 124-5; (4) My Inputs to the 'Getting in the Gap' and 'Japa' Technique, pp pp 125-7; (5) Integrated 'Getting in the Gap' Closeness to 'Source' or 'God' Meditation, pp 127-133; (6) Subsection "Meditation Now & Going Forward- A Potpourri of Choices", pp 136-142; (a) Choice in Meditation- Maintaining Silence, p 136; (b) Innovations in My Practice- Doing Nighttime Meditation, pp

138-9; (c) Doing Meditation in Beautiful Settings in the Outdoor Environment, pp 139-142.

The Rationale Behind My Meditation Practice

One of the best works on this subject that the author has come across, which is very readable for the public, happens to be, "Secrets of Meditation, a Practical Guide to Inner Peace and Transformation," by davidji. The book explores a variety of reflective processes to help take one's mind off its daily routine of dealing with mundane worldly affairs, including thoughts, into a mind profile of reflection with quietude. Meditation awakens us to deeper, spiritual levels through the stillness of the body and mind through routine practice. Taking time daily to go within and access the pure awareness of being brings a person from activity to silence, from individuality to universality. Meditation represents a bath of the mind, allowing it to be refreshed and rekindled. This process increases one's capacity for love, peace, well-being, and happiness through creativity. Regular time spent in stillness and silence can open one up to the real depth of Universal essence and consciousness that lies within each of us. It should be noted that the historical personages and authors Henry Wordsworth Longfellow and Henry David Thoreau were both emphatic on the need for quiet space and time each day (or regularly) for every person to reflect by connecting to their Infinite part ('essence' or 'Soul') within themselves.

Regularly feeling the depth of this pure, unbounded consciousness has allowed me to spiritually progress to ever-expanding awareness, openness, deeper empathy, greater clarity, and an expanded connection with our 'Source' or 'God'. It has also clearly helped me through the process of healing from the early in-life difficulties that I once encountered. Reflecting on my case, plus becoming aware of the whole subject of child-related sufferings throughout the world, led me to the regular practice of meditation. Quoting davidji from his book, "Secrets of Meditation":

'Our moods, feelings, and emotions are multidimensional interpretations based on our conditioning--most of it is probably imprinted into our subconscious before we reach our teens'.[72]

This statement was certainly verified from major parts of my prior work on the effects of childhood challenges from mistreatment with their negative carry-over effects into adulthood. davidij's book "Secrets of Meditation, a Practical Guide to Inner Peace and Transformation", was designed to be a meditation owner's manual. The book begins by explaining the basic benefits of meditation, that there is scientific evidence that meditation can be an effective tool for stress management, pain relief, restful sleep, cognitive function, physical and emotional well-being, as well as getting us closer to our Source (or God). The fight-flight response is discussed in conjunction with ego, especially the 'fight' aspects which can amplify the destructive effects of a person's ego when it affects the physical and/or emotional well-being of others. The subject of ego is discussed as part of Chapter 4, Theme 2 herein. Meditation helps us to alleviate conflicts generated by the various human processes when associated with the ego.

What in a nutshell does the process of meditation do? According to davidji, we were all born enlightened, and when we die, we will all become the same way. But, from the time of birth, we have all been layered over with perspectives, interpretations, and conditionings that have almost entirely covered the initial purity, perfection, and pure consciousness that we had before birth. Since our birth, we have all had a lifetime of conditioning and 'cleansing' from parents or caretakers, siblings, aunts, uncles, grandparents, teachers, clergy, spouses, exes, coaches, bosses, and the like—layers upon layers of conditioning.[73] By the time we have reached mid to advanced age, we have all traveled far from that initial moment at our birth of perfect, pure, and Infinite enlightened perfection. But that Infinite, perfect part of each of us, (i.e., our core or 'Soul'), is still 'the each of us' at the center of our consciousness and existence, beneath all the layers of our human conditionings. Meditation permits a person to see visages of their pure, unconditional loving self, which gives each of us a deeper understanding of our real position in life relative to the eternal Infinite State. [note.73] Another quote from davidji:

> 'Each time you meditate, you get the opportunity to reach back and peel back more layers of that lifetime of conditioning, and you can dip your toes in, dip your fingers in—and reconnect to your unconditional self— your pure, whole, perfect, enlightened self. And each time you dip your toes in, you take back a thimbleful of stillness, and each time you dip your fingers in, you bring back a tweezer full of silence; each time you surrender to who you truly are in meditation, you take back an eyedropper full of your unconditional self'.[74]

There are many paths to oneness through meditation. The author davidji describes meditations lasting for days or weeks, to just simply 20 minutes or so per day. Of all practices, meditation is the easiest and most effective to experience present-moment awareness in an alert state, but also at the same time, a state of stillness and silence, bringing unity of one's physical self (emotion & ego) with their spiritual self.

The author davidji explores various meditative processes such as: **(1)** biofeedback, visual meditation, and sound meditation, which utilize various wavelengths such as beta, alpha, theta, delta, and gamma; **(2)** energy meditation, including the seven chakra centers of the body; **(3)** sensory meditation which uses one or more of the five senses to fully experience the present moment, e.g., listening to sounds, soft gazing, inhaling aromas, tasting, feeling with the hands (massage), and Yoga; **(4)** Buddhist meditation through practicing the guidelines of the 8-fold path in daily living while having an understanding of the 4 noble truths, leading a person to a higher level of consciousness and Nirvana; **(5)** mantra meditation (including primordial sounds) through repetitive sound vibrations, helping to suppress the volume of typical thought patterns from daily life, e.g., sounds such as: 'OM', or

'AHM' (the hymn of the Universe); or 'AH' (the sound of birth, life, and death*); or 'AREM' (the sound representing a particular birth month/year); **(6)** chanting meditation, e.g., Gregorian chants done by Trappist monks, or the experience davidji describes of drifting down the Mekong River in Northern Cambodia on a boat listening to one Buddhist monk after the other doing their individual meditative chanting along the shoreline.[75]

In summary, davidji suggests that there is 'no one shoe that fits all' concerning the best meditative process to choose or follow, as long as the practice induces stillness, peace, and a closeness to the unconditional loving Infinite Source or Spirit.[76] He has experienced and practiced almost all of the ones suggested above, and he presently focuses on a couple of these in his current active practice (refer to his website: www.davidij.com). Each person can develop their own methods, whichever they feel most comfortable with. One should be open to experimentation. I will very shortly explain my practice, which has changed and evolved somewhat over time.

Although I highly praise and recommend davidji's contributions and suggestions, along with Wayne Dyer's mentioned below, for getting one started in learning about the field of meditation and practice, there are quite a few other excellent works that have been published recently on meditation practice and techniques. What follows are 3 examples of books on recent 'best seller lists' for the reader to consider.

* Alternately, W. Dyer suggests … 'AH'… as a manifest of 'Japa' or the sound and name of God (p 118).

Current Examples of Meditation Processes and Techniques

Books:

(1) "Practicing Mindfulness, 75 Essential Meditations to Reduce Stress, Improve Mental Health, and Find Peace in the Everyday", by Matthew

Sokolov, Althea Press, Emeryville CA., 2018. The work stresses mindfulness applied to meditation which benefits or has meaning for a person (1) to have a better focus on the present moment; (2) to be able to see or visualize clearly or have clarity; (3) to let go of judgments; (4) to have an equanimous or balanced approach; (5) to allow everything to belong; (6) to cultivate mental awareness; (7) to have patience; (8) to be kind to and forgive oneself.[77]

Mindfulness in meditation can help a person (a) to reduce depression or PTSD (Post Traumatic Stress Disorder); (b) to curb angst, anger, and panic attacks; (c) to have feelings of contentment and ease; (d) to improve memory and focus; (e) to have physical health benefits; (f) to improve creative problem-solving abilities; (g) to have less loneliness; (h) to have better self-esteem. [note 77] Essentials in the proper practice of Mindfulness Meditation include: (1) making the time available (see Note* below); (2) creating a regular space or place; (3) having the intention to practice; (4) having a consistent practice (see Note* below); (5) sharing meditation with friends; (6) keeping a journal or notes for a record. [note 77]

The principal part of Mr. Sokolov's work consists of 75 practical and unique Mindfulness Meditation exercises, divided into 3 subsections: (I) 25 Basic Mindfulness Exercises; (II) 25 Feeling Overwhelmed Exercises; (III) 25 Mindful Moods Exercises. [note 77]

Note*: Of all Mr. Sokolov's six essentials to the proper practice of Mindfulness Meditation, the most challenging one for me (and probably for many folks) to achieve with any consistency has been 'making the time available' each day to carry out the meditation. For me (as well as for many others), preset times get easily compromised with the typical mundane pressures of daily living despite strong intentions to regularly meditate. So, a different tact was tried by me starting a few years ago by taking another activity that I do regularly, e.g., outdoor jogging, or dishwashing following the evening meal, and tagging onto the end of either one of those activities a 20-minute meditation. Other people that I know 'tag' their meditation onto the tail-end of their daily 'lunch hour' or 'work break'.

In this regard, another time for doing meditation has emerged for me over the past couple of years as increasingly important: doing my meditation at nighttime in bed just before falling asleep or upon awakening during the night. This is indeed quite unusual and new to the discussion in the meditation field. I have found that at nighttime with the prime habit and goal of sleep is the best time for minimal disturbing mundane activity or pressures to distract a person from doing their regular meditation. Really! As part of doing meditation at night, I've learned to quietly whisper mantras (with mouth open or closed) instead of using an out loud voice, to not disturb my partner. More on nighttime meditation, pp 138-9 below.

(2) "Practical Meditation for Beginners, 10 Days to a Happier, Calmer You", by Benjamin W. Decker, Althea Press, Emeryville CA., 2018. This work gives clear detailed instructions for 10 different styles and formats of meditation as part of a 10-day program to help determine a meditation practice that works best for each person. The teaching methodology covered within the book follows Mr. Decker's successful teaching workshop practice in which he has educated numerous meditators nationwide. The 10 different styles and formats of meditation for the 10-day program include: (1) Zaren Breath Awareness; (2) Open Awareness Meditation; (3) Mindful Observation; (4) Mindful Eating; (5) Observing Your Emotions; (6) Walking Meditation; (7) Body Scan Meditation; (8) Mantra Meditation; (9) Sitting with Difficult Emotions; (10) Lovingkindness Meditation.[78]

Each of the 10 meditation styles or formats is fully explained along with the benefits of using each regularly, what specifically one needs to do to utilize each successfully, how one gets started in utilizing each style/format, and what progress notes one should make and keep as a personal record. [note 78] Overall, this work appears to be an easy guide written by a professional meditation educator for any novice to meditation, or even for a more seasoned meditator such as myself to obtain a good overview of major meditation styles proven effective for consideration in their meditation practice.

(3) "The Daily Meditation Book of Healing, 365 Reflections for Positivity, Peace, and Prosperity", by Worthy Stokes. Rockridge Press, Emeryville CA. 2020. This represents a work on meditation for healing and transformation that is less about perfecting the attention of the mind, and more about devoting oneself to opening the door up to the power of possibility. This involves freeing the instincts of one's bodily bio-neurological makeup affected by their prior conditioning from past experiences, by developing a greater consciousness that embodies the very essence of that person's being. [79] No one meditation process or practice is best for everyone to follow. Each person's presence is sufficient and represents to them a great gift of life. A person's simple, sacred wish to feel safe and secure, to cultivate hope, joy, and compassion is more than sufficient to make a valid and positive change in their overall bodily chemistry. [note 79]

Each person's courage and ability to heal have great potential. Transforming one's inner world through meditation causes something special to happen, namely that the electrical field around the heart along with the neural pathways carrying energy and intelligence throughout the body begin to operate more efficiently. Also, one becomes a more conscious being when their nervous system starts to do something deeply mystical and magical, which touches everything in one's life with a radically new and freedom-providing approach. [note 79] The mainstay of the work consists of 365 beautifully and simply stated, brief, easy-to-read, and understand meditation narratives, reflections, or affirmations, one for each day of the calendar year. These written meditations focus on possibilities for healing pain from past difficulties, as well as relief from stresses from other 'in-life' experiences and challenges that we all typically have or will face. [note 79]

It is highly recommended that any reader interested in learning more about the 'fruits of meditation' seriously investigate any (or all) these three well-written books. Of course, many other fine works on meditation have been published which can also be considered.

It should be stated that it was not the intention of my work herein to offer an all-encompassing research treatise on the background, fundamentals, and practices covering the entire meditation discipline. Rather, my intent here is more focused and is based upon two major components. These are composed of **(1)** Themes Focusing on Love from a Universal Perspective as a backdrop to Meditation Practice (Ch. 2 to 5) by presenting **(a)** an understanding of worldly types of love in contrast with Infinite Love; **(b)** proofs of Infinite Love along with the existence of a Heavenly State; **(c)** 'derailments' in achieving real true love in this life, e.g., negativity, fear, evil, and human ego; **(2)** Select Meditation Techniques, Processes, and Narrative Healing Meditations (Ch. 6 and 7) specifically covering **(a)** 'equality' of all people as a key 'apriority order and factor' in the meditation process with its healing influences; **(b)** priority meditation fundamentals with select practices, techniques, and processes, with related discussion; **(c)** 100 unique narrative meditations focusing on worldly and Infinite Love realities as representing 'springboards' for healing in this life.

Meditation Techniques That Began and then Added to My Practice

Transcendental Meditation

A well-known meditative technique first learned by me back in the mid-1980s was Transcendental Meditation (TM),[80] which I utilize occasionally now in my meditation practice. This was taught by a Transcendental Meditation teacher who was properly trained and qualified to do this. The process involves relaxing in a comfortable chair, closing the eyes for one minute, and while keeping them closed commencing to say out loud, or silently under one's breath, a repetitive mantra sound (e.g., 'AREM'). This was specifically given to me by the teacher, supposedly suited for a particular birth month or time of the year. The instructions were to repeat this mantra in a relaxed slow fashion every few seconds for a period of 15 to 20 minutes, and at the same time to gently let pass through the mind whatever thoughts come up (and many do). Regular repetition of this mantra helps to both relax the person and substantially cut down on the number of stray thoughts coming into the mind. This helps us connect to our inner Infinite essence ('Soul') or 'God' within. note 80 At the same time, it helps us to communicate with God directly. At the end of the meditation session, it is advised to open one's eyes only very slowly, taking up to a minute. I have found that utilizing this process relaxes and refreshes me as if I had taken a 20-minute nap.

Special Note on Transcendental Meditation (TM): it should be noted that my ethereal experience (pp 64-8 herein) in 2006 at Singing Beach, along with several follow-up ethereal experiences over the next several years, occurred in conjunction with the use of key aspects of TM. It was primarily used at that time as a mind-settling and silencing process to try to substantially slow down the vast number of stray thoughts that were typically coming into and cluttering my mind.

Subsequent Meditation Techniques Learned and Utilized

The 'I AM Wishes Fulfilled Meditation'

Wayne Dyer has produced a CD sound recording, "I AM Wishes Fulfilled Meditation," which was available through www.hayhouse. com or from www amazon.com.[81] This has recently become available as an e-file download to one's computer, tablet, or cell phone. The sound recording consists of (1) a voice introductory part by Wayne; and (2) two separate 20-minute sound recordings produced from research originally done by James Twyman. These recordings are composed of sounds consisting of many different frequencies based on the original 'Moses Code' representing signals and symbols of the words of God, originating from Moses and the surrounding ancient culture several thousand years ago. Wayne specifically re-produced these sounds from James Twyman's research into beautiful sound recordings for use in meditation and relaxation. note 81 I would sit in my favorite chair and listen to either or both sound recordings and just let my mind and imagination wander. I have found that over recent years these recordings have especially relaxing, restful, and insightful feelings/thoughts along with other good effects.

The 'Getting in the Gap' and 'Japa' Technique & Meditation

Another important meditation technique has been offered by Wayne Dyer in his book, "Getting in the Gap, Making Conscious Contact with God through Meditation", with its accompanying "Getting in the Gap Meditation" CD, (Hay House, Inc., Publishing; hayhouse. com). This is best available now as an e-file for electronic devices. The 'Getting in the Gap' technique can be effectively utilized as a process to significantly reduce thoughts from coming into a person's mind as well as a stress-reducing process.[82] Both Wayne and davidji, who are both meditation experts, have suggested that each of us has 60,000-80,000 or more thoughts that cross our minds each day, much like a rambling freight train. The author davidji suggests that without worry we should simply let them gently come and go, and continue with whatever we are doing, even if it's meditation. However, Wayne suggests a process to cut down the number of stray thoughts by getting us into the 'gap' or 'blank space between the thoughts', which brings us into direct contact with the Infinite 'Source' or 'God'. At the same time, this produces within us a peaceful & restful state of mind.[83]

Getting us into the space between thoughts, or the space between actual words or alphabet letters, or the space between musical notes (with their beautiful sounds) brings us into contact with ethereal space, which links us to our Infinite connection. Wayne claims that getting in the space between the two thoughts, words, or letters brings tranquility and peace, and getting in the space between the musical notes brings richness and beauty to the musical sound. He has used this 'Getting in the Gap' technique, including the use of 'Japa', as one of his most effective meditation techniques. I've discovered the same. I encourage any interested reader to refer to his book "Getting in the Gap, Making Conscious Contact with God Through Meditation" with the "Getting in the Gap Meditation CD" or e-file. I've found the CD an excellent primer to get one into the 'Get in the Gap' spirit.[note 82] According to him, 'Japa' presents the actual sound of God as ... 'AH'... which is also indicative of the actual name or calling of God. He points out that in many worldly languages and cultures the use of... 'AH'... as alphabet letter parts of certain words with their typical verbal sound, (e.g., 'Allah', 'Jehovah', or 'God') represent the presence and name of 'God'. The out loud voice sound of... 'AH'... brings on the reality of God's All-Loving, Peaceful Presence, along with His Healing, Clarity, & Spirit. [note 82]

In his book, "Getting in the Gap, Making Conscious Contact with God through Meditation", with its accompanying "Getting in the Gap Meditation" soundtrack, Wayne utilizes a meditation process that involves the use of the beginning part (9 words) of the 1st sentence of the Lord's Prayer: 'Our Father Who Art in Heaven, Hallowed Be Thy Name'. This meditation process is explained and demonstrated below with the following **Steps** in **capital letters** and **Sub-steps** in **numbers** [note 83]. It tries to closely follow the format & content suggested by Wayne in his book and soundtrack. This process is best done with the eyes closed as much as possible.

Before starting the meditation, you should get as comfortable as possible in whatever position that appeals to you (e.g., sitting up, lying down, in a yoga position, or your favorite chair) and put your hands face-up on the lap, with the forefinger and thumb of each hand barely touching each other so you can make an imaginary circuit between the words you are reading (or hearing) here and your heart....Then....

Step (A)...Sub-step (1)- Starting with the first two words in the first sentence of the Lord's Prayer, while shifting the head slightly to the left of the center, clearly imagine the word 'Our' on the left-hand side of your mind very briefly (3 seconds). Then **Sub-step (2)** while shifting the head slightly to the right of the center, clearly imagine the word 'Father' on the right-hand side of your mind very briefly (3 seconds). Then **Sub-step (3)** while shifting the head back to the center, focus on the mid-point of the imaginary blank space between the 2 words 'Our' and 'Father' and just rest there briefly (5 to 7 seconds*). Feel the peace of the Gap, the blank space made up of silence between 2 words. Then, slowly take a deep breath, and then exhale it while doing 'Japa' by saying out loud the sound of … 'AH'… until the breath runs out. Then **Sub-step (4)** with a continued focus on the mid-point of the imaginary blank space between the two words 'Our' and 'Father', slowly take another deep breath, and then exhale it while doing 'Japa' again by saying the sound out loud of … 'AH'…. until the breath runs out. Then **Sub-step (5)** if any thought enters your mind, or you choose to do so, return to the sound of … 'AH'…. on exhaling breaths 2 or 3 more times. This should keep you in the gap, the space between the two words 'Our' and 'Father'. Then:

Step (B)…Sub-step (1)- Taking the 2nd and 3rd words in the first sentence of the Lord's Prayer, while shifting the head slightly to the left of the center, clearly imagine the word 'Father' on the left-hand side of your mind very briefly (3 seconds). Then **Sub-step (2)** while shifting the head slightly to the right of the center, clearly imagine the word 'Who' on the right-hand side of your mind very briefly (3 seconds). Then **Sub-step (3)** while shifting the head back to the center, focus on the mid-point of the imaginary blank space between the two words 'Father' and 'Who' and just rest there briefly (5 to 7 seconds*). Feel the peace of being in the Gap, the blank space made up of silence between 2 words. Then, slowly take a deep breath, and then exhale it while doing 'Japa' by saying out loud the sound of … 'AH'…. until your breath runs out. Then **Sub-step (4)** with continued focus on the mid-point of the imaginary blank space between the two words 'Father' and 'Who', slowly take another deep breath and then exhale it while doing 'Japa' again by saying out loud the sound of … 'AH'…. until the breath runs out. Then **Sub-step (5)** if any thought enters your mind, or you choose to do so, return to the sound of … 'AH'…. on exhaling breaths 2 or 3 more times. This should keep you in the gap, the space between the 2 words 'Father' and 'Who'.

Completion of **Steps (A) and (B)** above is sufficient for a shorter up to 10-minute mini-meditation. Wayne's book and CD or e-file sound recording indicate that a person can engage in a longer meditation, i.e., up to 20 minutes by adding the following **Steps (C) thru (E)**:

Step (C)…Sub-step (1)- Taking the 3rd and 4th words in the first sentence of the Lord's Prayer, while shifting the head slightly to the left of the center, clearly imagine the word 'Who' on the left-hand side of your mind very briefly (3 seconds). Then **Sub-step (2)** while shifting the head slightly to the right of the center, clearly imagine the word 'Art' on the right-hand side of your mind very briefly (3 seconds). Then **Sub-step (3)** while shifting the head back to the center, focus on the mid-point of the imaginary blank space between the two words 'Who' and 'Art' and just rest there briefly (5 to 7 seconds*). Feel the peace of being in the Gap, the blank space composed of silence between 2 words. Then, slowly take a deep breath, and exhale it while doing 'Japa' by saying out loud the sound of … 'AH'…. until the breath runs out. Then **Sub-step (4)** with continued focus on the mid-point of the imaginary blank space between the two words 'Who' and 'Art', slowly take another deep breath and then exhale it while doing 'Japa' again by saying out loud the sound of … 'AH'…. until the breath runs out. Then **Sub-step (5)** if any thought enters your mind, or you choose to do so, return to the sound of … 'AH'…. on exhaling breaths 2 or 3 more times. This should keep you in the Gap, the space between the two words 'Who' and 'Art'.

Step (D)…Sub-step (1)- Taking the 4th and 5th words in the first sentence of the Lord's Prayer, while shifting the head slightly to the left of the center, clearly imagine the word 'Art' on the left-hand side of your mind very briefly (3 seconds). Then **Sub-step (2)** while shifting the head slightly to the right of the center, clearly imagine the word 'In' on the right-hand side of your mind very briefly (3 seconds). Then

Sub-step (3) while shifting the head back to the center, focus on the mid-point of the imaginary blank space between the two words 'Art' and 'In' and just rest there briefly (5 to 7 seconds*). Feel the peace of being in the Gap, the blank space composed of silence between 2 words. Then, slowly take a deep breath, and exhale it while doing 'Japa' by saying out loud the sound of ... 'AH'.... until the breath runs out. Then **Sub-step (4)** with a continued focus on the mid-point of the imaginary blank space between the two words 'Art' and 'In', slowly take in another deep breath and then exhale it while doing 'Japa' again by saying out loud the sound of ... 'AH'.... until the breath runs out. And then **Sub-step (5)** if any thought enters your mind, or you choose to do so, return to the sound of ... 'AH'.... on your exhaling breaths 2 or 3 more times. This should keep you in the gap, the space between the two words 'Art' and 'In'.

Step (E)...Sub-step (1)- Taking the 5th and 6th words in the first sentence of the Lord's Prayer, while shifting the head slightly to the left of the center, clearly imagine the word 'In' on the left-hand side of your mind very briefly (3 seconds). Then **Sub-step (2)** while shifting the head slightly to the right of the center, clearly imagine the word 'Heaven' on the right-hand side of your mind very briefly (3 seconds). Then **Sub-step (3)** while shifting the head back to the center, focus on the mid-point of the imaginary blank space between the two words 'In' and 'Heaven' and just rest there briefly (5 to 7 seconds*). Feel the peace of being in the Gap, the blank space composed of silence between 2 words. Then, slowly take a deep breath, and exhale it while doing 'Japa' by saying out loud the sound of ... 'AH'.... until the breath runs out. Then **Sub-step (4)** with a continued focus on the mid-point of the imaginary blank space between the two words 'Art' and 'In', slowly take in another deep breath and then exhale it while doing 'Japa' again by saying out loud the sound of ... AH.... until the breath runs out. And then **Sub-step (5)** if any thought enters your mind, or you choose to do so, return to the sound of ... 'AH'.... on exhaling breaths 2 or 3 more times. This should keep you in the gap, the space between the 2 words 'In' and 'Heaven'.

*As the meditator becomes more accustomed to 'Getting in the Gap' and staying there, they will be able to increase their time of 'Being in the Gap' without a multitude of distracting thoughts coming into mind.

Completion of **Steps (A), (B), (C), (D), and (E)** above would constitute an approximate 15-to-20-minute intermediate-length meditation. The full meditation would constitute adding the 4 **Steps (F), (G), (H),** and **(I) to any one of the 5 Steps (A) thru (E)** above. These would continue the usage of the Lord's Prayer 1st sentence. For **Step (F)** take the next Lord's Prayer two-word pair: 'Heaven' and 'Hallowed' and follow any one of **Steps (A) thru (E), Sub-steps (1) thru (5)** above... For **Step (G)** take the next Lord's Prayer two-word pair: 'Hallowed' and 'Be' and follow any one of **Steps (A) thru (D), Sub-steps (1) thru (5)** above... For **Step (H)** take the next Lord's Prayer two-word pair: 'Be' and 'Thy' and follow any one of **Steps (A) thru (D), Sub-steps (1) thru (5)** above... For **Step (I)** take the next Lord's Prayer two-word pair: 'Thy' and 'Name' and follow any one of **Steps (A) thru (D), Sub-steps (1) thru (5)** above. [note.82 or 83] Completion of all **9 Steps (A) thru (I)** above would constitute an approximate 25-or-so-minute meditation.

Wayne has indicated that anyone who engages in a significant part of the above meditation is well on their way to experiencing a valuable trip through the gap (the space between thoughts or words) and is entering the presence of Divine Energy thru the repetition of the effortless sound of .... AH.... He says that this sound has allowed his mind to keep out all thoughts from entering it, and has brought bliss, joy, and fulfillment knowing that he's made 'conscious contact with God'. [note. 82 or 83]

Further Techniques & Innovations Advancing My Practice

Preparatory to Meditation: Exercises to Consider. It is suggested that any of the following can be used:

1. Focusing on Equality- Actually (physically) raising your hand to take off that imaginary hat you might wear representing

an important role you play in real life, e.g., being a parent or guardian, boss, doctor, lawyer, teacher, leader, guru, politician, etc. This would demonstrate an actual feeling of the reality of equality amongst all of us. We have each been born with a perfect 'Soul' or Infinite eternal essence part. This translates a chief concept of the Infinite 'One' within this life by recognition of equality for all of us, which represents a golden key to 'open the door' to heal from any life difficulties or sufferings that any of us have endured. We have all been born equal to love and be loved, (despite what some might claim), but subsequent life on this planet has largely eroded that equality somehow.

When we suffered past life difficulties, whatever these might have been, we were often not respected nor considered equal by those in the environment around us. But, from an Infinite perspective via each of our spiritual essences or 'Souls,' we were (and still are) equal, even though our bodies did not feel equal then and may still not now due to the past difficulties we endured when we were young. But we are equal <u>now</u> due to: (1) awareness of our individual 'Soul' or perfect spiritual essence that has always accompanied us; (2) despite our past difficulties, each of us as combined body, mind, and 'Soul' have always been equal with everyone else (their combined body, mind, and 'Soul') who has ever existed; (3) the past suffering is over and will not return; and (4) we are unified as 'One' with everything in the Universe, to be Infinitely Loved without any reservations or negativities in the eyes of our All-good Infinite Creator or God.

2. Focusing on Making Repetitive Relaxing Sounds- After taking a deep breath, make vibratory sounds (either with the voice out loud or quietly under the breath with mouth open or closed): OM.........as you breathe out until your breath is exhausted. Some say this as AM.........as you breathe out until your breath is exhausted. Repeat this process for 1 to 2 minutes i.e., repeatedly

taking in a deep breath, and saying OM......... or AM.........
(either with the voice out-loud or silently under the breath with
mouth open or closed) ....as you breathe out until your
breath is exhausted. (See (4) below re. 'Using 'Japa' to Refresh',
the sound or name of God as ...AH...)

3. Relaxing the Mind and Body- This is done in association with
    slow, conscious rhythmic breathing in and out, at the same
    time consciously imagining a relaxation of the muscles and
    areas of the body (one at a time). This starts with slowing down
    or relaxing the mind with all of its stray thoughts, and then
    imagining a relaxing of the (1) top of the head; (2) eyes area;
    (3) jaw-mouth; (4) neck area; (5) top of back, shoulders, arms,
    hands; (6) chest; (7) heart and circulatory system; (8) lungs and
    breathing system; (9) stomach, intestines, liver, spleen, prostrate;
    (10) lower back; (11) lower abdomen; (12) thighs-upper legs;
    (13) knees; (14) lower 2 legs to feet; (15) the body as a whole,
    everything imaginatively and physically relaxed, including body
    and mind.

4. Using 'Japa' to Refresh- Involving the use of the sound of
    God as... AH... as discussed in Wayne Dyer's book "Getting
    in the Gap, Making Conscious Contact with God through
    Meditation" and its Meditation CD (discussed above pp 117-
    122). As a preparatory exercise to meditation, we should first
    take 5 to 10 seconds to get into a relaxed mode, either sitting,
    standing, or lying down, and then take a relaxing deep breath
    and say out loud the following sound (or more quietly expressed
    as a whisper under your breath, mouth open or closed*) ....
    AH.... until the breath runs out. Then take another relaxing
    deep breath and repeat the out loud sound (or quietly whisper
    under your breath, mouth open or closed) .... AH.... until the
    breath runs out. Then take another relaxing deep breath and
    say out loud the sound, or with a quieter whisper of .... AH....

until the breath runs out. Then repeat this process 4 to 6 more times, i.e., taking a deep breath and then exhaling while saying out loud or in a quieter whisper of …. AH…. initiating contact with Infinite 'Source' or 'God'.

*Instead of the out loud voice of …AH…, a 'quieter' approach has been used whereby the person can more quietly whisper … AH… under their exhaling breath (with the mouth open or closed). See item # (3) discussed in more detail on lower p 126 or 1st full parag. p 132** below.

My Inputs to the 'Getting in the Gap' and 'Japa' Technique

This continues the discussion (from pp 117-122 above) on the 'Getting in the Gap' and 'Japa' Technique and Meditation which was offered by Wayne Dyer in his book, "Getting in the Gap, Making Conscious Contact with God through Meditation" together with its Meditation soundtrack. During my recent meditation practice utilizing Wayne's technique, I have discovered several ways or inputs that I feel would enhance the overall effectiveness of using this technique in meditation. These consist of **(1)** as part of the 'Getting in the Gap' process of blocking thoughts from entering a person's mind, instead of using whole words (each made up with multi-letters), using single capital letters (bold font) in 2 letter pairs, e.g., **A B, B C, C D, D E, E F, F G** etc., and focusing on the blank space in-between each 2 letter pair; **(2)** increasing the usage (repetitions) of 'Japa' during meditation, (i.e., 'Japa'- an out loud or quieter under breath sound of …AH…); **(3)** in doing 'Japa', instead of using an out loud sound of …AH… on exhaling breath, doing it as a quieter whispering of … AH … on exhaling breath (with the month open or closed); **(4)** a 'Hand and Fingers Squeezing Process' is offered to utilize together with the 'Getting in the Gap' and 'Japa' technique.

The rationale behind these inputs: for **(1)** above, focusing on the blank space between 2 capital letters (bold font) rather than the blank space between 2 words (each made up of multiple letters) could amplify the effectiveness of thoughts being blocked from coming into one's mind. That is, a person's ability to focus on the blank space could be sharpened and increased by using 2 single capital letters (bond font) rather than using 2 words (made up of multiple letters). Doing this could enhance the blocking effect of stray thoughts from coming into a person's mind. Using words (w. multi-letters) could reduce a person's ability to effectively focus on the blank space between 2 words. This is due to the total space taken up by **(a)** blank space itself between the 2 words, **(b)** blank spaces between each letter in the 2 words, and **(c)** the space taken up by the letters in the 2 words. This total space could distract a person from full focus on the blank space between the 2 words. Rather, it seems to me focussing on the blank space between 2 capital letters (bold front) is less impinged and clearer. The reader (in their meditation) can compare this effectiveness (Wayne's use of words (in the Lord's Prayer) in his 'Getting in the Gap' and 'Japa' Meditation, pp 118-122 above, with my use of capital letters (bold font) in the Integrated 'Getting in the Gap' Closeness to 'Source' or 'God' Meditation, pp 127-133 below.

For **(2)** above, where it is appropriate in meditations, to increase the repetitions of 'Japa' (an out-loud voice or quieter whispering) of ... AH.... on exhaling breath, further enhancing the blocking effect of thoughts from coming into their mind and provide them an increased peaceful and restful state of mind with 'Source'. For **(3)** above, when doing 'Japa' as part of one's meditation routine (particularly at nighttime before sleep or after awakening), the out loud voice of... 'AH'.... can be expressed as a quieter whispering under one's exhaling breath of ... 'AH'.... This should not disturb our partner. For **(4)** above, using the 'Hand and Fingers Squeezing Process' (***pp 132-3) in association with the 'Getting in the Gap' and 'Japa' techniques could help to enhance the blocking effect of stray thoughts from coming into a person's mind.

This author has spent considerable time and effort over the past several years experimenting with Wayne's technique, and as a result, has developed several key refinement inputs discussed just above that would help people to 'Get in the Gap' readily and stay there. These strategies should allow any person to more easily slide into and stay in 'the space between the letters or thoughts', 'the space between musical notes', or 'the space between whatever'.... i.e., 'that blank space of nothingness' that readily brings us into direct contact with Infinite 'Source', or 'God'. Time spent in that blank space or 'in the Gap' would have significant and positive implications for us in this life, i.e., feelings of great ease, peace, clarity, euphoria, joy, and freedom, along with physical and/or mental/ emotional healing. I think and feel that adding my few refinements would enhance Wayne's already significant contributions in applying the 'Getting in the Gap' and 'Japa' techniques to the meditation process. His efforts have resulted in significant healing implications for many people in the world, making all his work truly worthwhile.

The following meditation combines my few input suggestions with Wayne's technique and meditation (from pp 117-122). Similarly, as above, one's eyes should generally be kept closed during the meditation. This will enhance any person's "Getting in the Gap" closeness to our 'Source' or 'God'.

Integrated 'Getting in the Gap' Closeness to 'Source' or 'God' Meditation

Step (A)...as a quick 'warm up' or 'starter' to our meditation, take a few seconds to get into a relaxed mode, either sitting, standing, or lying down, and then take a relaxing deep breath and then exhale it and do 'Japa' by saying the sound out loud, or quietly whispering under one's exhaling breath with the mouth open or closed ... 'AH'.... until your breath runs out. Then take another relaxing deep breath & then exhale it doing 'Japa' by saying the sound out loud, or quietly whispering under one's exhaling breath with mouth open or closed ... 'AH'.... until the breath runs out. Then take another relaxing deep breath and do 'Japa' again by saying the sound out loud, or quietly whispering under one's exhaling breath with mouth open or close ... 'AH'.... until the breath runs out. Repeat this process 3 to 5 more times, i.e., take a deep breath and then exhale it while saying out loud, or a quieter whisper of ... 'AH'.... until the breath runs out. Then:

Step (B)...Sub-step (1) Taking the first capital letter pair **A B** (bold font) while shifting the head slightly to the left of the center, clearly imagine the letter **A** on the left-hand side in your mind (focusing on the letter **A** very briefly), and then while shifting the head slightly to the right of the center, clearly imagine the letter **B** on the right-hand side in your mind (focusing on the letter **B** very briefly), and then shift your head back to the center and imagine a wide blank space in-between the capital letters **A B** (bold font), focusing on the mid-point of that imaginary blank space to block out stray thoughts from coming into your mind and just rest there for 5 to 7 or so seconds*. Feel the peace of being in the Gap, the blank space between 2 letters. **Substep (2)**- With continued focus on the mid-point of an imaginary blank space between the 2 letters **A B** (bold font) to block out stray thoughts, slowly take a deep breath and do 'Japa' by saying the sound out loud**, or quietly whisper on exhaling breath with mouth open or closed ... AH.... until the breath runs out. Then **Sub-step (3)** with a continued focus on the mid-point of an imaginary blank space in between the letters **A B** to block out stray thoughts, slowly take another deep breath and do 'Japa' by saying the sound out loud, or quietly whisper under one's exhaling breath (mouth open or closed ... AH.... until the breath expires. **Sub-step (4)**- repeat the Sub-step (3) guides 3 to 5x (incl. 'Japa'). Feel the clarity of bliss in the Gap.

Step (C)...Sub-step (1) Taking the next capital letter pair **B C** (bold font) while shifting the head slightly to the left of the center, clearly imagine the letter **B** on the left-hand side in your mind (and focus on the **B** very briefly), and then while shifting the head slightly to the right of center, clearly imagine the letter **C** on the right-hand side in your mind (and focus on the **C** very briefly), and then while shifting your head back to the center and imagine a wide blank space in-between the capital letters **B C**, focusing on the mid-point of that imaginary blank space to block out stray thoughts from coming into your mind and just rest there for 5 to 7 or so seconds*. Feel the peace of being in the Gap, the blank space between 2 letters. **Sub-step (2)**- With a continued focus on the mid-point of an imaginary wide blank space in between capital letters **B C** (bold font) to block out stray thoughts, slowly take a deep breath and do 'Japa' by saying the sound out loud**, or quietly whisper on one's exhaling breath with mouth open or closed ... 'AH'.... until breath runs out; and then **Sub-step (3)** with a continued focus on the mid-point of an imaginary wide blank space in-between letters **B C** to block out stray thoughts, slowly take another deep breath and do 'Japa' by saying the sound out loud, or quietly whisper on exhaling breath (mouth open or closed) ... 'AH'.... until the breath expires. **Sub-step (4)**-repeat the Sub-step (3) guides 3 to 5x (incl. 'Japa'). Feel the clarity of bliss in the Gap.

Completion of steps **(A), (B), and (C)** above is sufficient for a 10 to 12 or so minute mini-meditation. Using any number of up to an additional 6 two-letter pairs **C D, D E,** through **H I** below will: (a) lead to a longer meditation; (b) better help a person during the day from difficult emotions or situations; (c) help a person to prevent thoughts from coming into their mind; (d) help a person to get back to sleep at night.

Step (D)...Sub-step (1) Taking the next capital letter pair **C D** (bold font), while shifting the head slightly to the left of the center, clearly imagine the letter **C** on the left-hand side in your mind (and focus on the **C** very briefly), and then while shifting the head slightly to the right of center, clearly imagine the letter **D** on the right-hand side in your mind (and focus on the **D** very briefly), and then while shifting your head back to the center, imagine a wide blank space in-between the capital letters **C D**, focusing on the mid-point of that imaginary blank space to block out stray thoughts from coming into your mind and just rest there for 5 to 7 or so seconds*. Feel the peace of being in the Gap, the blank space between the 2 letters. **Sub-step (2)**- With the continued focus on the mid-point of an imaginary blank space between the capital letters **C D** (bold font) to block out all stray thoughts, slowly take a deep breath and do 'Japa' by saying the sound out loud**, or quietly whisper on one's exhaling breath with mouth open or closed ... 'AH'.... until the breath runs out;

and then **Sub-step (3)** With continued focus on the mid-point of an imaginary blank space in-between capital letters **C D** to block out stray thoughts, slowly take another deep breath and again do 'Japa' by saying the sound out loud, or quietly whisper on one's exhaling breath (mouth open or closed) … 'AH'…. until it expires; **Sub-step (4)**- repeat the Sub step (3) guides 3 to 5x (incl. 'Japa'). Feel the clarity of bliss in the Gap.

Step (E)…Sub-step (1) Taking the next capital letter pair **D E** (bold font), while shifting the head slightly to the left of the center, clearly imagine the letter **D** on the left-hand side in your mind (and focus on the **D** very briefly), and then while shifting the head slightly to the right of center, clearly imagine the letter **E** on the right-hand side in your mind (and focus on the **E** very briefly), and then while shifting your head back to the center, imagine a wide blank space in-between the capital letters **D E**, focusing on the mid-point of that imaginary blank space in-between the capital letters **D E** to block out stray thoughts from coming into your mind and just rest there for 5 to 7 or so seconds*. Feel the peace of being in the Gap, the blank space between the 2 letters. **Sub-step (2)**- With the continued focus on the mid-point of an imaginary blank space between the capital letters **D E** (bold font) to block out stray thoughts, slowly take a deep breath and do 'Japa' by saying out loud**, or quietly whisper on one's exhaling breath (with mouth open or closed) … 'AH'…. until the breath expires; and then **Sub-step (3)** with a continued focus on an imaginary blank space between capital letters **D E** to block out stray thoughts, slowly take another deep breath and do 'Japa' by saying the sound out loud, or quietly whisper on one's exhaling breath (mouth open or closed) …. AH…. until it expires. **Sub-step (4)**- repeat Sub-step (3) guides 3 to 5x (incl. 'Japa'). Feel the clarity of bliss in the Gap.

Completion of Steps **(A), (B), (C), (D), and (E)** above would constitute performing an intermediate up to 18-to-20-minute meditation. One can extend the meditation beyond this to include up to 4 additional steps: **(F), (G), (H). (I)** which would utilize capital two-letter pairs **E F, F G, G H, H I,** and follow the format of any of the **Steps (A) thru**

(E), Sub-steps (1) thru (4) above for each additional capital 2-letter pair. Completion of all 9 Steps **(A)** thru **(I)**, which includes the 9 capital 2-letter pairs **A B** through **H I** would constitute a full up to 25-to-28-minute meditation.

From this, a very special and powerful spiritual door can be opened, and a pathway directed to our 'Source', 'Higher Power' or 'God' through any of the following: **(a)** an effective blocking of random thoughts from coming into one's mind; **(b)** the person's intention of making 'conscious contact with God and all His Infinite Love'; **(c)** the person's awareness (thru feelings) of Infinite Love being present within their 'Soul'; **(d)** memories/experiences of Infinite Love having occurred in one's life. A combination of any of these leads a person toward creating a very special resonance (or clarity) and closeness to our Infinite 'Source' or 'Spirit' & Its Ever-Loving/healing presence. Plus, this reality represents a powerful meditation.

Special Ending Note. Doing 'Japa' really helps to control many of the disturbing/distracting thoughts from typically entering our minds daily. In addition, I've found the 'Hand/Fingers Squeezing Process' useful in controlling the numerous thoughts that invade my mind. Although not a formal part of the above meditation, if incoming distracting thoughts continue as a problem, any person can experiment with this process 'on their own' within this meditation, or try it elsewhere in other meditations. See *** below on pp 132-3 which fully explains the 'Hand/ Fingers Squeezing Process'.

* The actual blocking of all thoughts from coming into one's mind can be very difficult, particularly as the time length increases while they are 'In the Gap'. At the beginning of performing the 'Getting in the Gap' meditation, a meditator should start with a lower time expectation goal for keeping stray thoughts out of their mind, e.g., say 5 to 7 or so secs. Then, as they gain experience with doing 'Getting in the Gap' and staying free of invasive thoughts, the time length goal can be increased, e.g., 10 to 12 or more secs.

** An outloud sound of …'AH'…. seems most effective but can be disturbing to folks around us (particularly with our partner at night). Instead, …'AH'…. can be whispered more quietly (with mouth open or closed) under one's exhaling breath. In my meditation practice, I've discovered that a quieter whispering of …'AH'…. on the exhaling breath can be very effective (or nearly equal) to the out loud sound of …'AH'…. In all my readings, this quieter whispering (of mantas) has not been suggested, thereby making this novel.

*** The Hands/Fingers Squeezing Process (read through before doing so). Keeping out all stray thoughts for even 10 or so seconds can be difficult. As thoughts begin to penetrate your mind, do the following (for each alphabet capital letter pair)- Begin by holding both your 2 arms/hands apart in front of you at an approx. 90-degree angle, and then slowly squeeze each hand (fingers included) until they are tightly (but reasonably) closed, and keep them closed for at least 6 seconds while slowly counting (out-loud or quietly whisper to yourself)… 1, 2, 3, 4, 5, 6 (1 second between each count) …then slowly open the hands up. What helps while doing the 'hand closing/keeping them closed/ hand opening' process is gripping with each hand the corner of a small bed or couch pillow, a foot sock, or a handkerchief. Repeat this 'hand closing/keeping them closed/hand opening' process 2 more times (for a total of 3 times) for each capital 2-letter pair (e.g., **A B**, etc.). While doing this process 3 times, imagine and think (with intent) that you are **blocking** all thoughts from entering your mind. During the 3rd repeat time of doing this process (while slowly re-opening your hands), say out loud or whisper to yourself **'and making conscious contact with God and all His Infinite Love'**, and then briefly (for 20- 30 secs.) think of notable Infinite Love insights or experiences you've either gained from this book, or you've had in your life. Examples of my own include:

<u>Insights</u> **(1a)** I AM the name of God who lies within me as my perfect spiritual Soul, composed of Infinite Love; **(1b)** I AM unified with everything in the Universe, including all people (via their spiritual

Soul), as 'One', under the All-good God; **(1c)** Thereby, I AM 'equal' with all other people who have ever existed.

Experiences **(1)** Joys of experiencing a white coral-lined (looking like small Birch-barked trees) on the backside of a beach in Fiji in 1987, producing unparalleled euphoric feelings, pp 61-2; **(2)** sudden spiritual re-awakening at home in June 2004, pp 11-12; **(3)** sensational 2-hour ethereal experience on a summer day in July 2006 at Singing Beach, Manchester-by-the-Sea, MA, giving me unparalleled pleasure, euphoria, and joy, pp 64-8.

The Story of My Meditation Regimen Up to the Present

My principal learning tool with spiritual evolvement has been best garnered through continued regular practice of meditation with its resulting intuitions and insights that have emerged and evolved over time. Many of these intuitive insights have been presented herein within the Themes in Part I (including Chapters 1 to 6) and the 100 Narrative Healing Meditations in Part II. For most folks, the key is to be totally 'open' to all possibilities as to which meditation processes and techniques will work best in their pursuit of regular practice. Each person will react/adapt differently (i.e., no one shoe fits all or for everyone). Also, important is to have the willingness to be free and flexible in experimenting with different meditation processes and techniques (with their possible applications and combinations), while making appropriate adjustments in each person's meditation practice to best align with their spiritual growth needs at a particular point in time. My situation has changed and evolved somewhat over time (which continues even now), helping to make my meditation practice more regular, worthwhile, and effective.

At the start of my meditations in recent years, I become relaxed in my favorite chair, perhaps doing one (or more) of the four preparatory to meditation exercises listed above …(p 122-5), or none of them depending on my state of mind or feelings at the time. Then, as introduced earlier in this Theme in the narrative part, 'Subsequent Meditation Techniques Learned and Utilized', p 116-7, my daily practice has utilized (though a bit less frequently recently) either or both of the 20-minute sound recordings from Wayne Dyer's, "I AM Wishes Fulfilled Meditation CD", available (also as an e-file) through www.hayhouse.com or from www amazon.com.[note 81] As stated earlier in this Theme, these recordings consist of sounds of many different energy frequencies based on the original 'Moses Code' representing signals and symbols of the words of God, coming from Moses and surrounding cultures long ago. These signals and symbols (as sounds) were re-produced by Wayne into beautiful sound recordings for his and others' meditation practices. [note 81]

Until very recently, my meditation practice has consisted of regular listening to these 2 sound recordings. Often, two 20-minute meditations were conducted daily listening to the contents of both sound recordings. I would just listen and allow my mind to wander wherever it might go, taking in thoughts that simply come and go. At times I would reflect/meditate on the significance of certain spiritually based thoughts that would come into my mind, or refer to written narratives or notes, and then let the thoughts go. From regular daily listening to these recordings, I have evolved both spiritually and as a human person in the following ways: (1) limiting stress- when breathing out (i.e., exhaling), I consciously think (with intent)… to relax…and then with imagination, to feel…relaxed….throughout my body/mind; (2) limiting stress- to consciously think and feel 'I am completely free of all pressing worries'; (3) to have feelings of ease, contentment, and peace, without pressure for material gain; (4) to be less judgmental, instead to have compassion for others and their life difficulties; (5) to have more patience and kindness toward self; (6) to transform my current conditioning based on negative holdovers (e.g., from past abuse or grudges) into accepting and forgiving true love. In summary, a desire to feel spiritual and steadfast in bringing about newfound hope, joy, and compassion is more than enough to make important, positive changes in my life.

The author davidji utilizes other sound recordings for meditation: www.davidji.com,[84] as does the author Eben Alexander, M.D.: www.ebenalexander.com.[85] In the process of embarking on a meditation program, the reader can consider any of these or any other sound or other processes for their meditation that are found by them to be intriguing, peaceful, and relaxing. The reader is encouraged to do their research and experiment as to the most appropriate and useful sound process or other types of meditative accompaniment that would seem useful in their meditation practice. This represents an important key for any meditator's success in instituting regularity in their practice (e.g., to do their meditation daily).

In my meditation practice over the past several years, I have increasingly alternated the use of Wayne's CD sound recording, "I AM Wishes Fulfilled Meditation", with the usage of the 'Getting in the Gap' and 'Japa' Techniques from his book and CD. His published book, "Getting in the Gap, Making Conscious Contact with God through Meditation", and it's accompanying 'Getting in the Gap Meditation' CD emphasizes the use of 'Japa'. The book and sound CD (now available as an e-file) are available through either Hay Publishing Inc. or Amazon. At times I've utilized both the "I AM Wishes Fulfilled Meditation" and the "Getting in the Gap Meditation" soundtracks on the same day. However, my meditation practice has evolved to include, with more emphasis and frequency, principal aspects of his 'Getting in the Gap' and 'Japa' techniques. These are presented in the 'Getting in the Gap and 'Japa' Meditation, pp 118-122.

In the process of utilizing Wayne's 'Getting in the Gap' and 'Japa' techniques in my meditation practice, several significant innovation inputs of mine have emerged, which if any of them could be integrated with Wayne's technique, might enhance these techniques overall positive impact when utilized in people's meditations. These inputs were explained above in the subsection narrative 'My Inputs to the 'Getting in the Gap' and 'Japa' Technique', pp 125-7. Several of these inputs were integrated with Wayne's 'Getting in the Gap and 'Japa' Meditation', (pp 118-122), with the combined result being my re-write, namely the Integrated 'Getting in the Gap' Closeness to 'Source' or 'God' Meditation, (pp 127-133) above. Utilizing Wayne's meditation work along with my added inputs has allowed me to get a greater closeness to the Infinite Spirit ('God') with Its Infinite Love. This reminds me of the closeness to the Infinite Spirit I obtained from the ethereal experience in July 2006 at Singing Beach, Manchester-by-the-Sea, MA, pp 64-8.

Meditation Now & Going Forward - A Potpourri of Choices

- Clear Choice in Meditation: Maintaining Silence - I like the idea of 20-minute meditation periods, and when the time is available, two of these are done daily. Silent meditations (without an out-loud voice, mantras, or sound recordings) will often utilize at the same time my silent reading of any of the 100 Narrative Healing Meditations in Part II, Ch. 7, or narrative Themes in Part I, or Epilogue Final Notes near the end of this work. On these occasions, my meditation is done with as much silence as possible. There are times in my life when feelings would indicate that silence is indeed 'golden' and represents a healing meditation in and of itself. During or preceding my silent meditations, I will read through spiritually oriented narratives, which help to block out many everyday stray thoughts that typically come into a person's mind and, at the same time keep one's mind spiritually centered. At the same time (as reading), I will write down a few 'keynotes' and 'related feelings' from the reading. Then, for the remainder of the meditation, I maintain total silence and reflect on the spiritual meaning of my written notes and feelings.

Or... at the beginning of a 20-minute meditation, I would first read through (silently) a particular narrative meditation of my choosing (i.e., any of the 100 Narrative Healing Meditations in Part II, Ch.7, or book Theme or any other narrative book part). While doing the reading, I would write down on paper a few 'keynotes' or related 'feelings' from the reading, and then listen to Wayne's sound CD recording, "I AM Wishes Fulfilled Meditation", or his "Getting in the Gap Meditation"

CD, or some other spiritual sound recording, at the same time reflecting on the key ideas and feelings expressed in my notes. Then I would conclude by adding to my notes any significant concluding thoughts and retain these notes as a record.

Or... if the surroundings are still and quiet, I might forgo listening to any meditation sound recording or doing any narrative reading, and instead do a mini meditation using Exercise (4) "Using 'Japa' to Refresh', pp 124-5. This is part of Subsection Subtitle 'Preparatory to Meditation Exercises to Consider', (p 122-5). One can enhance its effectiveness by adding repetitions of 'Japa'. This will help to provide relief from various life stresses. The meditation consists of **Step (1)** taking 5 to 10 seconds to get relaxed by either sitting down, standing, or lying down and then slowly take a relaxing, deep breath and do 'Japa' out loud (or quietly whispering under exhaling breath, mouth open or closed) ......AH......until the breath expires. Then **Step (2)** slowly take another relaxing deep breath and do 'Japa' again out loud (or quietly whisper under exhaling breath, mouth open or closed) ......AH...... until the breath runs out. Then **Step (3)** slowly take another relaxing deep breath and do 'Japa' by saying out loud (or quietly whispering on exhaling breath, mouth open or closed) ......AH......until the breath runs out. These actions take approx. 1 min. Then **Step (4)**, repeat the Step (3) guidance 4 to 6 more times, (including 'Japa'). This takes 1-2 more mins. Repeating 'Japa'...AH... enhances body/mind relaxation, giving greater clarity of mind and closeness to our 'God'.

Or... I might focus during a silent and quiet period on certain spiritual concepts or thoughts to reflect upon during a meditation. For example: **(1)** what 'spirituality' really means in my life now and how it can help me; **(2)** what the 'afterlife' is all about and its potential meaning to me in this life; **(3)** how the spirituality (or lack of it) of others has affected me in the past, and how that is affecting me now; **(4)** listening to the Lord Jesus's along with Infinite Love's message within me and what this means now; **(5)** reflecting on the ethereal Infinite Love experiences I've had in my life and how they affect me now; **(6)** how the power of God or Infinite Love can help me now; **(7)** the meaning of 'the Magic of Love' at Christmastime to me now.

Or... from recent innovations in my practice, doing nighttime meditation in bed just before falling asleep, or in bed upon awakening during the night (see 1st full parag., p 113). As a suggested example for this meditation, one can try and select (for their regular usage) from 2 Option possibilities:

Option (1)- the person follows the guidelines for each of the following: **(A)** Do a quick 'warm up', by referring to and doing **Step (A)**- pp 127-8 above; **(B)** Use of capital letter pair **A B** (bold font) by referring to and doing **Step (B)...Sub-step (1) thru Sub-step (4)**- p 128 above; **(C)** Use of capital letter pair **B C** (bold font) by referring to and doing **Step (C)...Sub-step (1) thru Sub-step (4)**, p 128-9 above. These are all part of the Integrated 'Getting in the Gap' Closeness to 'Source' or 'God' Meditation, pp 127-133. Option 1 will take 10 to 12 mins.

Or..Option (2)- the person follows the following guidelines: **Step (1)**- become relaxed by taking a slow deep breath, then exhale it at the same time saying ('Japa') out loud or quietly whispering to themselves ... AH.... until the breath runs out, and then repeat these Step (1) guidelines (including 'Japa') 5 to 7 times, or more*. **Step (2)**- take capital letter pair **A B** (bold font) and imaginatively place the letter **A** on the left side of the person's mind (2-3 secs.) and then the letter **B** on the right side of their mind** (2-3 secs), then move to the center of their mind and focus on the blank space in between the capital letter pair **A B** for 8 to 10 seconds, trying to block out stray thoughts from coming into their mind. Feel the peace of being 'In the Gap', the blank space between the 2 capital letters. **Step (3)**- If distracting thoughts start to penetrate one's mind, perform the 'Hand-Fingers Squeezing Process' (see*** pp 132-3 above) and then proceed to Step (4) below. If distracting thoughts do not penetrate one's mind, disregard the 'Hand-Fingers Squeezing Process' and go directly to... **Step (4)**- take a deep breath then exhale it while saying out loud or quietly to oneself the ('Japa') …. AH… until the breath expires. Repeat Step (4) 3- 5 times. Option 2 takes up to 10 minutes.

Option (1) and Option (2) can be lengthened: for **Option (1)** by adding capital letter pairs C D, D E, E F, and following the guidelines suggested for either one of **… Step (D) or Step (E)** pp 129-130, for each capital letter pair. Adding these 3 capital letter pairs extends the total time for Option 1 to approx. 20 minutes; for **Option (2)** add capital letter pairs B C and C D and follow **Step (2) thru Step (4)** in the paragraph just above. Adding these 2 capital letter pairs extends the total time for Option 2 to approx. 15 minutes.

* I've found via experience that falling asleep at night (or back to sleep upon awakening) is enhanced by increasing the number of the 'Japa' …. AH…. repetitions from 5 to 7x, to a higher level of 10 to 15x, or a bit higher. Doing higher levels of 'Japa' repetitions has at times allowed me to fall asleep even before proceeding to **Step (2) thru Step (4)** above. Higher levels of Japa repetitions accentuate body-mind relaxation, and at the same time increase the blocking effect of distracting thoughts from entering one's mind, inducing the person to fall more quickly asleep.

** While lying on your back in bed trying to establish the capital letter **A** on the left side of your mind briefly, and then the capital letter **B** on the right side of your mind briefly, do the following: **(1)** holding your left hand to the immediate left of your head, take the 1st index finger (being next to the thumb) of your left hand and physically draw with that finger an (imagined) emboldened capital letter **A** on a nearby sheet or blanket. Then, **(2)** hold your right hand to the immediate right of your head, take the 1st index finger (being next to the thumb) of your right hand and physically draw with that finger an (imagined) emboldened capital letter **B** on a nearby sheet or blanket. Repeat these two steps once or twice to solidly implant the capital letter **A** on the left side of your mind, and the capital letter **B** on the right side of your mind.

Or… from recent discoveries in my practice, the ebullient effects of creating notable peaceful, restful, and euphoric feelings when meditation is conducted in beautiful settings in the outdoor environment, or indoors in naturally induced conditions. Examples include being by an ocean shoreline with the sights and sounds of breaking waves; on an elevated promontory viewing mountain peaks splashed in-between by adjoining lowland passes dressed in vegetative colors mixed with exposed rocks; being by a lake or riverine waterbody with its calm, shimmering, or flowing waters; at night a clear night viewing upward in the sky at the moon, planets, stars, and celestial outer space; or presence in an indoor planetarium. Particularly relevant here would be the restful and peaceful aftereffects from the views and sounds of flowing water in rivers/streams, and especially falling water in waterfalls, resulting in a relaxation that creates exhilarating, peaceful, restful, and euphoric feelings. My favorite outdoor waterfall site centers on annual retreat visits to Niagara Falls on the Niagara River at both Canadian & New York, USA overlook sites located on the river edges (see Ch. 1, Theme 3, pp 15-17). Favorite indoor waterfall sites are at Mohegan Sun Casino Uncasville CT, and St. Vincent Hospital, Worcester MA. My favorite ocean shoreline site is at Singing Beach, Manchester-by-the-Sea, MA (pp 64-8; & Subs. 7(D) Medit. 5, pp 177-8).

What an <u>ideal</u> way to end Ch. 6, Theme 2, 'The Science of Meditation Practice', by actually going to your favorite outdoor spot or viewing pictures or videos of it via your smartphone or having memories of it, at the same time doing a special meditation following the guidance as offered below. This closely follows the format given in the Integrated 'Getting in the Gap' Closeness to 'Source' or 'God' Medit., pp 127-131.

Step (A)- (w. eyes open*) First get 'warmed up' by taking a few seconds to get relaxed, then take a slow deep breath and exhale it while saying 'Japa' out loud or quietly whispering to yourself … AH…. until your breath runs out, then repeat the breathing guidelines (incl. 'Japa') 4 or 5 additional times. **Step (B)**- (w. eyes open*) Take the capital letter pair **A B** (bold font) and shift your head slightly to the left of the center, clearly imagining the letter **A** on the left-hand side in your mind (focusing on the letter **A** very briefly), and then shift your head slightly to the right of the center, clearly imagining the letter **B** on the right-hand side in your mind (focusing on the letter **B** very briefly), and then shift your head back to the center and imagine a wide blank space in-between the capital letters **A B,** focusing on the mid-point of that blank space trying to block out all stray thoughts from coming into your mind, and just rest there for 7 to 9 secs. or so. Feel the peace of being in the Gap, the blank space between 2 letters. **Step (C)**- (w. eyes open or closed*) While continuing to focus on the blank space between **A B** (bold font), slowly repeat 4 or 5 times breathing in and then exhaling breath saying the sound of 'Japa' ...AH.... Feel the clarity of healing serenity & bliss being in the Gap. Then for **Step (D)** Take the next capital letter pair **B C** and repeat the **Step (B) and (Step (C)** guidelines just above (incl. eyes open vs. closed). Then for **Step (E)**- Take the next capital letter pair **C D** and repeat **Step (B) and (Step (C)** guidelines just above (incl. eyes open vs. closed). Then for **Step (F)**- Take the next capital letter pair **D E** and repeat **Step (B) and (Step (C)** guidelines just above (incl. eyes open vs. closed). Then for **Step (G)**- Take the next capital letter pair **E F** and repeat **Step (B) and (Step (C)** guidelines just above (incl. eyes open vs. closed). Completing **Step (B) & (C)** guidelines for 5 capital letter pairs, **A B** thru **E F**, takes approx. 20 mins.

*(eyes open vs. eyes closed in meditation) From many readings, I've rarely seen this formally addressed, inducing me to raise the question. It seems many experts in the meditation field would suggest that a meditator's eyes be kept closed throughout their meditation to prevent activity or thought distractions. This would include Wayne Dyer. I pose a bit differently, depending on the situation. For example, a valuable part of experiencing any waterfall site is both the sight (via seeing) and sound (via hearing) of falling waters. Included also would be the occasional sight/sound of moving (river) or wavelet (lake) waters. Also, pertinent here would be meditations conducted in the presence of most other outdoor wonders of nature. Certain other meditations might also favor sight with the eyes, e.g., viewing videos or relics in churches; or use of other senses, e.g., hearing sounds (mantras), or smelling (aromas).

However, certain other meditation formats, (e.g., TM, a meditation on 'Spirit', or focusing on blank spaces), may be better served with eyes closed, limiting possible distractions during meditation. Whereas sound is difficult to control, views (with eyes) can be readily controlled by simply opening them vs. closing them at will.

Or... from a very recent and surprising discovery: googling via cellphone or computer: 'Wayne Dyer, Morning, Daytime, or Evening Meditations'. What appears are Front Covers of Wayne Dyer's available Sound Recordings and Books. 'Key moments' of various Sound Recordings are available online for folks to sample. Recordings & books are also listed for purchase. Regular access to 'Key moments' has invigorated my meditation possibilities. I invite the book's reader to share my joy.

Or... as a closing for this sub-section, all folks who practice meditation need to strive to look for improvements in their meditation techniques and practices that will help them (particularly with regularity in their practice). For myself, recent years have been spent experimenting with several techniques that have been found quite interesting and useful, with suggestions offered to improve certain applications of these techniques. One great example is doing meditation in the presence of natural environmental surroundings. Another is doing meditation at nighttime before falling asleep, or upon awakening at night. I have found nighttime (for me at least) to be the best time for meditation, the daytime often being too busy with mundane tasks. Then too, repeating the 'Japa' sound of ...AH.... on exhaling breaths helps one to initially fall asleep or more readily return to sleep upon awakening. This improves one's overall sleep performance, and thereby their health. 'Japa' also facilitates our journey both to and 'in the Gap', the space between our thoughts, by blocking many of the thoughts that typically clutter our minds each day. This is key to 'opening the door' to make conscious contact with 'God', allowing in all of His Love and healing realities to anyone.

CHAPTER 7- 100 NARRATIVE HEALING MEDITATIONS

Introduction

The following 100 Narrative Healing Meditations which make up **Part II, Chapter 7** are sub-divided into **9 (emboldened) Subsection 7(A) to 7(I) Titles**. The reader should first look at the list of **9 Subsections 7(A) to 7(I) Titles** below and choose up to several **Subsection Titles** of interest to them. After choosing the **Subsection Titles** of interest, the reader should refer to the list of *italicized specific Meditation titles* under each **Subsection Title** and select the specific Meditations of interest to them. Each *Meditation title* attempts to succinctly explain the overall purpose/content of the meditation. Immediately following each *Meditation title*, a page number is listed to locate and find the beginning of the meditation narrative.

Chapter 7, 100 Narrative Healing Meditations covers almost all the topics and concepts discussed in the narrative Themes covered in Part I, 'The Background to My Meditation Practice', Chapters 1 to 6 (pp 2-142). It is highly recommended that each reader familiarize themselves with the contents of the Themes.

As a suggested strategy to select and utilize any of the 100 Narrative Healing Meditations, there is no one prescription or strategy for the reader to follow*. Each reader will be different according to their interests, past lifetime experiences, and current mind dispositions.

*One possible strategy to suggest is **1(a)** Select 1 to 2 of the **9 Subsection 7(A) to 7(I) Titles** of particular interest to the reader from the **Subsection 7(A) to 7(I) Titles with Accompanying Meditation Titles List** (pp 146-152 below); **1(b)** For each of the **Subsections 7(A) to 7(I) Titles** selected, check off in pencil *Meditation Titles* of particular interest; **1(c)** Read through the selected Meditations within the text and prioritize them; **1(d)** Try utilizing top-priority selections as part of the reader's meditation practice. **2(a)** To consider additional **Subsection 7(A) to 7(I) Titles**, refer again to the **Subsection 7(A) to 7(I) Titles with Accompanying Meditation Titles List** (pp 146-152 below) and select up to several additional **Subsection 7(A) to 7(I) Titles** beside those selected in step (1a) above. **(2b)** Then for each newly selected **Subsection 7(A) to 7(I) Title**, check off in pencil *Meditation Titles* of particular interest. **(2c)** Read through the selected Meditations and prioritize them. **(2d)** Try utilizing top-priority selections as part of the reader's meditation practice. **(3)** To consider additional **Subsection 7(A) to 7(I) Titles**, refer to steps (2a) to (2d) just above and follow the guidelines. Special Note: one can use a small notebook to record their notes on meditations they select.

Prenote to the 100 Narrative Meditations: The author has spent considerable time over the past several years collecting and collating these diverse pearls of wisdom and translating them into 'to the point' narrative writings. The 'beauty' of this collection of meditations is the particularly wide range of diversity of positive-oriented healing ideas and concepts that are covered within the 100 brief and concisely written narrative meditations. The author knows of <u>no</u> other book on meditation that offers such a diversity of rich, valuable ideas and strategies for healing. And they are so well-researched and presented! These 100 meditations are arranged into 9 Subsections: 7(A) Meditations that Get Us in the Mood; 7(B) Resources for Healing; 7(C) Understanding Love as a Many Splendored Thing; 7(D) Melding Worldly Love with Infinite Love; 7(E) The Power of Infinite Love within the 'Soul' for Healing; 7(F) Dealing with Past- Suffering and Trauma- Moving on in Life (a) Worldly; (b) Spiritual; (c) Worldly/Spiritual; 7(G) The Power to Change the Past via Imagination; 7(H) Dealing with Negativity, Fear, and Ego- Origins and Effects of each of these in Human Affairs; 7(I) Perfection and Wonderment of the Infinite Side.

The author's most favored narrative meditations that demonstrate strong positive tonality, along with potentially effective healing outcomes, come from Subsection 7(D)-Meditations 4, 5, and 6. These principally deal with actual interfaces between folks still in this life with departed 'Souls' they once knew and loved who are presently on the 'Infinite Side'. This would include parents and caretakers. The main emphasis in these 3 meditations is that all interfaces between folks from both 'Sides' should focus on past joyful events that occurred, which all enjoyed when they were together in this life. This would be in direct opposition to dealing with or emphasizing past negative feelings, thoughts, and acts that transpired between these same individuals in this life. The current emphasis on happiness shared by those on both sides helps those who are still on this side to heal from any past negative difficulties with those they once knew! For me, Meditation 5- *Worldly and Infinite Connect at Favorite Sites or Places for Healing, pp 178-8*, describes the great healing that has occurred between me & both my parents departed on the Other Side.

Subsection 7(A) to 7(I) Titles with Accompanying Meditation Titles Lists

Subsection 7(A) Meditations that Get Us in the Mood- 3 Meditations. pp 152-155.
Meditation 1- *Time of Silence as 'Golden' in One's Day.* p 152.
Meditation 2- *Focus in the Present Sense Enhances the Joy in Doing Activities.* p 153.
Meditation 3- *Defining the Architecture of a Fully Evolved Person: I AM all that I AM.* p 154.

Subsection 7(B) Resources for Healing. 3 Meditations. pp 155-159.
Meditation 1- *Identifying Worldly and Spiritual Resources for Healing.* p 155.
Meditation 2- *Human & Social Resources- Tools that Reestablish and Reassure Self-Confidence.* p 157.
Meditation 3- *Through Awareness, We Can Choose to Be Different in Feeling, Thinking, and Acting.* p 158.

Subsection 7(C) Understanding Love as a Many Splendored Thing- - 15 Meditations. pp 159-174.
Meditation 1- *Having Just Arrived Here in this Life, it is So Very Different.* p 159.

Subsection 7(F) Dealing with Past- Suffering and Trauma- 26 Meditations. pp 202-226.

Meditation 2(G)- *Origins & Effects of Fear in Human Affairs: Fear of Feeling Alone, Adults/Infants.* p 241.

Meditation 3(A)- *Origins and Effects of Ego in Human Affairs: Ego's Definition.* p 242.

Meditation 3(B)- *Origins and Effects of Ego in Human Affairs: Suggested Ways to Deal with Ego.* p 243.

Subsection 7(I) Perfection and Wonderment of the Infinite Side- 7 Meditations. pp 244-250.

Meditation 1(A)- *Healing Flow from Book Title: 'Meditation to Healing Freedom thru Infinite Love'.* p 244.

Meditation 1(B)- *Positive Words of God by Watching Your Words.* p 245.

Meditation 1(C)- *Forgiveness in Our Worldly State is Unneeded in the Infinite State.* p 246.

Meditation 1(D)- *Infinite Love, One Way of Defining It.* p 247.

Meditation 1(E)- *Contrasting Examples of 'this Side' with 'the Other Side'.* p 248.

Meditation 1(F)- *I AM Healed via the 'One' (or 'Source'), totally Composed of Goodness.* p 249.

Meditation 1(G)- *Incredible Infinite Wonders within the 'Core', the Home of Our Higher Power.* p 250.

The 100 Narrative Healing Meditations

Subsection 7(A)- Meditations that Get Us in the Mood

Subsection 7(A)- Meditation 1- *Time of Silence as 'Golden' in One's Day.*

One of the Marist Brothers in the high school in Miami, Florida which I attended and graduated from in 1963, used to start his morning group prayer with the following:

'Be silent and know that I am God'.
'Be silent and know that I am'.
'Be silent and know that I'.
'Be silent and know'.
'Be silent and'.
'Be silent'.
'Be'.

Henry Wordsworth Longfellow and Henry David Thoreau were both emphatic in expressing the need for each person to have a quiet space in their lives for silence, meditation, or prayer for a short amount of time each day. For me, this time in silence is best carried out by imagining myself being in wintertime nature, e.g., in Robert Frost's poem of 'being deep in the woods on a snowy evening, with miles to go before I sleep, and miles to go before I sleep'. Or imagining myself on a beautiful beach on a sunny warm day at Singing Beach, Manchester-by-the-Sea, MA, experiencing the warm summertime ocean water, viewing each wave crash onto the shore and recede backward, watching seagulls and sandpipers abound, admiring a rock-strewn shore with glacially carved cliffs surrounding the back of the beach at the east end, with people all around relaxing and enjoying these scenes also. And, at the heart of these scenes, our 'Source', 'God', or 'Universal Consciousness' is an integral core and cause for all this wonderful creation.

Just spend 5 to 10 minutes in silence, relaxing the muscles in the body one-by-one, and imagining (or going to) your favorite scenic spot, witnessing, and enjoying all your favorite scenes in a panoramic fashion, or viewing your favorite scene from your video camera or smart-phone recording. No conflicts, simply feeling relaxation, peace, joy, healing, freedom, release, and invisibly a piece of God's Infinite Love.

Subsection 7(A)- Meditation 2- *Focus in the Present Sense Enhances the Joy in Doing Activities.*

Focus for a few minutes on a favorite natural scenic place of yours. Either go there to experience it again in person or imagine it in your mind (viewing pictures or a video can help). This place could be on a seacoast by the ocean at a beach, on a high promontory overlooking the ocean or mountains, by a lakeshore, or wherever natural beauty enthralls you. You could instead envision a favorite activity you particularly enjoy such as golfing, going to a ball game, playing tennis, fishing, or playing cards—whatever. With intention and imagination, place into motion this favorite scene or activity as occurring <u>now</u> (in the present time), and at the same instant savor all the enjoyment and pleasure of that scene or activity. Simply focusing on continuing enjoyment of that scene or activity now, without awareness or concern about 'the time clock' ticking by, extends and expands the 'pleasure' of the event by amplifying the overall enjoyment of the experience as actual time passes.

Focusing on savoring the enjoyment of an activity we are presently engaged with, without any concern over the passage of real-time, brings us closest to the true 'simultaneous' reality of the Infinite Side. 'Simultaneous' means that everything happens in the very same instant. With a focus on thinking and feeling the present while conducting a pleasurable feeling activity that consumes real-time, we call on the 'simultaneous' suggestion of the Infinite. What results is a relay of Infinite Love energy coming from our 'Soul' through our physical body and mind, creating a 'Nirvana' feeling of heightened pleasure and enjoyment in whatever desirable activity we may be involved with. Even while doing a tedious task, by focusing on the present-time mode, we can complete the effort more readily and with greater ease. The key is forgetting about looking at our usual worldly time clock while doing any of these tasks!

Subsection 7(A)- Meditation 3- *Defining the Architecture of a Fully Evolved Person: I AM all that I AM*. (In-text: 'I' refers to the author; 'I AM', as the name of God who lies within each of us as our 'Soul')

What I have recently come to realize is that all the positive and negative experiences that have occurred in each person's life, both in their prior history as well as the present, represent 'building blocks' in creating a truly positive architecture as to where each of us is at presently. What this is saying is that each of these things did not occur randomly or by happenstance, but rather they occurred as the dynamic part of a Divine Plan to get us to the development level where each of us is at a particular point in time. In other words, all of our experiences, both positive and negative including hardships and tragedies, have all contributed positively to building a more <u>highly</u> evolved human being, consisting of body, mind, and 'Soul'.

They say that age matures us and that as we age and experience more, we have a greater awareness of the realities of life as well as ourselves. We tend to remember more about the positive, enjoyable things and want to forget the negative memories. But the negative memories represent an 'equal' in the building of our total architecture of awareness and experiences, which make us more highly 'evolved' both as spiritual as well as bodily beings. We will carry this 'charge' and memory of our evolvement with us through all eternity. It is and truly will be the total of each of us, as well as part of all of us Unified as 'One' in the next life. As we all grow older in this life, we evolve forward toward the 'One', or 'God' of all-Love (Infinite Love) which makes up the entire Infinite Universe. Our lifetime progression reads: 'I AM all that I AM'.

Subsection 7(B)- Resources for Healing

Subsection 7(B)- Meditation 1- *Identifying Worldly and Spiritual Resources for Healing*.

One should call on and utilize all the 'helping' resources available to any of us for healing solutions to past lifetime difficulties, traumas, and tragedies. This would include both worldly (incarnate) and Infinite (spiritual) related resources, which can either be used separately or in combination depending on the individual's choice. Each of us should call on appropriate worldly 'helping' resources that have been made available for all of us to utilize while here in this life. These would include (1) awareness and consciousness about our past; (2) proper diet; (3) adequate exercise; (4) keeping a diary of past experiences; (5) fostering a love of self (including the 'child' within); (6) developing loving communities of supporting people to help us; (7) having loving relationships; (8) utilizing counseling therapy; and (9) use of medications under the proper care of professionals.

Additionally, my life experiences have resulted in the development of another dimension for healing, namely the awareness and power of spiritual healing. Yet I feel that both worldly and spiritual strategies can be utilized, either separately or infused together. Either way, the principal goal for each person is producing the most effective healing for themselves from the after-effects of past life difficulties, which will provide them with greater fulfillment and happiness during the remainder of their lives.

Dr. Alice Miller, an author of many books on early-in-life sufferings of children, expressed in her work, "Free from Lies, Discovering Your Own True Needs":

> 'My belief is that no therapy can fulfill the wish that many people probably harbor: the wish to be able, at long last, to solve all the problems they have been confronted with so far. This is impossible because life repeatedly confronts us with new problems that can re-awaken the memories stored away in our bodies'.[86]
> Dr. Miller has had doubts that any worldly therapy can provide total healing.

This is precisely why I have embarked on the spiritual quest for total healing, namely, to fill in the gaps and void left behind by the various worldly human processes, while being extremely useful for getting one on a solid road to recovery, may not result in complete healing for them.

The spiritual component for healing is best summarized from my review of Florence Shinn's work, "The Magic Path of Intuition:"

> 'Let the bright white dazzling light of Infinite Intelligence shine from within each of us, (i.e., via our 'Soul'), casting out forever from our mind all doubts, fears, and negative memories from the past, filling our total body and mind with Source's (God's) Infinite Love, light, positiveness, warmth, peace, happiness, guidance, and healing'. note 63

Subsection 7(B)- Meditation 2- *Human and Social Resources- Tools that Reestablish and Reassure Self-Confidence.*

Awareness- that the past pain(s) from any mistreatment did occur, and that the victim needs to take 'the bull by the horns' by clearly admitting this convincingly to themselves before admitting it to others. At the same time, they must put the negative carry-over memories and effects of this past pain aside by crafting positive feelings, thoughts, and actions toward themselves and others, which will improve the victim's future. This is aided by the belief and feelings that the past pain is over and essentially will not return.

Regain Love of Self- Each victim of past mistreatment needs to resurrect a sense of personal reassurance and love of self to counteract the negative after-effects of guilt, self-debasement, lack of equality, and lack of personal self-respect. Re-establishing a sense of positive empowerment is most important for past suffering victims, as each of these people is entitled to and perfectly worthy of being happily alive and productive for themselves as well as for others around them. The victim needs to develop a love of self by appreciating their beautiful body and mind, their work occupation, hobbies, and interests in their lives.

Enlightened Support- Having or finding an enlightened supporter who understands and cares for the troubled victim, without defending in any way whoever caused the past trauma to affect the victim. This supporter is someone that the formerly mistreated person especially likes and can identify with, who has total sympathy for the victim's story. The supporter provides comfort and support to the victim, who may have gone through similar life experiences and can wholly identify with what the victim suffered through in the past.

Social Interaction- Developing a social structure to form a loving and supportive community of family, friends, and whomever else that is reassuring to the person who has endured past painful experiences. This will present consistent positive interactions between people, helping to resurrect and maintain hope and trust for the formerly troubled victim. Family or people whom the person is close to or lives with and interrelates with on a day-to-day basis are particularly crucial in best helping the victim.

Counseling Therapy- Working with a therapist who is sympathetic towards the person who has endured past painful experiences, who is not necessarily sympathetic with the perpetrator(s) who likely caused the past pain. Reassurance must be given to the person who suffered the past pain that they were very likely not responsible for their past suffering, that instead blame should be cast on the perpetrators. Also, repressed pain from the painful memories needs to be expressed and released from the victim's mind.

Written Diary or Journal- This is a record that explains in as much detail as necessary the mistreatment or trauma history, i.e., what, when, how, and by whom, with related emotions and feelings both then and now.

Subsection 7(B)- Meditation 3- *Through Awareness, We Can Choose to Be Different in Feeling, Thinking, and Acting.*

I reflect on the past experiences with the Australian-born priest, Father John Bettridge, emphasized in my first book, "Love and the Infinite, Healing from Childhood," as well as mentioned within this book. Any repetition is simply because of its great importance. One of the main concepts Father John spoke of (also discussed earlier by Neville) is recognizing the power of <u>awareness</u>. Once we become aware of something, through our free will, we can choose to change by thinking and acting differently behavior-wise. Awareness of past mistreatment earlier in a particular victim's life can have carryover effects of learned pain that is embedded in their subconscious mind, which can re-emerge later in their lives as aggressive, 'get-even' emotions and feelings, resulting in negative or malicious acts towards others or back upon themselves. Through awareness, free will, and conscious choice, prior abuse victims can choose to feel and act differently, to instead think and act more positively and lovingly towards others as well as themselves.

Subsection 7(C)- Understanding Love as a Many-Splendored Thing

Subsection 7(C)- Meditation 1- *Having Just Arrived Here in this Life, it is So Very Different*.

Can you fathom via the imagination of something so sweet, fresh, precious, innocent, and little, with all its loving beauty and glory, having just come from the warm protective cocoon of its mother's womb? This small package of love having just arrived here in a completely new, threatening, and strange place, towered over by images of large and very strange-looking beings, with the loving touch and contact of one image (its mother) and total dependence on her for nourishment, acceptance, trust, kindness, and unending love. Just before being in mother's womb, this tiny packet of Love's prior existence was embellished in Infinite Love's glory, euphoric pleasure, acceptance, and permanence, without any concern, fear, or doubt for its protection, or any possibility there for Love's loss, denial, or even question.

Things seem so different here: this newly arrived tiny package does not feel safe nor have the assurance of love or protection like it always felt and had back in its prior Infinite State of existence. This new little being feels separated and alone in the Universe and, at the same time, very fearful. Indeed, this seems so strange and scary. Besides being so small and in an undeveloped physical state, it is unable to do anything to help sustain or protect itself.

> 'See me as I am now: so little, helpless, fearful, cold, hungry…things that were not true back in my recent past Infinite Life. Instead, there I had all the comforts and surroundings of unchallenged love. I find myself crying so very often here, feeling so lonely, confused, and fearful in this alien world. Part of me (my Infinite Spirit) reflects on and calls forth from whence I have recently come, to please come and return, restore, protect, and love me as I once was'…

Subsection 7(C)- Meditation 2- *Why We Came Here to This Life: To Discover New Love*.

Coming into this life, we came from an Infinite experience of total, complete, and painless Love as Infinite Spirits, into a contrasting bodily (incarnate) form with physical senses, emotions, and feelings (including pain). We started our life here as tiny fetuses within another incarnate being, to be born innocently with total dependence on our worldly caretakers to help us physically and mentally to survive, grow, and mature. We would experience both positive and negative experiences and learn through building blocks of awareness and maturation what true unconditional love contrasting with conditional love was through the development and use of our bodily capabilities. This process of learning about the many aspects of love in this life would be quite different from a Love (Infinite) that was 'permanent' and an 'automatic given' as it was back on the Infinite Side.

While our spirits were still back in that Infinite State, this offered us a 'challenge' or an 'adventure' to embark upon here, with the caveat that once the different kinds of love were discovered and experienced by our human senses and feelings in this new worldly state, it would add tremendous dimensions to our already inherent understanding of the many beauties of Infinite Love in that State once we completed our journey here. Love within our life here would mostly offer conditional love, a love that would be frequently given and then taken away according to human free will. From experiences with various dimensions of love here, we (each of our spirits) collectively as 'One' upon return to the Infinite State will re-engage in a truly <u>higher</u> energy state of awareness, joy, bliss, and embellishment with Infinite Love's rewards as compared to what we had before coming on our worldly journey here.

Subsection 7(C)- Meditation 3- *Life's Search for Meaning through Discovery of True Love*.

Victor Frankl's book, "Man's Search for Meaning," presented a real human eye view of typical life experiences in Nazi concentration/death camps where Frankl endured the most horrific conditions for 2½ years during the early to mid-1940s. It seems that his desire to once again experience and love other people both on an individual and collective basis was chief in his mind, which drove him to endure extreme limits to survive until the day when liberation would finally free him from the camps. In summary, his book says that the main purpose here in this life is to find or re-find and experience what true <u>love</u> truly is, no matter how big or small, despite how profound the negative experiences that we must encounter here.

Upon entering a prison camp Frankl was immediately separated from his wife who was pregnant and subsequently knew nothing about her whereabouts or health. It was only after liberation 3 years later that he learned she had rapidly deteriorated and died within several months along with her fetus after being separated from him. The following account from his book reveals his love and search for her:

> 'But my mind clung to my wife's image, imagining it
> with an uncanny acuteness. I heard her answering me

and saw her smile, her frank and encouraging look. Real or not, her look was more luminous than the sun which was beginning to rise'.[87] 'A thought transfixed me for the first time in my life, I saw the truth as it was set into song by so many poets, proclaimed as final wisdom by so many thinkers. The truth—that love is the ultimate and highest goal which man can aspire to. Then I grasped the greatest secret that human poetry and human thought have to impart, that the salvation of man is through love and in love. In a position of utter desolation, when man cannot express himself in positive action, when his only achievement may consist of enduring his sufferings in the right way—an honorable way—in such a position man can, through loving contemplation in the image he carries of his beloved, achieve fulfillment'.. [88]

Subsection 7(C)- Meditation 4- *Removal or Surrender of 'Barriers' which Prevent Love/ Forms of Worldly Love.* (In the text: 'I' refers to anyone)

The writings of American psychiatrist David R. Hawkins, MD., point out that while we are here in this (worldly) physical state, we must surrender all resistances and negative human feelings that block love from adsorbing us, and thereby allow in the radiant, spontaneous energies of love to permeate and transform our overall being into a true love state.[89] Many of us have encountered love-denied, love-withheld, or love-loss experiences during our lives, resulting in walls of 'resistance' being built around us, preventing the great physical joys of present-day love-sharing with others. We must surrender those barriers and walls, and put in their place true, lasting love to replace the love lost from our difficult pasts. This 'surrender' requires a great change in a person's intention and effort (as discussed later). Surrendering those walls of resistance and replacing them with currently available love in the present sense represents the chief key to unlocking the doors to truly embellish and enjoy the joys within this physical life.

Love in its pragmatic form is largely a product of this physical life, which is often 'conditional', (i.e., if you will do this or that for me, I will love you, but if you don't, I won't). Love in its potentially true, 'unconditional' form, (i.e., I will accept you for everything you are, no matter who you are, or what you have been through), is as close and pure to Infinite Love as we can experience in this life. Dr. Hawkins suggests that true love can come in many forms: romantic love or love of relationship; love of family and friends; love of pets; love of freedom and country; love of attributes, talents, skills, or enthusiasms; love of hobbies or favorite activities; love of work and career; love as acceptance or forgiveness; love as appreciation or kindness; love of groups, fraternal bonds, or 'buddies'; love as affection or loyalty; or love as maternal love. note 89

Subsection 7(C)- Meditation 5- *Contrasting Worldly Love to Infinite Love- (Conditional vs. Unconditional vs. Infinite)*. (In the text: 'I' refers to anyone)

In this human life, our body through its senses, emotions, and ego largely experiences conditional love, and much less often unconditional love. Conditional love is the rule of thumb in this physical life: 'If you do this or that for me, I will love you, but if you don't I won't'. This includes many aspects of romantic love. Our bodies and minds are programmed and 'hard-wired' into this reality, which is inculcated into all of us from the moment of our birth into this life. This type of love is susceptible to being easily given and then readily taken away, and only given back when certain stipulated conditions or requirements by the love-giver are met by the supposed love recipient. Unconditional love is a relatively rarer occurrence in this life: 'I will love you for what you are, no matter what you've done or endured, what you've said, how you've performed, no matter what your feelings are, how you look, what you possess materially, or what you represent'. This is pretty much the maximum conception of unconditional love, coming anywhere close to Infinite Love, that our bodies, senses, and minds are capable of perceiving or doing in this life.

Unconditional love is an occurrence in this life that is rare and intermittent and can come and go according to certain human situations, but <u>Infinite Love</u> always was, is now, always will be, and can never, ever be taken away. And, the vastness of Infinite Love is indescribable from our human language or perception perspective, in that the euphoria, pleasure, joy, acceptance, and freedom feelings generated from this Love are so much greater in comparison to the euphoria, pleasure, and joy from the best worldly unconditional love that can ever occur in our lives. This incredible and incalculable Infinite Love is what we will all have waiting for us at the end of this life at our next stop, the Infinite State.

Subsection 7(C)- Meditation 6- *Comparison of Infinite Love with Worldly Love*.

From what Dr. David Hawkins describes as true love here in this life, can we fathom the difficult-to-imagine dimension of Infinite, totally accepting Eternal Love we will all face after this life? The Infinite Love State is where we all emerged from before this life, an Infinite wonder of totally accepting and encompassing love, way beyond anything indicated by Dr. Hawkins or suggested by anyone else within this life, even the best of love in an unconditional sense (i.e., the best romantic relationship here). Dr. Hawkins mentions that love here can be conditional or unconditional, and if conditional, can be temporary, i.e., here today, and easily 'taken' away or gone tomorrow as so often happens with most typical love interactions and experiences between people in this life.

But with Infinite Love, it is not only perfect, omniscient, and comprising everything in the Universe, but it is, always was, always will be, cannot <u>ever</u> be taken away, and is far superior with far greater warmth and euphoric joyful pleasure as compared to the best romantic relationship here in this life. A love that is untrammeled and is part of an Integrated Universe of 'God', that can never be 'judged' as taken away like love can be in this life, nor held accountable for people at the end of their lives as Heaven versus Hell for all eternity as is typically taught by various worldly religious systems.

Subsection 7(C)- Meditation 7- *Contrasting Worldly Love Experiences to Enhance Infinite Love Joys at Our Next Stop*.

If we can just imagine for a moment our existence before being born into this life when we all thrived under the embellishment of Infinite Love back in the prior Infinite State consisting of a perfect state of acceptance, euphoria, warmth, joy, and understanding, merged under an umbrella of Universal Love. All Love and acceptance within that perfect Spiritual State were a 'given' in that they didn't have to be 'earned' (i.e., 'worked for'), nor could this Infinite Love ever be taken away like worldly love typically is in this life. Nor could the Love be held accountable for a later-on 'judgment day' as is taught by Western religious traditions that happen at the end of this physical life.

Somehow, Infinite Wisdom fathomed that an even higher joy and euphoria of the Infinite Love State would be envisioned and created by experiencing, via worldly physical life, contrasting imperfect love that wasn't a 'given' in that it had to be 'worked for' or 'earned'. Also, this worldly love could be conditional, intermittent, or lost temporarily, yet gained back through various emotions, promises, and love acts within this life. The physical experience of love as conditional and intermittent with 'coming and going', versus more consistent and longer-lasting unconditional love, would represent a contrast that would expand and enhance our overall appreciation for the totality of all Love in the Universe. Through Infinite memory, this contrast would enhance the overall understanding, dimension, pleasure, joy, and euphoria of the Infinite Side (including Infinite Love itself) once we arrived back there at the end of this life.

Subsection 7(C)- Meditation 8- *Analogous Comparison of Property* *Landscaping Differences with Love Differences.*

I would like to offer an example of viewing contrasting property landscaping differences as actually enhancing the pleasure of viewing bounteous and beautiful landscaping. Then I would like to relate this comparison to contrasts between conditional and unconditional love experiences in this life and how the comparison of these will enhance the euphoria, pleasures, and joys of Infinite Love when we arrive at our next stop, the Infinite State.

This example comes from a meditative-contrast experience recently encountered while visiting friends in Northern California. I happened to be outdoors doing my daily routine jogging exercise, this time through an exclusive housing neighborhood where we happened to be staying. It was determined that day to have no remorse nor ego desire over the fact that I absolutely could not financially afford to own one of these fine properties. Rather, I was simply admiring the different architectures of the properties, as well as the types and amounts of landscaping and vegetation around each property while cruising through various neighborhood streets. Some properties had a plethora of vegetation and trees, with a rich combination of leafy and/or evergreen hedges neatly trimmed, with evergreen, eucalyptus, oak, maple, fruit, nut, and palm trees of various varieties scattered throughout the property. Other properties offered little if any vegetation or trees except some grass, walls, and pavement.

It struck me that visually contrasting the properties having little or no vegetation and trees with those having an abundance, greatly <u>enhanced</u> the pleasure and joy of viewing the properties with bounteous vegetation and trees. Without this contrast, I would not have developed this enhanced pleasure from viewing the abundant vegetation and treed properties. I liken this to experiencing the contrast between (untrue) conditional and (true) unconditional love in this life, and how memories of these differences (contrasts) of love here will greatly enhance the overall spiritual joys of the higher ordered Infinite Love each of us will experience upon our return to the Infinite State.

Subsection 7(C)- Meditation 9- *What Near Death Experiences (NDEs) Teach Us about the Infinite Love State*.

A significant part of the wisdom and dimension of Infinite Love is the reality that 'forgiveness' for errors or sins committed, or things left unaccomplished during this worldly existence is completely unnecessary and absent in the Infinite State, including our entry into that State. New York Times Best Selling Author, Anita Moorjani, discovered during her Near Death Experience (NDE) that despite all the emphasis in this life of a traditionally taught judgment day encounter facing each of us upon entry into the next life, this was false.[90] Our entry there will instead be accompanied by the opening of 'arms of love and acceptance', with nothing to judge nor forgive, and that all faults with associated 'guilt' and 'blame' typically encountered here are completely meaningless and non-existent there. [note 90] In other words, Infinite Love does not know of or identify with fault-finding, nor follow-up punishment for errors or faults committed here. For each 'Soul' entering the eternal state, what is put in the place of fear over errors, faults, or things not accomplished here with their consequences in this life, is the easy flow of entering the next life-state consisting of total Love, acceptance, perfection, euphoria, clarity, and warmth.

Each person mentioned in this work who came back to this life from a Near Death Experience (NDE) described an Infinite Force with overflowing Love that is near at hand, which is far greater than anything encountered here in this life. Each was convinced of a 'Source', 'Power', 'Great Spirit', or 'Father' of the Universe far greater than any of us here could <u>ever</u> imagine, just awaiting our eventual entry into its Paradise with open, loving, and caring hands. Also, this 'Source' is far more loving, giving, compassionate, and warm than any of us will ever encounter here. And we can bring about the realities of those loving feelings right here, right now, by each of us allowing via our conscious thought and imagination that His Infinite Love is currently freely available via our 'Soul', infusing our body and mind with His Healing Love.

Subsection 7(C)- Meditation 10- *Rationale for Folks Returning to this Life Following their NDE into the Afterlife.*

An interesting insight from the writings of the three authors: Anita Moorjani, Betty Eadie, and Eben Alexander, M.D., who each encountered Near Death Experiences (NDEs) on the Other Side, is that once they returned here each was convinced that <u>this</u> side was the best place to be at this point in their existence. Despite all the wonderful things they learned and encountered on the Infinite Side, life within this worldly realm in the present time context was the most desirable thing to be experiencing at this point, as each of them was thrilled to have made the decision (via free choice) to return to this life.

What was discovered is that perfection and Infinite Love making up the entirety of the Infinite State could be experienced in bits and pieces within this life through conscious awareness and imagination, the bodily senses, and emotions. Also, producing and experiencing tiny pieces of Infinite Love via unconditional love (romantic-related) acts here in this life is something fantastic that cannot be replicated within the Infinite State because of the human bodily feeling and emotional aspects applied to love here. Each realized they had unfinished 'business' back within this realm consisting of educating people about (1) the existence of great beauty and Love existing in the Infinite Realm; (2) the fact that Infinite Love can be replicated and experienced here even in 'bits and pieces'; (3) each person's Unity with 'Oneness' of everything in the Universe (via their 'Soul'); (4) that healing can occur here in this life through solid belief by each person in their being (via 'Soul') 'an integral part of the Unified 'Oneness' of everything in the Universe'.

Subsection 7(C)- Meditation 11- *Imagine 'Passing' from this Life into the Next (Infinite Life)*. (In-text: 'I' refers to the author; 'I AM' or 'I am' as the name of God who lies within each of us as our 'Soul')

And then, I imagine myself as just having 'passed' from this life, and having entered the eternal state of Nirvana, Eternity, Infinite Love, and Bliss. This provides my spirit with a 100% instant understanding of why we each came into this past human life and had to put up with the good along with evil and suffering, and exactly how this stacks up in an Infinite Universe of Wisdom consisting of so much Infinite Love and goodness. These are things that many of us have spent our entire lifetimes pondering over, with no definitive answers given. All our lifetime questions are instantly answered, such as why it seemed to us that evil far outweighed the good in this life when we were alternately told that the good far outweighed the bad. At almost the instant of death from this life, we are re-born and re-awakened, in that we completely understand all the answers to this question, as well as many others. All doubts and questions as to 'why we came here and had to suffer so much' are completely answered to the satisfaction of each of our 'Spirits'.

All worries about 'daily life' from my past worldly existence, including all things that were supposed to have been done and were not, including material things and gain, are gone, forgotten, and no longer relevant. This provides me with tremendous <u>relief</u>. I am One with all beings and all things in the Universe, acceptable and accepting, without any competition, separation, or individuation, which in my past life generated (via egos) competing rivalry with others to be the best. I meld and am equal with every being and thing in the entire Universe, which encompasses and transcends everything with Infinite Love. This self generates euphoric pleasure and joy of unimaginable magnitude, unlike anything ever experienced in human life. Everything that ever was or will be is present here via Infinite Love through eternity.

I AM Ageless,
I AM Boundless,

I AM All Love,
I AM Infinite Light,
and I AM finally free and released.

Subsection 7(C)- Meditation 12- *The Meaning and Feeling of 'Warmth', A Closeness to Infinite Love*

'Warmth' can be defined as both a sense and a feeling intertwined, that is, an almost blind feeling and trust by one individual for another individual, that no matter how bad or whatever circumstances the one individual has endured, that person is loved and accepted by the other person for all that they truly are. This truly represents an incredible feeling of total acceptance for a person by another human individual, the full feeling being defined as unconditional love, very closely bordering on the Infinite Love of God which is a completely euphoric love that just is, does not have to be earned, and can never be taken away.

Subsection 7(C)- Meditation 13- *An Author's True Experience with Infinite Love, Realized-Part I.*

Here is a pathway to <u>Infinite Love</u> found at Singing Beach on a summer day in 2006 (Ch. 3, Th. 2, pp 64-8).

I have it in my hand! A clear memory of the ultimate meaning of several past ethereal encounters as being Infinite Love. I can tell you what I think Infinite Love is. But to describe it in language terms is quite difficult because it is clearly an energy entity that is well beyond our physical state of understanding, yet so close to seemingly being a part of us. I know what conjugal love is: looking forward to it, the sharing, the good feeling and pleasure, and the wonderful effects both during and after sharing it, as true and big as love can be in this life. But the Infinite Love discussed here is far, far beyond that, the description and magnitude of which is so very difficult to define or even explain from our language contexts.

Infinite Love is so very strange to feel and endure, yet so completely trustworthy to be true and real, with complete confidence in its all-goodness with absolutely <u>no</u> competition or evil. This Love is truly incredible when compared with our normal human love contexts and expectations. We can best try to explain it via the memory of dramatic human feelings. And to receive it, (i.e., Infinite Love), one does not have to be rich, famous, successful, of high status, dependent on others, give to receive, or any other human thing. The only requirements are being open, humble, willing, and accepting, and it will simply be given. And, once you receive it, it will be yours for all times going forward, and it can never be taken away.

When I felt this Love with all its magnificence enveloping me with incredible euphoric and trusting feelings, I realized that despite my life with all its past challenges and doubts, these clearly did not matter. Also, everything going forward would be just 'fine' and for me, to not 'worry' at all about the past or the future. All that had happened to me in this life did not matter within this new trusting state I was temporarily visiting, while still being physically at my favorite location at Singing Beach in Manchester-by-the-Sea, MA on that summer day in 2006. These factors during these few brief moments made me feel so remarkably healed, released, and free. It was not like being in a new place, but rather awakening into a new and completely pleasurable reality or 'energy' state while still being in my familiar favorite worldly place. This produced great euphoria! During that day, all my bodily discomforts and mental anguish vanished. It felt like I could not ask for nor endure anything better while being at this wonderful place of relaxation and joy for myself and so many other folks. It felt like I was in a piece of 'Nirvana' or 'Heaven.

Subsection 7(C)- Meditation 14- *An Author's True Experience with Infinite Love, Realized-Part II*.

This follows Meditation 7(C), 13- After experiencing the 2006 ethereal encounter plus several follow-up euphoric encounters over the next few years, I slowly began to realize with increasing clarity the true nature and source of these highly euphoric feelings as being Infinite Love. As best as I can describe, this 'Infinite Love' is (or was) composed of (1) a love far greater than any or all combined worldly love; (2) feelings of complete release and freedom; (3) feelings of complete acceptance, peace, and clarity; (4) actual relief or healing from all pain and ills in this life; (5) a permanence that can never, ever be taken away; (6) being non-judgmental both now and at life's end; (7) ethereal joys far beyond all pleasures of this world. The combined energy of Infinite Love and joy generated from these aspects cannot be duplicated or exceeded by the totality of any or all worldly love with all its associated pleasures. And from human dimensions, these components of Infinite Love represent just the beginning. Might there be something else important that is missing?

From an ancient spiritual statement or proclamation, 'We are all Unified as One under an umbrella of Infinite Love and Goodness of God', the suggestion is made that everything in the Universe is merged under 'One', composed of all-goodness and all-Love in the Universe. But what about all the mistakes, misgivings, wrongs, and evil acts that have been produced by humankind? How is it even possible these be considered as included as any part of the spiritual proclamation 'all things being Unified as One under an Umbrella of God's all-goodness and Love'? This would indicate that this proclamation goes well <u>beyond</u> the seven Infinite Love components listed above. It would mean that God's Love must 'absorb' or 'absolve' all human mistakes, sin, and negativity under some sort of Infinite umbrella consisting of incredible 'Universal forgiveness, acceptance, understanding, and compassion'. This would truly represent an Infinitely driven 'forgiveness' that goes well beyond our very limited perception of worldly forgiveness, proving that God's Love for us is so much <u>more</u> than we ever thought possible or could even imagine!

Subsection 7(C)- Meditation 15- *Other Strands of Infinite Love Evidenced within Our Lives Here*.

Follows Medit. 7(C), 14- Other vestige signs of Infinite Love from human endeavors in this life could be:

a) Euphoric, joyful, and relaxing feelings and experiences while visiting and enjoying the beauties of nature such as ocean shorelines, beaches, rivers, lakes, mountain views, tropical areas, or anywhere where scenic beauty inspires a meditative, peaceful, and reflective feeling state. These represent the face of the 'Infinite' or 'God', experienced by viewing the perfections or wonders of nature. Similarly, this was experienced and expressed by St. Francis of Assisi during his time.

b) Loving relationships between males and females, and what typically happens at the beginning of most intimate relationships, i.e., the initial aura that many folks have with heightened euphoria, excitement, positive emotions, elation, joy, and in many instances, sexual attraction. This could be Infinite Love energy being interchanged between each person's 'Soul' in the new relationship.

c) Focus on the 'pop' music recording culture in America over past decades, with its numerous artist recordings focusing on love relationships portraying imagined themes of harmonious love, which attempt to overshadow typical troubled situations in many typical human-love relationships. These music creations that stir deep emotions could be simulated via vestige energy imprint memories stored within the music composer's 'Soul' from their prior Infinite State existence. These energies, perhaps imbued with Infinite Love, transmit via the composer's mind ideas for the creation of their music. Listeners of music feeling euphoric 'highs' may also be touching this same Infinite Love energy.

d) Exploration of all sorts in 'worldly life', including travel to or exploring new places, exploring new ideas, or writing books (maybe this book). Have you ever noticed how babies (infants) seem so enthusiastic about freely exploring by sensing and touching their new surrounding environment? Being brand new here, they carry a recent direct touch and connection with explorative and love-related energies from their very recent Infinite past.

e) Spiritual-type activities that many people engage in. These would include membership in religion, church, or other organizations with associated worship, prayer, or meditation along with raising funds, giving alms, or conducting programs to help the poor. These could well be vestige touches with Infinite Love.

f) The magic of Christmastime, when the presence of Jesus and Santa (their Spirits) are brought together to produce good tidings, good cheer, and hope for many people in the world. Perhaps touches of Infinite Love?

Subsection 7(D)- Melding Worldly Love with Infinite Love

Subsection 7(D)- Meditation 1- *Six Principal Reasons for Coming into this Life*. ('I' refers to anyone)

For the following reasons, I freely chose back in the Infinite State to come and enter into this life to fully experience a bodily existence along with its emotions, five senses, and ego: (1) to clearly contrast the perfection of Infinite life before my birth with the imperfections of this worldly life (particularly with love), thereby gaining greater appreciation for Infinite Love on the Infinite Side when I return there after this life; (2) to experience and feel the five senses: to see, hear, touch, feel, and smell; and the nine human emotions: to love, hate, have envy, warmth, compassion, joy, pathos, irony, and humor; (3) to experience my own ego in conjunction with the egos of other people; (4) to clearly recognize the difference between worldly unconditional love (i.e., I accept you for everything you are, what you do, and represent), versus conditional love, (i.e., 'If you do this or that for me I will love you, but if you don't, I won't'); (5) to re-discover my spiritual part or 'Soul' deep within me which is God that lives forever, but was put asleep within me at birth so I would not immediately recollect nor recognize it; (6) to re-connect with this perfect Infinite Loving 'Soul' part of me as I grew up and matured through awareness, consciousness, intent, meditation, or prayer.

Subsection 7(D)- Meditation 2- *Reasons for an Easy/Happy Transition from the Infinite State to this Life via Mother*.

A <u>smooth</u> transition from the perfect, Infinite State into this worldly, physical state is very necessary for any being's successful and happy transition from the Infinite Side. This requires a mother who translates to the infant that has just been born a piece of Infinite, unconditional Love that it has just left behind. In physical life, this type of love is called 'motherly love'. This love certainly mimics the unconditional Infinite Love left behind in the Infinite State, in that a mother unswervingly and unwittingly gives her love to a helpless infant for all that it is as a person in its brand-new physical state, not expecting anything from her baby in return. Every infant or child has a legitimate self-need to be noticed, understood, and taken for what and who they truly are by their mother. In the first few months of life, the child needs a mother to provide for all its needs and to be mirrored by her absolute love. Not receiving this fully from the mother in the infant's brand-new state of existence represents a double blow for that baby: (a) not receiving unbridled, unconditional love from the mother; (b) not being able to call on the spiritual powers of Infinite Love from within itself (via its 'Soul') or from the recently departed Infinite Side to help rescue it.

What often happens in this physical life is that the mother projects onto her baby all the frustrations and needs from deficits and negativities in her own life and sustains these grievances on the child throughout its upbringing, rendering the child a virtual slave to the mother. This represses the child's natural emotional development, needs, and expression as a human individual. Oppression and lack of respect for the child in the first few years of life as a real, separate person with uniqueness to be protected and fostered, results in life-long social and behavioral problems down the road in that same child's adult life.

Subsection 7(D)- Meditation 3- *Growing Toward the Divine by Experiencing Worldly Love*.

We grow toward awareness of the Infinite Spirit through emergent feelings of the essence of true love in this life via the human senses and emotions. We are here to grow toward God through a growing awareness of the Infinite Love that we came from before this human experience when we were still in the Infinite State. We are here in this worldly state to grow back toward the Divine by growing unconditional love with others through awareness and the experience of creating this love by sharing it with another or others, without any prior expectation of receiving that same love back from them. Any progress towards this here in this life is positive, and Infinite memory of this (via our 'Soul') only serves to build for us an enhancement of the joys and ecstasy of Infinite Love upon our return to the Infinite State. In essence what this is saying is that Love is God, and God is Love, and that this can be perceived, felt, and experienced via the practice of true unconditional love with others during this life. This truly builds us toward the joys of Infinite Love.

Pondering this further, what this means is that while we are here in this life, we should keep our feelings and thoughts on strictly the good and positive, which will help us to wade through all the negative and debasing things that we all must endure here. This will place each of us on an easy 're-entry' track to return to that joyful 'energy state' of Infinite Love and bliss once we conclude our life here.

Subsection 7(D)- Meditation 4- *Connecting Loves; The Living with Departed Souls We Once Knew*.

Through conscious awareness with intent and meditation, we can connect via our Infinite 'Soul' (or Spirit) with the Spirits of certain departed parents, relatives, or special persons we once knew who are now in the Infinite Love State. Enhancing connection with the Infinite essences of our parents and others is best done by returning to or imagining a geographical spot, location, or an activity where there was joy, fun, and positive times between ourselves and the various folks we once knew. This may well have contrasted with difficult or not-so-good encounters we experienced with certain of these folks earlier in our lives or later in adulthood. Happy memories create high-energy vibrations of positive thinking and feeling, instead of the negative or downside thinking and feeling modes created by unhappy memories.

This effort can be a good alternative to the more common practice of visiting former family members or friends at their actual burial-grave sites. Our parents or caretakers, relatives, and former friends we once knew in this life who are now on the 'Other Side' are available and awaiting our conscious connection with them. They are in a pure state of bliss consisting of Infinite Love, totally devoid of all the rules, culture, expectations, mindsets, and negativity from their former human lifetimes. They only have positivity and perfect Infinite Love to offer us, nothing else. Their Infinite Love (energy) connection with us can be translated through our spiritual essence (or 'Soul') as healing energy, giving each of us positive feelings of love, hope, peace, and healing. This can render spiritual as well as bodily and mind healing within each of us, particularly if we <u>believe</u> that this spiritual 'connection' with them can occur and that this connection will result in feelings of peace and healing for us. Better still, this peace/healing <u>has</u> already occurred.

Subsection 7(D)- Meditation 5- *Worldly and Infinite Connect at Favorite Sites or Places for Healing.* (In the text: 'I' refers to the author)

One of the most powerful meditations I have experienced is returning to an actual location that my parents and I along with close friends visited during the summer when I was a child. This was a place where everybody had fun and happy times together. For anyone, this place could be by a beautiful lake or pond, by a stream at a campsite, in a cabin in the woods, in a picnic area overlooking a stream or mountains, at a beach cottage near the ocean, or anywhere in this world where there is some sort of scenic beauty. This place would have special meaning for you, your caretakers, family members, and/or friends, in that it brought tremendous joy and happiness to all involved. Just returning or imagining going there and reminiscing at that very spot where you all congregated, where you and your parents and others sat, what was said: the jokes, the stories, the laughter, and joy, makes this positive intention connect your spirit with theirs and creates good feelings within you. Each time you return to revisit that favorite spot, this positive connection re-establishes, reinforces, and strengthens those good feelings.

For me, what is significant is returning to Singing Beach, Manchester-by-the-Sea, MA, as often as I can and sitting at the back of the beach on the east end, in front of a group of 60-foot high glacially carved rocks. This is exactly where my parents and I along with their two best friends Mary and Fernand would be together late in the afternoon when the sun's heat had receded somewhat. Reminiscing listening to them talk, all happy, having a great time enjoying the beach and surroundings as well as themselves, contrasts with the more usual challenging and negative encounters back at home. Just reminiscing on those happy times creates for me an intense connection with my folks spiritually. I can feel that they are there in spirit at that very moment. This brings feelings and emotions of intense ecstasy and joy, which at times brings tears to my eyes from joy (not sadness), bodily tingly pins-and-needles sensations, with a distinct feeling of healing. These are clearly vestige signs of Infinite Love. Each time I return to that spot and meditate there late in the afternoon, the feelings of spiritual connection with my folks get stronger.

Subsection 7(D)- Meditation 6- *Healing via Conscious Connection with Souls Known in the Past*. (In-text: 'I' refers to the author; 'I AM' as the name of God who lies within each of us as our 'Soul')

In a specific sense, the meditation process can make conscious contact with departed 'Souls' you once knew during their lives who respected and loved you. They may be family members, relatives, friends, work colleagues, or other folks you once knew. Through conscious intent,

178

this connects spiritual energy from your spiritual essence or 'Soul' with the departed essences or 'Souls' that you once knew and cared about. This energy can be returned to you through your 'Soul', bringing positive benefits to your physical and mental health. This meditation can focus on one's parents or caretakers, as well as 'special people', or as I call them worldly 'guardian angels' who especially cared for each of us while they were alive. I have used this meditation as one of my favorites, providing feelings of peace and tranquility, along with physical and mental health benefits.

For example, I meditate the following: I AM Infinite Love, Perfection, Healing, Good Health, and Peace through 'my 'Soul' to the spiritual essences of both my parents, along with the worldly 'guardian angels' who especially cared for and watched over me particularly when I was younger. For the worldly 'guardian angels'* that I once lovingly and joyfully knew in this life: Gramps (the grandfather on my father's side), Grammy (the grandmother on my mother's side), Auntie Flo (a babysitter I once knew), Brother Ben (my high school principal), Perry (my lifelong friend), and a waitress friend I met in Maine when I was only 7 years old in 1952. Then I imagine connecting with other 'special angel friends' I once knew in my prior Infinite State existence whom I currently in this life do not remember, who joyfully watch over me now.

Perfect physical and spiritual health comes to me from the Infinitely Loving healing energy of the departed Infinite Spirits of my parents, worldly guardian angels, and special angel friends I once knew during my past spiritual existence (but can't remember now), connecting through my 'Soul' to my body, translating healing energy throughout my present physical state.

While performing a series of relaxing 'in' and 'out' breaths, I mentally reflect on 'perfect health' for each of my major body systems from head to toe.

Then I meditate: 'I AM Perfect Health via the Infinitely Loving Energy of Spirits with whom I once shared love (identifying their names), who are all 'Unified as Lovingly 'One' or 'God' in the Universe'.

*The reader can develop their own set or list of people and worldly 'guardian angels' that they once knew and especially loved for their meditative connection.

Subsection 7(D)- Meditation 7- *Creating My Best Day Ahead by Thinking and Feeling Good.* (In the text: 'I' refers to anyone)

I desire when awakening to begin my day by thinking and feeling good, positive, happy, and healthy.

First, I must be completely forgiving to # 1 <u>myself</u>, and thereby love myself. I have had past conflicts with others which at times have been my fault. I disown all feelings of anger and guilt from my past. Only by completely forgiving myself can I open the door and begin to feel the real love of self.

Second, I completely forgive all those who have had negative, hurtful effects on me in my life.

Third, I promote sweetness, kindness, and love for my beautiful body and mind, and my pursuits. I see beauty and magic as I gaze at my eyes in a mirror and just rest there, feeling via my eyes a positive energy vibration coming from my perfect and loving spiritual core (or 'Soul'), which makes me feel good.

Fourth, I reflect on someone I love and look into their eyes, just resting there for a moment, and connect with their Spiritual core (or 'Soul') which then meshes with my own Spirit ('Soul'), producing a 'Nirvana' feeling of connecting two Infinite Loves of our 'Source' or 'God'.

Fifth, today I must resolve to live my life fearlessly. Any good or loving intention that I have or express towards another must be viewed through my eyes fearlessly.

Sixth, when I know that I am love, I don't need to work at being loving towards others, but rather by being true to myself by loving myself, I become an instrument of loving energy that gravitates toward others.

Then, I project sweetness and kindness toward all people whom I will deal with in the day ahead. Even if any of them might combat me, I will still forward love and acceptance to them.

Lastly and most importantly I meditate on the total dimension of the Source's (God's) Infinite Love. This consists of absolute and unimaginable love, joy, bliss, euphoria, and acceptance that is deeper and more voluminous than all the oceans in the world. Neville Goddard talked about Infinite Love as way beyond the most intimate loving relationship between two people in this life. [note 5] Betty Eadie's NDE placed her in Jesus's presence, where she felt a fantastic love unlike any love here, way beyond the best maternal, romantic, or any other love that she could ever imagine, and vastly more than all these combined. [note 22]

Subsection 7(D)- Meditation 8- *Accepting the Facts of Worldly Life with the Peace and Healing of Infinite Love*. (In the text: 'I' refers to anyone)

- I accept the fact that during my prior Infinite existence, I freely chose to enter this life to be born into a completely different dimension by experiencing a physical body.
- I accept the fact that I was born into this life as a helpless infant, totally dependent on others, i.e., caretakers, for all my needs including protection from all harm.
- I accept the fact that in being born, I lost all awareness of my spiritual, perfect core (or 'Soul') which has been with me through all eternity, including the earliest parts of my life.

- I accept the fact that I had to re-find and re-connect with my perfect spiritual core or 'Soul' during my adult life.
- I accept the fact that at times certain people in my life did not treat me well, and because of that, I endured mental and physical anguish at their hands.
- I accept the fact that I have had to face those who mistreated me and tell them that they were at fault and not me for having generated the negativity that has affected me (even up to now).
- I accept the fact that I am releasing all feelings of guilt from within my mind that I was the cause of these mistreatments, as others were responsible for it, not me.
- I accept the fact that I have felt 'anguished' from past mistreatment, that this negativity was in the past and will not return, and instead, I need to think and act more positively going forward.
- I accept the fact that the greater good I do for others, the greater good that is returned to me.
- I accept the fact that I am blessed with healing peace throughout my body and mind from all past hurts by the power of Infinite Love of the Unified Universal 'One', 'Source', or 'God'.

Subsection 7(D)- Meditation 9- *Forgiveness Meets with Infinite Wisdom*.

The whole issue of forgiveness came to the forefront through recently updated news regarding the 1989 horrific Hillsborough, England tragedy at Sheffield Stadium where 96 people were trampled to death in a clearly overcrowded and poorly managed British football sports facility. For the victims surviving families, 'forgiveness' was finally realized after 30 years of the police and news media blaming the fans back then for having been drunk and creating a riot at that event. A recent high court inquest determined that the fans at that time were not drunk or at fault and were thereby forgiven, that instead the stadium authorities and police were to be fully blamed for the disaster.

This is just one example throughout history of the tremendous energy, time, and effort spent in human affairs on all aspects of forgiveness, with this being the engine that drives so much of the negativity that all of us endure in this life. There are so many examples of forgiveness: forgiveness for mercy at trial, the forgiveness of hatred/hurt, forgiveness for debts owed, forgiveness for sins, forgiveness for violence, forgiveness for abuse, forgiveness for wars, or forgiveness for genocides/holocausts. Each of us must meet some level of 'standard' or 'expectation' for forgiveness set by others, and if we fail to meet these we are scorned and made to feel simply 'awful'.

Let us meditate on the totality of what it might mean for all of us if we could agree that our societies and lives are overwrought with concern over forgiveness. How can we cut down on its emphasis? How does the next life Infinite State manage its affairs without a concept of forgiveness? What if there is no negative judgment at the end of this life invoking the need for forgiveness of our sins, indiscretions, or things left 'undone', that instead what awaits us is the open loving arms of our Infinite Source to greet us? Might it produce relief for us here that we will <u>only</u> feel euphoric Infinite Love upon entry into the Infinite State?

Subsection 7(D)- Meditation 10- *NDE Memories Bring Infinite Love from Heaven to this Life*. (In the text: 'I' refers to the author)

It is revealed in the book, "Heaven is for Real", by Todd Burpo, that his young son Colton at the age of four had a Near Death Experience (NDE) where he went to Heaven and afterward returned to his body and life in this world. Colton clearly identified a painting of Jesus by Akiane Kramarik as truly Him that he experienced from the many hundreds of images or pictures shown to him by his father Todd, who is a Pastor at Crossroads Wesleyan Church in Imperial, Nebraska.

Akiane came from a family that lacked religious emphasis or persuasion, but at a young age, she began to have ethereal, spiritual inspirations. These were translated within her as both an ability and insight to create beautiful works of art on various historical religious figures and scenes of note, without her having much of any religious training or background. At only age 8, she created the painting (below) of Jesus.[91]

Prince of Peace, Akiane Kramarik, Age 8
What God Comments. Art & SoulWork

When I view and reflect on Jesus's painting by Akaine, I am awestruck with the notion of having a 'best friends' conversation with Him about our lives, experiences, and challenges that each of us has faced, and would have absolutely no feelings of fear over sharing these with Him. This sharing would be at the same time as being in the presence of the Throne of 'Lord of the Universe', who is intertwined within and around each of us as a veil of unbridled Infinite Love and acceptance. In viewing the painting of Jesus more and more, I have a growing sense of clearly feeling His undivided attention just to me, as well as to billions of others either as passed spirits or still in this physical life who are vying for His undivided attention at the very same instant. This is one clear example of 'everything Unified as One under an Umbrella of Universal Infinite Love', in that He can give His undivided Infinite Loving attention both to me as well as billions of others at the same simultaneous instant.

Whenever I feel a current stress or a negative memory that is a relic of my past lifetime, I quickly turn to view this painting and feel peaceful true healing Love. I also know that others viewing this painting can result in their feeling the same real, true healing Infinite Love.

Subsection 7(E)- Power of Infinite Love Within the 'Soul' for Healing

Subsection 7(E)- Meditation 1- *I Go Within 'Soul' to Find Healing via Infinite Love- Part I*. (In title and text: 'I' refers to anyone; In the text: 'I AM', as the name of God who lies within us as 'Soul')

I go within the inner reaches of my conscience where my 'Soul' or spiritual essence resides near the physical heart area. This essence is eternally existing, and it represents complete peace, tranquility, truth, and harmony. I was not aware of this inner core during my early childhood, but now that I am aware of it, I call forth into the recesses of my 'Soul' for total tranquility and the healing of my body and mind. People only encounter my body which is merely a physical manifestation of this worldly life, which represents ego. But my true eternal self is spiritual, an Infinite everlasting, and perfect being. Since my eternal spirit is perfect, this means that I AM 'One' with the Universe. The energy of my spirit permeates my entire being, i.e., body, mind, and 'Soul', and thereby totally cleanses me of all calamities that have happened to my body and mind by restoring their excellent health. This healing is perfect. I surrender both body and mind to the wisdom and guidance of my Source (God), and thereby His purpose becomes mine. There are no remaining obstructions from past sufferings to flood my mind, only to allow unshakeable faith in the power and presence of His Infinite Healing Love to cure my present body and mind from the past harm that I have endured.

Subsection 7(E)- Meditation 2- *I Go Within 'Soul' to Find Healing via Infinite Love - Part II*. (In the meditation title, 'I' refers to anyone; in the meditation text, 'I' refers to the author)

An important part of this work draws upon our Infinite Source, or God, with its Infinite Loving Power as Spirit or 'Soul' within each of us living persons, to be fully recognized and believed. Once belief in this happens, through conscious intent, a person can initiate an Infinitely Loving and healing process to cure impacted parts of the incarnate body. This healing process includes the mind which has likely been 'hard-wired' with negative influences from memories of repetitive or dramatic hardships endured earlier in our lives. These negative influences have carried over into our current adult lives. The existence of Infinite Love and recognition of it within our 'Soul' along with a strong belief in 'feeling it' are real keys to initiating healing. Also, faith in our Infinite 'Source' via Infinite Love to heal is key in all spiritual aspects of healing.

I have experienced Infinite Love through meditation by first, via intention, going within to my 'Soul' where silence, Love, and quiet exist, and then contemplating Infinite Love's unparalleled depth and vastness that encompasses a limitless Unified Universe. During this meditation process, several ethereal episodes have occurred over the past 18 years in conjunction with being at an ocean beach for several hours on warm summer days. During these episodes, distinct feelings of unparalleled Love, warmth, and euphoria, along with associated 'Nirvana' feelings have occurred, including bodily tingly pins-and-needles sensations, and tearing of the eyes from feelings of euphoric joy, not sadness. To me, these combined sensations and feelings were unlike anything else imaginable within this human context and were clearly ethereal signs of Infinite Love.

Subsection 7(E)- Meditation 3- *The Lord's 'Promise' to Us from Neville Goddard's Work, "The Law and the Promise"*. (In the text: 'I' refers to anyone)

The 'Promise' is a concept in a narrative by Neville Goddard from his work, "The Law and the Promise." The narrative begins with the statement:

> 'All the world's a stage and all the men and women are merely players. The purpose of God's play, or through Jesus Christ's time on earth, was to transform man the created into God the creator. The play begins with the crucifixion of God (via Jesus) as man, and ends with the resurrection of man as God, with God ending up spiritually in man. God became as we are so that we might become as he is. God became man so that man might become first a living being and then a living spirit of God.'[92] God (via Jesus) took upon himself the form of man and became obedient unto death on the cross of man: 'I have been crucified with Christ. It is no longer I who live, but Christ who lives in me. And the life I now live in the flesh, I live by faith in the Son of God, who loved me and gave himself for me (Galatians 2:20).'[93]

His promises relate that he has become man, and in that act has forgotten (left) being God in the process of his human death, in the hope that man thus created would eventually rise as God and that through man's awareness and imagination would see the existence of God in himself (i.e., within his 'Soul') as man's spirit.[94] When we truly buy into the fact that His (God's) presence is within us (our 'Soul') as the Unifying Universal 'One' composed of Infinite Love, we can begin the healing process.

Subsection 7(E)- Meditation 4- *I AM Finally Free by Declaring all Past Negativity Null and Void.* (In the text: 'I' refers to anyone; 'I AM', as the name of God who lies within each of us as our 'Soul')

I hereby open my entire being consisting of body, mind, and 'Soul' to the total energizing and positive unconditional love of my Source (God), which heals my body/mind from any effect of negative thinking that has or may permeate into my mind. Therefore, this automatically heals my body/mind and protects me from all bad thoughts that may arise from the past. I think only positive and good thoughts in the present moment and project these same thoughts forward, making all the negative things that happened to me in the past 'null and void'. I know that at the center of me, i.e., within my 'Soul', I AM ageless, limitless, deathless, perfect, warm, happy, and equal, as this spirit permeates my bodily and worldly affairs now. When I become confused, unhappy, or worried again, I think only happy thoughts in the present, and I surrender all bad thinking and feelings derived from my past to the Infinite Source, the Great Spirit, or God. And in turn, through the perfect clarity of Him, I accept and allow His Infinite Love and healing to freely flow through my mind and body. I AM finally released and <u>free</u> at last!!!

Subsection 7(E)- Meditation 5- *'I AM' as the Name of God who Defines Me and Lies within Me as My 'Soul'.* (In the text: 'I' refers to anyone)

I ask for God's (or Source's) peace-loving, harmonious, and organizing presence.

I AM a powerful being composed of a spiritual core ('Soul'), fully capable through conscious mind intent of creating bodily healing.

I AM loved and cherished dearly, forever; I have nothing to fear; I can do no wrong; I am loved and accepted unconditionally.[95]

I AM principally in this life to find out what worldly love means by comparing Unconditional Love (no strings attached, i.e., I accept you for all you are and represent), with Conditional Love (strings attached, i.e., if you do this or that for me, I will love you, but if you don't I won't).

I AM also in this life to re-discover what became invisible or lost to my 5 senses when I was born, namely my Infinite Loving 'Soul' which has existed through eternity. This Infinite Love part of me was put asleep at my birth, waiting to be re-awakened and then arise.[96]

Let the Divine Design of my life flash into my conscious mind a Perfect Plan.

I AM God; I AM One; I AM Infinite Love; I AM Infinitely Loved; I AM not Judged.

I AM the Resurrection and Light.

I AM the Center of the Universe, and I AM an Impact on the Entire Universe.

I AM at Peace and Happy, and the Universe is at Peace and Happy.

I AM a Powerful, Magnificent, and Wonderfully Loving Force, and I Trust that All is Well.

I AM Already what I have been trying to Attain All My Life.

I AM Surrendering all Damaging Thoughts from Past 'Conditioning' and 'Mind Control'.

I AM Surrendering all my Fears by Allowing in my Source's Fearless and Peaceful Infinite Love.

I AM Forgiving Myself for Judging Me.

I AM a Beautiful Child of the Universe.

I AM in a State of Pure Consciousness and Pure Magnificence.

I AM Letting Go and Releasing all Attachments to any Belief or Outcome and am Trusting Uncertainty.

I AM Willfully Converging, via Intent, my Infinite 'Soul' with the Universal Life-Force Energy of 'One'.

Subsection 7(E)- Meditation 6- *The Voice, Power, and Love from Within Me.*[97] (In the text: 'I' refers to anyone; 'I AM', as the name of God who lies within each of us as our 'Soul')

I go within myself to my invisible, powerful, and invincible crucible, core, or 'Soul', where the Infinite Eternal Spirit of 'Source' or 'God' lies. Within this Spirit of mine lies the essence of the entire Universe where all goodness and law are evident. This internal place within me is completely peaceful and healing. It translates healing outward when I ask of it to my sore, inflamed, and shattered body and mind from any prior childhood or adult life love-denied or love-loss experiences, and harkens comfort and solace from within me. This represents Divine Law and Presence, and Its truth represents the unlimited power of creation through the Infinite Love of Spirit. I AM presently Love, I always have been Love, I always will be Love. The truth about my Infinite 'Source' or 'God' is Infinite Love for all of creation including myself, all people, and all things. This Infinite Love translates as equality for all people through everlasting love, without having to 'earn' love like here in this life. This is a Love that just is, that is permanently within me via Soul, which cannot be questioned, challenged, or taken away like typical love is so often in this life.

Subsection 7(E)- Meditation 7- *Infinite Wonder of 'Source' Transforms Goodness and Healing throughout My Being.* note [97] (In the text: 'I' refers to anyone; 'I AM', as the name of God who lies within each of us as our 'Soul')

I surrender both my body and mind to the 'Source' or 'God' within my inner 'Soul', and this transforms into healing throughout my entire physical being. This creates complete peace and freedom within me. I AM One with 'Source' with all its power, energy, goodness, and knowledge. My being comprises Universal knowledge, which is completely <u>good</u>. I AM repulsed by anything known as evil, badness, negativity, fear, or confusion, for my 'Source' does not know of these things because they are all regarded by Infinite Mind as unreal and untrue, as total goodness and Infinite Love pervades the entire Universe. This Love is fulfilled within me by being transferred throughout my being (body, mind, and Soul) right now. Through the process of translation, this love transforms into perfect knowledge, perfect health, perfect peace, perfect joy, perfect warmth, perfect happiness, and perfect love throughout my being. This helps me to relinquish all the false or negative materially based impressions, illusions, and sufferings of this physical world. I do not accept anything but the truth, which is always evidence of goodness that wholly defines the Infinite Wonder of the Universe, namely the Unified 'One', 'Source', or 'God'.

Subsection 7(E)- Meditation 8- *Connection with the Divine through Acts of Human Love*. (In the text: 'I AM', as the name of God who lies within each of us as our 'Soul')

Within this life, the will of 'Source' or 'God' is expressed through having fun, joy, and rendering service toward other people, which represents the good, the significant, and the constructive. All else, including all negative things and thoughts, are not permitted, or allowed to affect the good, perfect, spiritual, and quiet part of our being or 'Soul'. The chief precept and goal in this life is the fulfillment of true, unconditional love acts with others in this physical world, which is most easily carried out through conscious connection of our own all-good spirit or 'Soul' (within) with the all-good spirit ('Soul') of others with whom we are sharing our love. Through these acts, all doubts, suspicions, confusions, and fears are completely surrendered to the all-good healing effects of the Infinite Loving Spirit or 'God' within each of us. With this realization, we are each (as 'I AM') united with God. Healing freedom comes through sharing worldly unconditional love acts with others, which invites and allows Infinite Love from deep within the Divine to come into each of us (via our 'Soul') and flow or interchange between each of us.

Subsection 7(E)- Meditation 9- *Looking from the Inside-Going Out, rather than Looking from the Outside-Going In*.

Many people look at life from the outside going in, i.e., the external world affecting the inner view. We need to reverse that and rather look from the inside-going out, i.e., seeing ourselves as an integral part of a greater whole at the center of the Universe. As Anita Moorjani states in her work, 'Dying to be Me', we should go from finding solutions to life's problems and mysteries on the outside, i.e., seeing ourselves from books, drugs, doctors, experts, therapists, gurus, etc., to looking and reaching from within, i.e., from our own inner perfect spiritual essence, core, or 'Soul'.[98] She also states that people should view and regard all socially and religiously determined beliefs very critically with skepticism, and consider all of their prior beliefs and prescriptions suspended.[99] Instead, people should open themselves up to all possibilities. The 'magnificence' of each of us exists at the center of our consciousness, i.e., our center of Oneness (our essence or 'Soul') which is composed of the Infinite, and at the same instant being the center of the Infinite. This center of the Infinite is not outside of ourselves, out in space somewhere.

Just as Anita did during her NDE, once each of us can recognize our magnificence and perfection (our 'Soul) as being an integral and Unified part of the 'One', 'God', or 'Infinite Perfect Universe', and not part of an external or separate God away from us, then each of us can be physically and mentally healed. This would well relate to how she was cured of her cancer.[100] Included in this is having strong faith and belief that the spiritual perfection within each of us (i.e., our 'Soul') coalesces with everyone else's spiritual perfection (their 'Soul'), which makes all people equal and part of the Unified spiritual perfection of the 'One' (or 'God') in the Universe.

Subsection 7(E)- Meditation 10(A)- *Identifying the 'God Within' in Promoting Healing Miracles-Introduction*. (In the text: 'I' refers to anyone)

I go within myself to this infinitesimal piece of me known as 'Soul' that has always existed—it was always, is now, and will always be. This 'Soul' essence wholly represented me before this life and was perfect, existing in a purely Infinite Love State devoid of any of the imperfect love experiences with the associated pain that all of us experience in this life. Each of us will immediately return to this perfect Infinite Love State at the conclusion (our death) of this life. Experiencing true unconditional love versus imperfect conditional love in this physical life will greatly enhance the appreciation of our permanent home, namely the perfect Infinite State composed of Infinite Love when each of us returns there. This is the prime reason why we are here, to learn this and adapt our lives to the eventual return to this Infinite Love reality.

Our existence in this life represents only a 'smidgen' of the totality of our eternal presence and existence. Our 'Soul' or small spiritual piece of each of us near our physical heart area represents perfect love, perfect euphoria, perfect acceptance, perfect and pure peace: truly it is God! Despite the imperfections and resultant suffering endured by this life's physical body and mind, our 'Soul' is in a perfect non-suffering state. When each of us dwells on our 'Soul' through awareness, prayer, or meditation, it consumes and infuses our entire physical body and mind with an enveloping feeling and reality of euphoria, acceptance, pure love, and peace, unlike any other love experienced in this human life. Our 'Soul' has enormous potential for healing power.

Quiet moments to reflect on chief points in this meditation:

(1) Our 'Soul', being near our physical heart area is composed of perfect love, euphoria, and peace.

(2) All 'things of this world' (materially) are illusional and transitory (i.e., temporary).

(3) Awareness, intent, and positive belief in healing via 'Soul' can (or will) cure body/mind maladies.

Subsection 7(E)- Meditation 10(B)- *Identifying the 'God Within' in Promoting Healing Miracles- Past Suffering & Pain*. (In the text: 'I' refers to anyone)

My past has consisted of pain from love-denied or other difficulties during earlier years of my life before now, which I have had little accounting for until very recently through awareness of my mind. I have learned and embedded pains that have had, and continue to have, negative carryover effects during my adult life, which have caused considerable unhappiness and consternation during much of this time. I have principally projected these negative carry-over effects from prior sufferings onto myself creating stress, restlessness, angst, and unhealthy habits. Plus, at times I have unwittingly projected these negative effects onto others with whom I have interacted and interrelated with. All these things have negatively impacted my physical body and mind during my adult life. Through present conscious awareness and intent of mind, I can empower myself to divest away from these negativities with their bad effects on me and others. And I can come out into the 'light of sunshine' by embracing positive thoughts, emotions, and intentions, plus engaging in enjoyable activities with others now. Also, I can develop new true unconditional love relationships with others now, replacing all the love-loss experiences from the past.

Quiet moments to reflect on chief points in this meditation:

(1) I am aware that true love denied to me in the past has created problems in my present adult life.

(2) I can divest my mind away from past pain by coming out into 'the present light of sunshine' through positive thinking and engaging in good and enjoyable activities with other people.

(3) I am replacing love denied in the past by enacting new true love acts with others now.

Subsection 7(E)- Meditation 10(C)- *Identifying the 'God Within' in Promoting Healing Miracles- via Healing Sounds*. (In the text: 'I' refers to anyone; 'I AM', as the name of God who lies within each of us as our 'Soul')

*Suggested sound accompaniment: 'I AM Wishes Fulfilled Meditation' CD (or e-file); or introduction (or 2 parts) in the 'Getting in the Gap Meditation" CD (or e-file) by Wayne Dyer, PhD., Hay House Publishing. [101]

As I listen to these relaxing, beautiful sounds and embrace them, they begin to cast aside all the negative memories with their past and present effects on my body and mind. With these sounds, I emerge into the Infinite, warm light of sunshine which begins to first immerse my inner Soul with Infinite Light and Love, and then disperses healing warmth, light, and Love energy throughout my tired body and stressed mind. This relaxes and relieves stress in much of my present body and mind. For the 'Lord' takes His time, this renders within me a slow but definitive healing to these injured body and mind parts. The healing is translated through the wisdom of eternal Infinite Love which can never be taken away, unlike common aspects of this-life love (i.e., conditional, or even unconditional) which can be so frequently given and then taken away. This Infinite Love is translated from an Almighty Source of all Love via my 'Soul' essence, acting like a 'transmitter' radiating and transferring its Infinite Love and warmth throughout my entire body and mind, rendering a slow but definitive healing. This healing is released through my bodily being through solid faith and <u>belief</u> in the healing process. This healing represents the action of the Infinite Almighty speaking to me through Its (His) soothing healing power coming from my 'Soul' to my stressed body and mind.

Quiet moments reflecting on chief points in this meditation:

(1) Euphoric, eternal, Infinite Love given or provided to me can never be taken away.

(2) Infinite Love can be defined as 'I am loved and cherished forever; I have nothing to fear; I can do no wrong; I am loved and accepted completely without any reservation; I am completely comprised of Love'.

(3) I believe that Infinite Love is radiating a healing warmth throughout my stressed body and mind.

Subsection 7(E)- Meditation 10(D)- *Identifying the 'God Within' in Promoting Healing Miracles- I AM Healed & It Lasts*. (In the text: 'I' refers to anyone; 'I AM', as the name of God who lies within each of us as our 'Soul')

I have the intention of having faith and belief that I AM healed from all past negativities and their negative after-effects on me. In other words, I AM emphatically saying: not that I wish or want to be healed, but rather that I AM <u>already</u> healed.

As I desire and ask for the continuation of this healing to last, I must repeat (aka daily) this intent and askance through prayer and meditation. I know that my continued healing condition in this life is contingent upon the intent, belief, and communication within myself that the healing will continue to last. This includes a continuing commitment to absolute faith and belief in the healing process, and the power of Almighty 'Source' to continue providing His healing through the auspices of my inner 'Soul Power'.

Quiet moments reflecting on chief points in this meditation:

(1) Each of us should not say 'I wish or want to be healed', but rather say, 'I AM already Healed'.

(2) We need to have faith that healing from 'Source' via 'Soul' to body-mind will continue to last.

Subsection 7(E)- Meditation 11- *Healings Attributed to St. Francis of Assisi.* (In the text: 'I' refers to anyone)

As St. Francis of Assisi in the 12th Century A.D. wrote and prayed: 'Lord, make me an instrument of thy peace. Where there is hatred, let me sow love; where there is injury, pardon; where there is doubt, faith; where there is despair, hope; where there is darkness, light; where there is sadness, joy. Oh, Divine Master grant that I may not so much seek to be consoled as to console, to be understood as to understand, to be loved as to love. For it is in giving that we receive, it is in pardoning that we are pardoned, and it is in dying that we are born into eternal life.'

I ask the Lord to make me the instrument of His well-being. My body has taken on a state of unwellness during my existence in this physical world, and I pray to be re-connected to the stream of the Lord's perfect well-being. There is a piece of God within me, i.e., my spiritual 'Soul', and therefore I know the Lord's healing power is within me, and through this perfection within me is the wish to have my body and mind healed. I turn my mind quietly toward the Lord and His total Infinite Unconditional Love for me. Through this, I quietly, gently, and lovingly affirm that the uplifting, healing, and strengthening power of His Spiritual healing presence is steadily flowing through me and healing me right now.

I pray this knowing that God or the Lord represents for me: Infinite Love, perfect forgiveness, compassion, happiness, warmth, abundance, clarity, and peace and that He loves and accepts all people in the world just as he loves and accepts me, as I accept and love all people too.

Subsection 7(E)- Meditation 12- *Healings Attributed to Brother Andre of Montreal, and Jesus of Nazareth.*

Healing can occur when the many splendors of love that David Hawkins describes, (Subsect. 7(C) Medit. 4), are shared with other people in an unconditional loving sense. On the other hand, Infinite Love, Universal Wisdom, 'Source' or 'God' can <u>directly</u> heal without any need to involve other people. This can come about through a person's unshakeable faith and belief in the power of Infinite Love, Universal Wisdom, 'Source', or 'God' from within themselves (i.e., via their 'Soul') to heal. In other words, each of us is composed of 'You are God' (U. Andersen), which in and of itself can facilitate our own healing.

Brother Andre from Montreal called on this same concept to teach his many ill friends who came to visit him for healing when he asked each of them to completely forget and cast away all their past negativities, regrets, and fears from their past life experiences. Instead, he told them to concentrate on the vast well of Infinite Perfection and Love which was available from within each of them (i.e., their 'Soul').

Jesus of Nazareth, long ago, taught from the very same perspective in that each person at that time who came to him for healing was told to completely turn away from all their past depravities, imperfections, or sins, and instead focus on the internal goodness and perfection that existed 'within' themselves (i.e., their 'Soul'). Forgoing their depraved past along with unshakeable faith and belief in the Infinite Power and Love of God from within each of them to heal resulted in healing for many of these folks! Let us strive through the ease of silence, prayer, or meditation to surrender via faith and belief to the healing power of 'God' through our 'Soul' to bring healing to our physical body and mind. Better still, let us presume that this healing has already occurred.

Subsection 7(E)- Meditation 13- *Our Spiritual Guardian Angel, A Valuable Partner for Each of Us*.

Each of us has a Guardian Angel which is purely spiritual (i.e., an energy or vibration), without having any name, body, voice, or any other physical characteristics. This Angel is part of the invisible 'God' within us (via our 'Soul') which has been with each of us throughout eternity. During our lives, it is a vital part of our spiritual entity (or 'Soul'). It is a separate entity within each of us which is ours alone. This angel mainly influences us through small clues, inspirations, and thoughts, which are all mostly gentle and 'subtle'. It is our spiritual guide, mentor, and our best friend spiritually, like a Divine life coach.[102] This entity is always available to assist each of us if we consciously and willingly choose to make the effort to connect with it.

Our Guardian Angel helps to steer us on a useful, lighted, and spiritual course in our worldly lives. This entity comprehends invisible threads that fuse us with Universal consciousness and purpose through its connection to each person's Higher Self.[103] This angel <u>can</u> be reached through the meditation process, which opens the door, away from the typical lifetime 'clutter' we all encounter. It is acceptable if we give our angel a 'name' but keep this strictly to ourselves. Our angel is a spiritual partner whose only desire is to manifest a beautiful, fully realized human being in this world. This is our inner spiritual guide that links both the human and the Divine. It represents the 'God' within each of us. It is a 'communication link' that through meditation creates quiet thoughts to arise as if coming from 'somewhere' else strangely. It fulfills our highest desires properly by keeping our Soul's compass on track. [note 103]

Subsection 7(E)- Meditation 14- *Calling on 'Archangel Power' to Facilitate Healing for Us*.

Follows Subs.7(E), Medit. 13- We can ask our Guardian Angel to help guide us to other Angels (namely, Archangels) who can help us to heal.[104] Examples of Archangels are:

(1) <u>Sandalphon,</u> the Guardian. Strengths: trust and reliability. He is visualized by people as wearing sandals. He has feet to ground in this world and his head to the sky in Heaven, bringing a river of Infinite Love and healing from Heaven to us. He manifests calmness in asking us to trust in the Love of Divinity. He offers masculine, brotherly, and gentle support with Love. He once experienced a human life long ago in Hebraic times as 'Elijah'. At times, he needs the help of other Archangels to rid evil in human affairs.[104a]

(2) <u>Auriel,</u> the Companion. Strengths: tender loving care and mending hurts. She is 'of the earth' and is the partner of Sandalphon, and by this can combine qualities of both masculine and feminine. She is competent and assured in self-knowledge. She supports the Divine Mother role. Auriel can nurture and soothe our 'inner child' from past hurt and encourages feelings of emotional security and strong self-worth within us as adults. She reassures and supports us to feel 'comfortable' in all that we do.[104b]

(3) <u>Raphael</u>, the Healer. Strengths: healing and reassurance. She is the principal healing Archangel who is the architect of the message: 'I am the River of Divine Healing flowing over the Earth'. She is the world's 'Angel of Healing' who has all the medical insights, knowledge, and healing remedies. She provides a gentle soothing balm, i.e., a warm, loving energy of healing. Her love gives reassurance to help unwind tensions, anxieties, worries, and negativities. She can also help to bring families back together.[104d]

(4) <u>Zaphkiel</u>, Understanding. She works with Raphael. Strengths: Infinite Love and compassion. She is called the 'Angel of Contemplation'. She represents the Divine Mother, supporting the Queen of Angels. Thinking about her is blissful. Many healers have found that along with Raphael related to healing, Zaphkiel can also help heal physical or psychological maladies rooted in older family-related issues going back in time. She soothes various hurts in life.[104f]

(5) <u>Zadkiel</u>, the Comforter. Strengths: abundance, generosity, and enthusiasm. He provides us with a direct connection to the boundless abundance of the Divine. Saint Germain, an Ascended Master, is said to have utilized insights from Zadkiel, e.g., by activating Zadkiel's violet flame, a healing energy that dispels human negativity. Do pleasurable things in life and move toward abundance, as the Universe overflows with it.[104h]

Subsection 7(E)- Meditation 15- *Strength of Faith in the Power of Mind Over Body*.

Throughout history, there have been selected places in the world where people have congregated to specifically heal from physical and mental illnesses. Eric Von Daniken, a historian-archeologist, has written at least several books on the 'ancients' or civilizations of the past. One of his discoveries is evidence that 'contacts' occurred over past eons between us humans and terrestrial beings from beyond Earth. Also, his writings give convincing evidence that over thousands of years, people have visited certain sacred 'places of healing' or 'healers' to cure bodily maladies of all sorts.[105] Examples of places or healers include 1) Thebes in ancient Egypt (Amphiaraus); 2) Temples to 'Apollo' in ancient Greece; 3) Sanctuary of Asclepius at Epidaurus, Greece (Aesculapius); 4) Jesus of Nazareth; 5) Lourdes in Southwestern France; 6) Brother Andre (André Bessette, C.S.C.) from Montreal. Strong evidence exists that many healings occurred at each site or through each healer. [note 105]

Von Daniken contends that the sick visitors who came to these sites or healers often utilized the process of 'autosuggestion' in facilitating their healing. Autosuggestion can be defined as a 'repeated suggestion to oneself of a wish or desire arising from within one's mind which focuses on a narrow point to affect one's thinking and bodily functions', i.e., 'narrow point' meaning devotion to a personage such as Mary, Jesus, Andre, or to a 'God'; or a particular healing place; or the healing process itself. [note 105]

Another self-healing person, Paramahansa Yogananda, from India during the early 1900s has stated: 'God has endowed each individual with potential faith, free will, conscious reason, and common sense to help themselves from all suffering', i.e., 'God needs each person's power through their self-will to heal themselves', or that 'strength of faith in the power of mind over body' is key to a person's self-cure*.[106]

*see a similar discussion: 'God helps those who help themselves' in Subs. 7(F) Medit. 3(A) p 223.

Subsection 7(F)- Dealing with the Past- Suffering and Trauma

Subsection 7(F)- Meditation 1(A)- *Moving on in Life, Worldly: The Past is Not Our Fault; Choose Differently from the Past.*

We need to look squarely at the facts, and if true, admit to ourselves that specific past mistakes, failures, tragedies, or difficulties associated with people that we have been involved with were often not caused by our fault, but were instead the fault of these other people. Blame by others that we were the prime reason for creating their unfortunate circumstances is very often unjustified. Our human minds (via ego) and our world cultures have tended to permit or allow throwing the blame of others for negative occurrences back onto us as scapegoats. We tend to take these things 'personally' in a negative fashion, when in fact other folks in our lives are very often self-projecting their frustrations and failures onto us by totally blaming us for their unfortunate circumstances. This 'self-projection' of their frustrations onto us cannot be reconciled to help make us feel better until the clear fact that, instead of us, they are fully to blame is clearly established in our minds. Until this happens, we will continue to be dragged down by the negativity of 'poor me' thoughts and feelings and are likely to act these out by projecting viral energies as destructive thoughts or acts upon ourselves or toward other people.

I often reflect on prior experiences with an Australian-born priest, Father John Bettridge, who was a psychologist-counselor. The principal concept he stressed was that via awareness and our own free will, each of us can choose to change by thinking and acting differently behavior-wise. Concerning the 'self-projection' problem above, we can change our feelings and behavior once we become aware that we have been consciously blaming ourselves for something another person did that they are blaming us for. That is, they have been 'self-projecting' onto us their guilt feelings for being 'the blame' for having caused the matter to happen. With this assumption, we can declare our innocence and by this thereby <u>choose</u> to think, feel, and act more positively and lovingly towards ourselves as well as others.

Subsection 7(F)- Meditation 1(B)- *Moving on in Life, Worldly: Focusing on the Positive Sense of Self.*

Therapists today often define personal empowerment as seeing oneself as a valid, positive, and worthwhile individual, to be vibrantly alive and positively contribute to their surrounding world and people. This helps to elevate one's importance from that person's standpoint, as well as from others they might be trying to help. One of the major themes in the work herein is the need for each person to develop (via emotion) a love of self through appreciation of their interests, hobbies, skills, work, merits, as well as positive contributions toward helping others. This resurrects a psychological state of mind for those who have had difficult or abusive-ridden times during their lives, giving them a more positive sense of self-worth and a vibrant spirit of gladness to be alive. Within this light, another theme to remind ourselves of the after-effects coming from a difficult past is once we become <u>aware</u> of our painful past and how it has been negatively affecting us in the present, we can change our attitudes and behaviors. Through intention, we can project a more positive and loving attitude toward ourselves and others, and in this way dissociate from our past endured difficulties and memories with all of their present follow-up negative effects on us.

Subsection 7(F)- Meditation 1(C)- *Moving on in Life, Worldly: Conditioning from Childhood Follows Us in Adult Life*.

Our early conditioning from a significant number of parents generally taught us a fear of failure and that we would not make it or succeed, which trained us to be critical and dissatisfied with almost everything, resulting in negativity towards ourselves and others. This funneled into our need as we grew up to have to listen to others much of the time to get suggestions or commands of action from them. And from others' prescriptions, to establish judgments such as 'this is good versus this is bad' or 'this is black versus white', which further fostered in us the need 'to be right' rather than 'feeling good' about dealing with any of life's typical problems. From the standpoint of early-in-life or even adulthood challenges, these negative tending prescriptions have impinged on many people's abilities to perceive and experience the true fullness and awareness of just 'who they truly are'. Real healing from 'not knowing self' re-establishes a true fullness of self-knowingness through positive thinking and emotions, leading to the enactment of pleasurable relations and activities between oneself and others in self-respecting, loving environments.

The principal insight here is the importance of <u>self-love</u>. What this means is developing a strong, positive feeling of trust and appreciation for one's beautiful body, mind, work, hobbies, and other enjoyable interests they have in this physical life. This is not necessarily manifested by overly pampering oneself with material things. Rather, this self-love associated with strong feelings of loving belief in oneself represents the easiest doorway to one's spiritual Infinite Loving part, or 'Soul', which is key in healing leftover hurts from former life difficulties or traumas. (See Subs. 7(F)- Meditations 2(A) to 2(L), *'Moving on in Life, Spiritual'*, pp 212-223).

Subsection 7(F)- Meditation 1(D)- *Moving on in Life, Worldly: Being Vibrantly Alive; Creating a Happy Child Within*.

Each victim of past mistreatment or abuse by another person needs to resurrect a sense of personal reassurance and love of self to counteract the negative abusive after-effects of guilt, self-debasement, lack of equality, and lack of personal self-respect. Via attitude, the victim must restore the feeling and power in their positive sense of self-worth, that they are somebody fully worthy of 'being' vibrantly alive in this life to be listened to and respected.

Another important avenue for enhancing a love of self is remaking or remolding any unhappy child who went through difficulties earlier in their life. Besides poor treatment by parents or caretakers, people can endure all sorts of other earlier life difficulties or tragedies such as the death of parents or siblings, illness or disease, poverty, large families, wars, environmental disasters; or a later-on in-life divorce, or an end to a long-term relationship. Any of these can certainly create an unhappy 'tonality' that can persist for the rest of a lifetime for any victim of former difficulties. Often an adult person's unhappy child that lies 'within' them awaits to spring forth as a <u>happy</u> child. One way of remaking that unhappy child into a happy child is by re-doing some of the fun things remembered from long ago which on occasion made that child happy then. Or even doing more recently discovered fun things would be helpful in the remaking of any currently unhappy child, or for that matter the remaking of any adult person from their recent life difficulties. These fun things can be done now in the context of the complete absence of any worries or fears from whatever childhood or other adult-life restrictions or conditions this person once endured. All these past life restrictions and difficulties are gone and should not return. This should provide real healing, release, and freedom.

Subsection 7(F)- Meditation 1(E)- *Moving on in Life, Worldly: Hard-Wiring of Pain in the Mind from Early Traumas*.

We have learned that human evolution over eons of time generated the weird after-effect from repeated early-in-life abuse and/or traumas of hard-wiring or inculcating emotional memories of the pain and hurt in the unconscious mind of the child victim. This pain often re-emerges or reappears much later in that person's adult life as a rage or urge to 'lash out' pain or abuse upon themselves or innocent others such as their children, family members, work colleagues, or friends. Negative carry-over effects can also result from adult-life divorce, relationship breakup, other difficulties, or tragedies. Via awareness, the past victim must re-program their mind to prevent or block these urges to 'lash out' the hurt, which only continues and exacerbates their suffering. Hurt toward the victim can include self-inflicted depression. Instead, through awareness and intent they can <u>choose</u> to do just the opposite by thinking and acting more positively and lovingly towards themselves and others, thus instituting healing for any past victim.

Perhaps the principal reason why we are here in this life is to experience fetus birth, with follow-up physical and mental development to successfully overcome the barriers and adversities that many of us endure early on (or even later) in our lives. This results in evolution from our past difficulties into blossoming our adulthood through increased awareness, positive thoughts, intentions, and actions to better ourselves, our families, and the world community. With difficult childhoods or even later-on adult-life difficulties, this means overcoming barriers created from these past negative encounters by crafting solutions through awareness, knowledge, and strategies revealed in this work or from otherwise worldly resources. This particularly includes forming new, true loving relationships with others …(Subs. 7(F) Medit. 1 (F), 1(G), & 1(H) below). These strategies and resources will lead toward successful healing from our negative past.

Subsection 7(F)- Meditation 1(F)- *Moving on in Life, Worldly: Need for Developing New Loving Relationships*.

People from past difficulties need to develop a sense of personal reassurance and love of self to overcome the negative follow-up consequences of lack of personal self-respect, lack of equality, and self-debasement. Re-establishing a sense of positive empowerment is most important for past suffering persons, as each of these individuals is entitled to be perfectly worthy of being happily alive and productive for themselves as well as for others around them.

People who have experienced socially related lifetime tragedies or difficulties need to develop contacts and a support structure resulting in a loving and supportive community of family, friends, and whomever else that is reassuring to the past suffering person. This would provide a mutually supportive social structure that consistently presents positive interactions between people, helping to resurrect and maintain hope and trust for the former suffering individual. People or family whom this individual is close to or lives with and interrelates with on a day-to-day basis are particularly important in best helping the victim to resurrect trust in other individuals.

Finding an enlightened supporter who especially understands and cares for the past traumatized person is also important. This supporter can be a therapist, a friend, or even a member of one's family. This person is someone that the past sufferer likes a lot, appreciates, and can identify with, who has total sympathy for the victim's story. This supporting person provides comfort and support to the victim and is available for frequent contact and consultation with them. This supporter may very well have gone through similar life experiences or circumstances and can therefore wholly identify with the person's feelings and reactions as to what they endured in the past. This supporting person can also help to identify others in creating a 'social architecture' of additional loving and helping people for the victim.

Subsection 7(F)- Meditation 1(G)- *Moving on in Life, Worldly: Past Love has Departed, but New Love is Available.* (In the text: 'me', or 'I' refers to anyone)

It is usually best to completely surrender all hopes that the love lost or denied to a person during their past life experiences will ever return to them from former caregivers, partners, or whomever in this life. This lost/denied love is most often or likely gone forever. The wishing game of hoping that this love might return to the love lost/denied victim via a past caregiver or partner has likely, in a subconscious manner, contributed to imagining love coming back from the former person, or coming from other persons in imaginative contexts. Also, the hope of this past love returning has generated doubts, suspicions, and 'built walls' that have cordoned off new unconditional love that perhaps has been made available to the past victim in more recent contexts. This person could have used this new love (if it was available) to help heal from their traumatic and difficult love-loss past. The person-victim needs to believe that genuine, unconditional love can be rekindled from others <u>now</u> and that this love will truly substitute for the love denied or lost from their past experiences. By presenting themselves as true love, any person who has lost love can more readily or easily invite and receive reciprocation or the return of true love from others.

The past is gone, it touches us not and will not return, and the present is here and with us now. The past cannot hinder us from looking forward, which is all within the present (i.e., now). Focusing on the present helps us to release the past, and this yields freedom. For me to successfully pursue finding the new true love that I deserve, I must <u>surrender</u> by relinquishing the past with all its disappointments, creating the new 'present' dawn of day with all its anticipated, positive, and happy 'future' possibilities.

Subsection 7(F)- Meditation 1(H)- *Moving on in Life, Worldly:* *Forming New Love Relationships*. (In 1st paragraph: 'I' or 'my' refers to the author; in 2nd paragraph: 'I', 'myself', or 'me' refers to anyone)

A principal awareness I have discovered through attempts to recover from my past life difficulties is that past love-denied or lost can be re-discovered or rekindled by finding new unconditional love with others in the present-time context. This can be done by first extending love to others, and through this receiving love back from them to me in return. This can be a viable alternative to love that was either denied or lost long ago. The false hope of recovering the love lost from people of long ago creates a barrier or <u>block</u>, which prevents a person's efforts in finding and rekindling true replacement love with others presently. Surrendering all hope of recovering lost love from folks in the past removes that block, allowing love to flow more easily back and forth, leading a person forward in finding new unconditional love now. Once this block is removed, the key to moving on to capture new love is producing a love exchange between people that is true and unconditional, that as closely as possible resembles Infinite Love.

This unconditional love needs to flow back and forth between people without having to force it, no matter what the giver and receiver might have done or represented to whom in the past. <u>Faith</u> that this new love replaces the former love denied or lost, helps to lessen all doubts and mistrust generated by any former failed or lost relationships and lessen the hurt/loneliness from the prior love-loss situation. Once I can convince myself of love and appreciation for my beautiful physical being, then I can more easily and happily project this joy outward from myself to better embrace meaningful love coming from others by receiving real love from them back to me. This strengthens the new love relationship and helps to facilitate healing for any victim who has endured emotional wounds from the past.

Subsection 7(F)- Meditation 1(I)- *Moving on in Life, Worldly: Contrast Feelings of Love- Author's Story*.

It is well remembered that back in 1952, at age 7, Mother and Dad took me on a vacation trip to a fishing camp in Middle Dam, Maine. There was a waitress who served us our meals with whom I developed a strong affinity and liking; she really seemed to care for me somehow. She was enthralled with my interests then, e.g., my mica rock collection, growing plants, and following the weather. These specifics, along with her genuine concern for my 'uniqueness' meant something highly special to me then, which can still be identified through my feelings today. Back then, I could not remember ever having had a caring feeling like that towards me from a woman, and because of that, it was so wonderful to sense and experience this.

Somehow deep inside me, there was a genuine human <u>warmth</u> coming from her that up to that time had been completely missing, particularly from my mother. Following the departure from that fish camp stay, I had tears and tormented feelings because of having to leave that waitress and the temporary 'warmth' she had offered, at the same time I had to repress that wonderful experience into my subconscious mind. This was because I was re-entering my mother's frightful ongoing realm of non-warmth strictness during my childhood for literally what was felt at that time would be forever. The bitterness of leaving the waitress and losing that small piece of unconditional love was so excruciatingly painful at that time, and memories of that even now bring on the same intense emotions and tears from the true love that I felt at that time had been lost. But the overall experience with that waitress gave me a 'compass' and 'roadmap' in my life to search for and hopefully find new and real, satisfying love relationships to replace the love that I assumed had been lost forever.

Subsection 7(F)- Meditation 1(J)- *Moving on in Life, Worldly: Release of Past Difficulties Providing Healing Freedom*. (In the text:

'I am', refers to any person, as well as the name of God who lies within themselves as their 'Soul')

Our goal in this life should be #1 happiness, and to achieve that we must be completely aware of all the past influences in our lives, including childhood, and how these have affected how we think, feel, and act in our current adult lives. As Father John Bettridge has stated (earlier herein): 'We can change our attitudes and behavior by choosing (or re-directing ourselves) to feel, think, and act differently'. Real freedom comes through our awareness and intent to leave behind all the dark, negative, competitive, and ego-centered aspects of our past lives and come out into the present 'light of sunshine' to fully express and capture the prospective positive happiness of the 'new dawn of day'. This is ours to choose and fully embrace now in creating a brighter future in our lives.

Let us now imagine taking an inflated balloon for each of the past lifetime woes and negativities in our lives and releasing all of them at once into the air and watching them rise, letting their rising motion and the wind take them ever upward and away from us until we can see them no more. And what is left behind is our eternal loving self, composed of body-mind and an eternal Infinite part or 'Soul', which is filled to the brim with Infinite Love, power, clarity, warmth, light, and healing. Since 'I am aware that I am all Love', and that all my bad and difficult past is gone and will <u>not</u> return, I am finally fully released and <u>free</u> from all my past.

Subsection 7(F)- Meditation 1(K)- *Moving on in Life, Worldly: Removing Memory Blockages Providing Freedom*.

Repeated childhood or later-on adult traumas of many sorts often create (1) a split-off, blocked-off, or repressed effect on past emotions which become locked deep within the subconscious mind, creating inabilities for a person to consciously express their emotions in the present-day sense;[107] and/or (2) a burying of painful memories of love-denied emotions in the subconscious mind, creating negative prompters or follow-up feelings such as sadness, depression, negativity, restlessness, angst, envy, or hatred.[108] Either or both of these can often produce the same effect in forming blockages that create inabilities to readily and properly feel and express present human emotions of all kinds, including love. And, since normal adult conjugal intimacy involves an ability to express and share highly charged/felt emotions, any antecedent repression or blockage affecting emotional expressions can lead a person to be unable to <u>fully</u> engage in and enjoy elated intimate emotions of tenderness and pleasure with another person. This prevents a couple from maximally sharing and enjoying these mutually.

Reawakening and releasing long-blocked-off emotions and feelings from past early-life traumas or adult life difficulties begin the process of regaining one's ability to have positive feelings of pleasure, closeness, and tenderness, which are all components for the successful sharing of intimate relations. Releasing and expressing long blocked-off emotions can be aided by: (1) talking with someone who can understand what the traumatized person has endured, (i.e., a therapist, friend, relative, or even a lover); (2) writing a diary recounting the past difficulties with the 'players' involved, fully expressing and releasing feelings both then and now; (3) via awareness, reminding oneself that these early life or adult life difficulties are over and will <u>not</u> return; (4) developing new unconditional love relationships with others now (in present time).

Subsection 7(F)- Meditation 2(A)- *Moving on in Life, Spiritual: Acquiring and Building Faith, Part I.*

Acquiring and building faith involves developing belief in a Higher Power, the organizer behind all existence in the Universe. Our Higher Power does not exist as some sort of entity out in space somewhere but instead exists within each of us as our 'Soul' which is perfect at its core, which also exists in everything throughout the Universe as living Infinite Intelligence. This perfection is the key spiritual identifier for initiating all physical and mental healing in this life. Belief in this is essential to begin the healing process. Faith is the way to achieve or manifest this belief. Faith is achieved through feelings, not the five senses. Feelings are the doorway to the living Infinite Intelligence, or 'Soul', or the spiritual perfection within us.

In the work, "Three Magic Words", Uell Andersen describes his experience as a college student in the 1930s at Stanford in California when he had serious discussions with his college chaplain about belief in a God or Higher Power. At that time, the young Uell stated that he was a non-believer in this Higher Power or God, that it was all a myth and mistake, and no proof could dissuade him from this opinion. His chaplain simply stated: 'Well Uell, I see the Creator (God) everywhere, within me, within you and everyone all around us; and I see the Creator in the brook outside the office here, with the birds in the air, with animals, in the meadow across the way, in the trees and landscape beyond, and at the seashore'.[109] This natural surroundings part is similar to what St. Francis of Assisi perceived/expressed during his lifetime.

Subsection 7(F)-Meditation 2(B)- *Moving on in Life, Spiritual: Acquiring and Building Faith, Part II.*

Continuing from Subsection 7(F), Medit. 2(A) above- Uell Andersen began to grow spiritually through the assimilation of the meaning from his chaplain's statement, to begin recognition of faith through his feelings about the increased perception of the significance and meaning of what had been said. Namely, that Infinite Intelligence (or God), Infinite Love, and Perfection can be found everywhere throughout the entire world and Universe. Faith begins through our basic feelings that there is something outside of ourselves, (i.e., our physical body with its five senses, and ego), something way beyond, far more powerful, far more meaningful, far greater, better, and longer lasting. We must strive to feel and believe that this Infinite Intelligence truly exists, as it cannot be proven through the five senses. Without unshakeable <u>faith</u> in the healing power activated through the Infinite 'Source' (or God), healing through any spiritual process is virtually impossible. Brother Andre Bessette from Montreal has suggested:

'That opening up our hearts to God takes time and patience, that faith and sanctification don't occur like a 'bolt out of the blue', but that God or Infinite Spirit is always close to us. The launch pad for our meeting God is rooted in the willingness to be loved by God exactly as we <u>are</u> without any masks or makeup. This is true humility. This is the only way of opening ourselves to God and His goodness, and in doing so to allow each of us to be transformed by His Love'.[110]

Subsection 7(F)- Meditation 2(C)- *Moving on in Life, Spiritual: Healing the Afflicted.*

With the spiritual perfection of Jesus, his healing was done by revealing and identifying with the spiritual perfection that exists within each person who was afflicted whom Jesus was attempting to help. He was attempting to help that person by encouraging that the buried pains, hurts, and afflictions from the past within that person should be forgotten, and that the 'real you' within each person is both good and perfect. Turn to the spiritual self and perfection within you (i.e., your 'Soul') and regain your physical or mental health. The way to help heal a friend who has a physical health affliction: from the recognition of your own spiritual perfection, reach out in meditation to the spiritual perfection within your friend and declare that they are healed of their affliction. Jesus facilitated the healing of thousands of people during his time, and Brother Andre Bessette, who promoted building the Cathedral of St. Joseph in Montreal, healed thousands there during the early part of the 20th Century.[111]

Both Jesus and Andre tuned into their absolute faith that Infinite Intelligence and Power accomplished this work. At the same time, they tuned in to the imperfections, (colloquially known as 'sins'), within each of the ill persons they were attempting to heal. Then both convinced these individuals that they should forget and forgive these personal weaknesses by recognizing the Infinite Perfection and Love that existed within each of them, and then stand up tall and 'move on' with their lives. These 'sins' or 'weaknesses' represented negativity in these people's lives that both Jesus and Brother Andre were attempting to purge. These two healing folks believing in the sick victims' need to recognize Infinite Healing Power from within themselves (i.e., via 'Soul'), coupled with convincing them to forget their past imperfections, mistakes, or 'sins', resulted in healing by curing their bodily and/or mental afflictions.

Both Uell Andersen and Neville Goddard (covered earlier) have indicated that the chief message of all Jesus's teachings was: 'the good news I bring you is that the Kingdom of Heaven is within each of us' (i.e., via our 'Soul').

Subsection 7(F)- Meditation 2(D)- *Moving on in Life, Spiritual: Mankind as Arbiter of Its Own Fate.*

'I AM' or 'I am' is the self-definition and foundation of the absolute definition of God. 'I AM' or 'I am' is the statement declaring and defining the Infinite Mind, or Infinite Intelligence. 'Let the weak say, I AM (or I am) strong' (Joel 3:10). Do not say things like 'I am weak, sick, feeling bad, tired', etc., but rather say 'I am strong, healthy, feeling great, or enthusiastic'. The 'I am' concept of oneself eventually becomes projected as an effect in that person's conscious world. The 'I am whatever' sends a signal to the subconscious mind, which is impersonal and unchanging, and this returns to the conscious world of that person as physical reality. The great discovery of cause reveals that, good or bad, man is the arbiter of his fate, and that his concept of himself determines the world he will live in, i.e., his actual thoughts will create his actual living conditions. To consistently believe and say 'I am healthy' brings good health, contrarily 'I am unhealthy or not well' produces poor health. 'I am strong', 'I am abundant', or 'I am loved', will bring about these positive things. [note 48]

Consciousness is the only reality that conceives itself to whatever is desired and said, which frees destructiveness from outside forces in life that would affect and dictate one's consequences. The womb of creation is the subconscious or Universal Mind of God, which receives signals from the conscious mind and sets about to create that reality back into the life of the individual who originated the idea. Feelings are the doorway to the 'Soul' or subconscious and are the principal communication medium to it. Subconscious (the Infinite/God) impressions (from feelings) determine the conditions of the world since they never fail to express what has been impressed on them by the conscious mind, and thereby set out to produce in the outer world the exact likeness of those feelings. note 49

Subsection 7(F)- Meditation 2(E)- *Moving on in Life, Spiritual: Emphasizing the Positive Instead of the Negative.*

Infinite Intelligence (or God) behind the Universe does not destroy nor manifest modes of destruction or evil upon itself. God, or the power behind the Universe, does <u>not</u> know of the existence of these negative things, even though many religious organizations teach that evil is a competing and opposite part of God's Universe. As Uell Andersen states in his work, "Three Magic Words", the 'Negative Prompters' or negative thoughts such as lack, limitations, unhappiness, guilt, fear, remorse, doubt, and loneliness, create feelings that block us from the proper use of the great faculties of power of our Great Infinite 'Source' ('God'). Thinking and thoughts should, as much as possible, disavow all negative thinking and instead dwell on the positive.

The power of a particular suggestion goes from the conscious mind to the subconscious mind and returns the same back into the conscious mind and physical life of the individual. The Universal Subconscious Mind has unlimited power for good and abundance, and the more faith one has in this, the more power is available to produce good and abundance in one's life. On the other hand, 'Negative Prompters' or negative thoughts are planted in our minds as mental coping mechanisms established to deal with memories of pain from past love denied to us. These human negations of love lead to fear, which then leads to hate, and ultimately leads to the creation of evil, affecting any person. What this is really saying is that the origin of all fear, hatred, and evil comes from humankind, not God.

Subsection 7(F)- Meditation 2(F)- *Moving on in Life, Spiritual: Everyday Dealings with Negativities of People*. (In the text: 'I AM', as the name of God who lies within each of us as our 'Soul')

Like myself, any of us who have faced a difficult past by developing elevated feelings and thoughts of release from that past can get easily pulled or dragged down again with the negative energies and acts of other people we typically associate with in everyday life. Through ordinary human interaction processes, any of us can begin to doubt ourselves as to the great truth of just who we truly are, namely that each of us is God composed of Infinite Perfection and Love. When we become intertwined and stressed out with other people's negativities, whatever the cause of them, we need to each temporarily withdraw and retreat from active engagement with these folks. Then, we need to remind ourselves of the <u>positivity</u> of the Infinite, Perfect Loving 'Source' that lies within each of us. But after a brief pause reflecting on this, we need to re-engage ourselves with others in our everyday matters with a renewed sense of positiveness. To help us return to that proper positive thinking and re-engagement mode, here is a 'fast track' overall thought with follow-up sample 'I AM' bullet applications discussed earlier*. The 'fast track' thought is: 'I AM Infinite Love, Power, Warmth, Perfection, and Peace throughout my Being for Clarity of positive thinking and feeling in overcoming the negative thinking and acts of others'. Follow-up shorter sample bullet applications include:

- 'I AM Infinite Love, Power, Warmth, Perfection, and Clarity for positive thinking to overcome the negativity of others.'
- or shorter: 'I AM Feeling Positive with Perfect Clarity to overcome other folks negativity.'
- or shorter still: 'I AM an Eternally Loving and Positive Person.'
  *Chapter 3, Theme 5, pp 73-5.

Subsection 7(F)- Meditation 2(G)- *Moving on in Life, Spiritual: High Energy Vibrations of Thinking and Feeling Good.*

The main wisdom indicated in the recent Wayne Dyer and Esther Hicks book, "Co-Creating at its Best, a Conversation Between Master Teachers", is that each person can reach alignment with the Source (or God) by achieving the high energy vibration of well-being by <u>first</u> thinking good, and <u>then</u> feeling good. This creates a law of attraction from these feelings, bringing into one's life the things a person most desires in association with those good feelings.[112] By being in alignment, a person becomes in synch with Source energy within themselves by having positive thoughts and feelings, which generates the energy of well-being, producing vibrations of least resistance (i.e., the easiest path) for Source to deliver a person's desired outcome. What this says is that each of us can be the creator or healer of our own reality.[113]

Everyone has access to the energy of well-being and vibrations of least resistance from the Source for healing, without the need for help from or respect for someone such as a counselor or a 'guru' type leader. However, a particular person of intense respect for the victim can act as a medium to help soften the negative feelings, resistance, or hatred a victim has towards someone else who was formerly abusive or cruel towards them. This allows soothing for any negative vibration or hatred the victim has, thus permitting healing and peace to readily flow from the Source, or God, to the victim.[114] Through the victim's focused concentration on the person of respect, the fear or hatred toward the former cruel or abusive person is allayed or vanquished, allowing healing energy from the 'Source' to flow to the victim more freely.

Subsection 7(F)- Meditation 2(H)- *Moving on in Life, Spiritual: The Infinite 'Well' of Love from Within.* (In the text: 'I' refers to anyone)

The best doorway to reaching the Infinite well within, (i.e., our 'Soul'), is through love and appreciation of our physical self, our beautiful body and mind, our positive abilities, work, hobbies, and related interests in this life. Just viewing our eyes from a mirror and resting there for a moment is one possible pathway to feeling our spiritual perfection within. Once we can convince ourselves of our positive self-worth for being alive by eliminating all guilt feelings from our difficult past, then we can more readily reach and tap into that inner well of spiritual perfection ('Soul') within. Self-love begins the process of healing, which is amplified by reaching within. It seems that connection with the Spirit within cannot be found through, or dictated by, any religious organization, person, or prescriptive system, but instead must be rendered through an individual's <u>intent</u> and conscious connection with the Source or God within themselves. This connection needs to be expressed with heightened energy and emotion of mental joy and happiness, in anticipation of God's Infinite Love and healing flowing via Source from each person's 'Soul'. The contact within should be made in a relaxed manner (not forced) and is best done through meditation.

Once I can convince myself of this love and appreciation through my beautiful physical being and connect with my Infinite Love well within, then I can more easily and happily project this joy outward from myself to better embrace meaningful love coming from others and receive real love from them back to me. The Infinite well 'within' is best expressed through my intuition of 'healing' as revealed in Florence Shinn's book, "The Magic Path of Intuition":

> 'Let the bright white dazzling light of Infinite Intelligence shine from within each of us (i.e., our 'Soul'), casting out forever from our existence all doubts, fears, and negative memories from the past, filling our total body and mind with Source's (God's) Infinite Love, warmth, happiness, guidance, peace, and healing'. note 63

Subsection 7(F)- Meditation 2(I)- *Moving on in Life, Spiritual: Despite My Past, I AM God and thereby I AM Equal.* (In the text: 'I' refers to anyone; 'I AM', as the name of God within each of us as our 'Soul')

I AM God, composed of an incarnate body with an eternal Infinite essence or 'Soul'. I go within myself to that Infinite essence where there is total acceptance, perfection, peace, love, and quietness. This essence has existed for all the past eternity, and although I have not always been aware of this, it is true. This essence was truly within me throughout my upbringing. My essence observed and felt all that happened to me then, including the good and positive including any kindnesses and love from my caretakers, as well as any unpleasant or difficult situations. Back then, I feared my caretakers not only due to any unkind treatment but also because they loomed so large and tall compared to my small body.

My Infinite being was equal with my caretakers before birth when I was back in the Infinite State, was equal with them at birth, and throughout my childhood, I AM equal with them now and will remain as such for all eternity. I have always been equal with all others because of my Infinite Spiritual essence ('Soul'), and we are all equal in that we have come from and are an integral part of the Unified Infinite Loving 'One'. But due to being so small and at times helpless and not treated well while being so young, inequality and lesser worth became hard-wired into my mind. But I was equal then and realizing these rights the inequality and lesser worth once felt, which makes me 'whole' again. I AM now calling forth to stand up tall by casting off any sadness from the past and moving on with my life joyfully. I AM calling on the power of Infinite Love from within me (my 'Soul') to arise, heal me, and set me free!

Subsection 7(F)- Meditation 2(J)- *Moving on in Life, Spiritual: Lack of Awareness of Our 'Soul' When We Were Little.*

Many spiritual writers lay the claim that our spiritual essence or 'Soul' accompanies us throughout this life, including childhood, and that this perfect spiritual essence is <u>not</u> dormant during our lives and can help us. If this is so, then why didn't this essence help rescue us from the challenges our physical bodies and minds endured when we were so little and vulnerable? We were clearly not aware nor cognizant of the existence of our spiritual cores at the very earliest stages of our lives. And our minds were not yet developed enough to consciously think or choose differently other than to 'weather' the physical and mental 'storms' that we each had to endure when we were so small, vulnerable, and defenseless.

Although we were aware of physical and mental (psychic) pain from a primitive survival standpoint, none of us had any cognizance at the earliest stages of life of our inner spiritual core (or 'Soul'). Nor were we aware that this perfect spiritual core or essence accompanied us and was witness to all the struggles we endured just to physically survive during those earliest stages of our lives. Yet that perfect part of us lay dormant during those early-life happenings, seemingly unable to help or come rescue us. Perhaps a possible explanation for this might have been our lack of mental awareness that we possessed a spiritual core or 'Soul' during those earliest stages of our lives. Had we been aware of it, we might have been able to make the conscious-awareness choice of calling upon this spiritual essence to assist us to better endure the discomforts or suffering, or even avoid these.

Subsection 7(F)- Meditation 2(K)- *Moving on in Life, Spiritual: A Piece of the Author's Life Story*.

Upon arriving in this life as a fetus in my mother's womb, my being (Infinite Spirit) had just left its eternal home of non-stop, unbridled Infinite Love with all its perfect joys, euphoria, and pleasures, to enter a new and challenging world here. I embarked on this 'new world' venture with Infinite Wisdom that the Love shared as 'One' back in the Infinite State would be experienced here in totally new and exciting ways through a physical body. My Infinite Spirit was truly looking forward to this new experience. Infinite Wisdom suggested there would be challenges to the physical body I was entering, the specifics of which were largely or completely unknown to me back in that dimension.

Dearest Mother: I have expressed painful emotions and feelings from what was experienced both during and following the earliest days of my life. It honestly felt like love was denied or lost from you back then. But I understand now how you suffered so much from Dad's escapades with other women outside your marriage. For that past, I feel so sorry for you. Due to these indiscretions, you were consistently not 'warm' with me and severely over-disciplined me at almost every turn during my earliest years. This resulted in negative carryover effects during my adult life consisting of periods of depression, false imageries, impatience, and angst, all of which have made me a real 'social loner' in relationships with people (including my first family) during my lifetime. But via awareness of my past, I have learned to completely forgive you by seriously attempting to forget all that unfortunate past.

I encapsulate my Love within your present Infinite State of perfect Love, peace, happiness, joy, warmth, and understanding. All negativities between you and me over both of our sufferings and pain earlier in my life are dissolved and forgotten under your present Umbrella of Infinite Love. Your Infinite Spirit and mine (via my 'Soul') are melded together, and this is twice blessed. All else matters little, including the need to forgive from the past because true Infinite Love has <u>already</u> healed all. This includes all my hurts. You presently have only Infinite Love to offer me, which is composed of only the good, which I completely surrender to.

Subsection 7(F)- Meditation 2(L)- *Moving on in Life, Spiritual: The Infinite Love of 'Soul' is Healing; Author's Event.*

An important part of this work draws upon our Infinite Source, or God, with its Infinite Loving Power as our 'Soul' within each of us living humans, to be fully recognized and believed, thus rendering healing for any part of the incarnate body. This includes the mind which has been 'hard-wired' with inculcated negative memories from repetitive and/or traumatic early-in-life difficulties. The existence and presence of Infinite Love or Divine Unconditional Love, and recognition of this Love within our spiritual essence or 'Soul', with a strong belief in 'feeling' it, are <u>real</u> keys to initiating healing. Unshakeable faith and belief in the power of 'Source' with Its Infinite Love to heal, and its presence within us are essential for spiritual healing.

I have very occasionally experienced Infinite Love (via 'Soul') after being on a beach by the ocean for several hours on a warm summer day, then meditating on Infinite Love's vastness which encompasses a limitless Unified 'One' Universe made up of the all-Love 'God'. Distinct sensations of unparalleled warmth, and euphoric joys, along with highly pleasurable 'Nirvana' feelings have occurred, accompanied by 'tingly pins and needles bodily sensations' and marked 'tearing' of the eyes. These were clearly peaks of joy, not sadness. The energy producing these feelings came from within me ('Soul'), not from some outside source. To me, these sensations and feelings of joy and Love were <u>unlike</u> anything I have ever experienced or even imagined within this human context and were clearly ethereal signs of Divinely inspired Infinite Love.

Subsection 7(F)- Meditation 3(A)- *Moving on in Life, Worldly & Spiritual: Reprogramming the Mind into a Radical New Reality.*

As Uell S. Andersen neared completion of his book entitled "Three Magic Words", the three words were revealed as 'You are God', meaning that each of us is comprised of God (via our spiritual 'Soul'). During the later stages of completing my prior work, "Love and the Infinite, Healing from Childhood", a similar set of 'magic words' came to my mind from the Scriptures and other past readings, namely that 'God helps those who help themselves'. In this regard, I reflect on the healing person, Paramahansa Yogananda, from India during the early 1900s who similarly stated: 'God has endowed each individual with potential faith, free will, conscious reason, and common sense to help themselves from all suffering'. Or restated, 'God needs each person's power through their self-will to help heal themselves,' or again restated, 'strength of faith in the power of mind over body is key in one's self-cure.' [note 106]

Earlier in this work is the story/metaphor of a Brazilian-native Matis chieftain which is presented in Wayne Dyer's book, "My Greatest Teacher". Namely, 'a snakebite doesn't kill, but what can is the snake's venom, unless the bite victim learns to release/extricate it from their system or assimilate/change it from being toxic into a medicine'. From this, a primitive yet highly evolved notion is applied that we can look at the most damaging and painful sufferings in our lives and turn these into our greatest teachers or gifts in healing ourselves. Wayne's book with its fictional life story of an Anthropology professor's lifetime misfortunes and eventual turnaround happens to closely mirror his (i.e., Wayne's) own true childhood and lifetime story of family abandonment by his father before his birth. Additionally, it mirrors Wayne's lifetime of hatred towards his father and despising over this, and ultimately (at his father's gravesite in Mississippi) a <u>total</u> surrender and decision change to complete absolution and love for his father, opening the door to psychic, physical, and spiritual healing for himself.

This represents an astounding example of a person convincingly reprogramming their mind away from past life difficulties to a completely different reality. Another dramatic example of reprogramming in Wayne's life was his follow-up healing response after being unexpectedly diagnosed with Leukemia, which followed an extremely stressful psychological event occurring during his life:

> 'This is how I choose to deal with my diagnosis of Leukemia, I choose to feel good, i.e., to feel God, and to offer unconditional love to everyone, including those who played a major part in any or all conflict dramas that once defined my life. I go by how I feel, and the truth is, I am well, I am strong, and yes, I am God, and I am resolving any (and all) conflicts with massive doses of God's unconditional love. This is what I choose to imprint on my subconscious mind, and this subconscious mind accepts as true what I feel as true'. [note 41]

Special Note- Reversing a lifetime of hatred and regret doesn't occur 'like a bolt out of the blue' but instead takes great personal courage, intent, and effort by the person to completely reverse their past lifetime of misfortunes and negativity into a completely different and positive paradigm.

Subsection 7(F)- Meditation 3(B)- *Moving on in Life, Worldly & Spiritual: Removing 'Poor Me', 'Have Pity on Me' Images*. (In the text: 'I AM', as the name of God in each of us as 'Soul'; 'I' refers to anyone)

- I AM (by telling myself) a very powerful and good person who is perfectly capable of standing up tall and declaring their rights as a perfect and everlasting constituted being.
- I AM deserving of full respect and love, fully capable of loving others and carrying out my favorite and enjoyable activities with them now.
- I now cast off all negativities projected upon me by others in the past as irrelevant, and at the same time replace these with kindnesses that have been shown to me as 'Pearls of the Universe'.
- Many sins and wrongs perceived by others that I supposedly committed are cast off and aside from me and are placed upon those who accused me of these things, as these so often represent 'self-projections' of their own mistakes and negativity that they have chosen to cast upon me.
- I AM a Treasure and Jewel of the Universe which is merged with all-Goodness, and Perfection.
- I AM completely worthy of being 'All that I AM' which makes me a truly evolved and positive being, namely with the Light of the Lord my God and the Prince of Peace.
- I AM He the Lord (Love), and He is me (Love), thereby I AM all Love, and this Love (through Him) can never be taken away from me!
- I will now lead my life going forward in Perfect Love, Prefect Order, Harmony, and Peace.
- I resolve to carry forward unconditional love acts as to how I will treat others in my life.

- I merge all my thoughts with the Infinite Love, Power, and Understanding of the Prince of Peace.

Subsection 7(F)- Meditation 3(C)- *Moving on in Life, Worldly & Spiritual: Hearing Our Feelings and Spirit from Within.*

Any concerned person must face their own situation and determine the relative happiness they feel at a particular stage of their adult lives, and if it is less than acceptably happy and satisfying, a more careful look inside themselves must ensue on their experiences and associated feelings from the past. This can be done before any outside therapy is sought, discussed with others, or admitted to others. One's feelings about unhappiness are key to focus on. Each of us needs to first <u>see</u> by examining and disclosing to ourselves about our past, <u>feel</u> just what this means to each of us, and then <u>act</u> in any helpful manner to positively address those feelings by re-orienting ourselves toward a brighter future with greater happiness and more fulfilling life. If the person suffered a difficult childhood, the best and most useful way of examining feelings is to ask the child still inside the older adult just how it feels now. If it feels sad, in angst, or just waiting 'to become alive', we need to surrender to the need to remake that unhappy child into a happy one who is glad to be alive. If our suffering involves past adulthood sufferings or difficulties, we need to get to the 'taproots' of our feelings and be determined with intention to move on by envisioning 'brighter days' feelings-wise by engaging with new loving people and sharing happy, pleasurable activities with them.

Also, from a spiritual standpoint, each of us needs to call on that infinitesimal piece within us, i.e., our 'Soul' with all its goodness, perfection, clarity, and Infinite Love, and (via our intention) allow Its healing power to be infused throughout our body and mind, removing any leftover hurts from past sufferings.

Clear awareness and recognition must register that the past with all its woes and oppressors is gone and will not return. Rather, the present is here, and a bright, positive future is yet to be. Through these efforts, we reprogram ourselves to think, feel, and act differently to create a happier, brighter, and joyful future.

Subsection 7(G)- Power to Change the Past via Imagination

Subsection 7(G)- Meditation 1- *Imagination as a Spiritual Sensation, Part I: Altering Our Past*.

Picture an image of a wish desired and give it the clarity and dimensions of reality by thinking mentally as if it were already a physical reality available and here now. For example, imagine that you are holding a rose in your hand, and sense how it would smell: you can sense the smell. This is a spiritual sensation, (imagining via sight, sound, smell or scent, taste, or touch). Now apply that to a particular wish, and vividly feel the presence of it as fulfilled. As for the past, (e.g., an adult-love relationship loss, or a difficult childhood), these seem inalterable, but the past is connected to the present because it (the past) still affects the present, therefore it can be altered.

Changing one's present life means changing the past through thought and imagination as to how or what it should have been.[115] This means that even if the past was regarded as bad or evil in the present time, going back into the past and replaying scenes as to how things <u>should</u> have been, (e.g., a good past relationship or a childhood filled with loving kindness and understanding instead of unkindness and mistreatment). This represents revision and revision results in repeal. Changing one's life means changing the past through imagination in the present time. The cause of any present evil (particularly thoughts) comes from unrevised scenes of the past. These unrevised past scenes can be altered by imagining in the present what should have been in the past, plus having a strong belief that what 'should have been' was actually 'as it should have been' during that past.[116] This can be the springboard for creating an actual new reality, e.g., a new and satisfying love relationship, or a recreated and 'happier child' within a past victim.

Subsection 7(G)- Meditation 2- *Imagination as a Spiritual Sensation, Part II: Author's Example of Altering the Past.*

Go back to before my existence in this life, before my mother became pregnant with me, and imagine when my Spirit or 'Soul' existed in the Infinite State without a physical body. My Spiritual Being was loved unconditionally, could not be judged, had no fears of God restricting love for me, could do no wrong, nor be punished mentally or physically. Also, there was no parental/caretaker oversight, conditioning, or mind control; nor earthly rules and inhibitions, people's egos to combat, or competitive thinking.

In coming into this life through pregnancy via my mother, I entered a whole new and challenging world in that my mother had a difficult pregnancy with me because she was highly stressed both physically and mentally while carrying me. This coupled with her continuing stress after birth, caused her to be emotionally angry toward me particularly during early childhood, resulting in her giving me little cuddling, loving, personal respect, or understanding at that time.

Instead, I now imagine that my mother had a very normal pregnancy and resultant birth with me, treated me well with loving and cuddling respect in those early years, that my father was supportive and faithful to my mother and myself during all my childhood, and all babysitters treated me well with respect. This means that living with my parents (or caretakers) through all those years was joyful, just like it was with them at Christmastime.

Imagining this kinder past has provided me with (1) relief and release, freedom, and healing from all the residual negative feelings of a past oppressed childhood; (2) my having forgiving, loving, and accepting feelings toward both my parents presently; (3) mental imagining of acceptance of love from them now.

Subsection 7(G)- Meditation 3- *Calling on Imagination to Change Our Past*. (In the text: 'I' refers to anyone)

We can recover from a difficult past by (1) imagining a much kinder and more loving past; and (2) replacing memories of our negative past with more positive present-day thoughts, feelings, and activities.

- I was born through a natural miracle of love and for a brief space of time, my needs were totally in another's care—life's offspring of love—God is love (Neville).
- I freely chose to come into this bodily life to fully experience an incarnate body with its human senses, emotions (including love), and ego, and awaken my perfect Infinite Spiritual part ('Soul').
- A good practice at the beginning of meditation is freeing everyone in the world including myself from blame, for the <u>law</u> is not violated: 'every man's conception of himself is going to be his reward'.
- The eternal body of man is all imagination, which is God Himself within me as 'Soul'. At my birth, God was put asleep within me, waiting to be reawakened as I matured through imagination as a life-giving spirit.
- Through our imagination and our affirmation, we can change our world and our future.
- The truth that is within us is governed by imaginative love.
- To dissolve a problem that seems real, remove your attention from it in consciousness and <u>feel</u> that which would be the solution to the problem, (e.g., use of the 'rose' example in Subs. 7(G) Medit. 1). Claim it in consciousness, not in words, but rather feel the quality of it in consciousness until you feel yourself to be it, i.e., lose yourself in feeling it and it will be given.

229

- I abandon all memories of my past undesirable life-state and mentally replace that negative past with thoughts for the new reality of a more desirable and pleasurable life-state.
- I am surrendering all my past negative conditioning and fears, and in its place am presently allowing in fearlessness and positiveness.
- All negative effects from my earlier life are abated as my life's compass is put on a positive future.

Subsection 7(G)- Meditation 4- *Focusing Our Imagination on the Dimensions of Infinite Love*. (In the text: 'I AM' or 'I am', as the name of God who lies within each of us as our 'Soul')

At this point, it should be clearly stated that focusing on Infinite Love as it was experienced by Anita Moorjani, Betty Eadie, Eben Alexander, M.D., and Colton Burpo in their respective Near Death Experiences (NDEs), and expressed earlier herein by Uell Andersen, Neville Goddard, Wayne Dyer, and Florence Shinn, represents a viable platform for (1) amplifying one's faith and belief in the existence of a Higher Power with an accompanying joyous afterlife; (2) healing any past hurts that still linger in our present lives. To bring these about, we need to focus our imagination on (a) just what this Infinite Love consists of, i.e., how pure, unadulterated, euphoric, warm, free, and available it might be; (b) the meaning of the phrase in Ch. 3, Theme 5: 'I AM Infinite Love, Power, Warmth, Perfection, and Peace throughout my Being for Perfect Health and Healing', i.e., I am an Infinite Power capable of healing myself from within (via 'Soul').

NDE accounts of unfathomable, unconditional Infinite Love making up the Infinite Side, indescribable from a language standpoint, have immensely bolstered my faith in a Higher Power. These accounts reveal that there is something very special to live for and eventually look forward to in the next life, which through awareness, imagination, and meditation can be tapped into while we are still in this life. We <u>don't</u>

have to wait to die and go to the next life to perceive/experience pieces of this Love (Subs. 7(C), Medit. (13, 14, 15)

Subsection 7(H)- Dealing with Negativity, Fear, and Ego

Subsection 7(H)- Meditation 1(A)- *Origin and Effect of Negativity in Human Affairs: The History of Negativity*.

Humans beginning long ago found out that they got more immediate human arousal and attention by putting something like a roadblock to survival with its consequences in a negative, threatening mode rather than in a more positive mode or framework. That is, it was much easier to get on an immediate track 'to get things done' in response to a threat with negative-based statements. In the primitive mode going back hundreds of thousands of years, human survival very often depended upon an immediate response, which was best and most easily produced by threatening and negatively stated prescriptions. This was interpreted through experience by early humans as the faster and more expedient way to get their survival-based needs most quickly attended to or accomplished.

Human experience determined that negative threats forced action, whereas non-threats or positive statements left the door open for human inaction or to countervail. The threat of death was the most extreme enticer to force or produce immediate life-saving strategies and actions. Many human cultures inculcated within their social structures, including methods in raising children, the threat and fear syndrome as the best survival methodology to actually 'get things done' or produce 'hard results'. Alternatively, the non-threat or positive pleading mode was 'softer', which left the door open for the human mind and decision-making and acting process to easily ignore or even avoid. As a result, the common use of the negative, threat, and fear-based mode became popularized and passed down through multitudes of generations over eons of time.

Subsection 7(H)- Meditation 1(B)- *Origin and Effect of Negativity in Human Affairs: Our Modern Culture*

Have you ever noticed the negative, drama-sounding, as well as cataclysmic slant to much of the news and media on radio, television, in newspapers, and on the internet? Disasters, murders, robberies, sexual perversions, and human attacks, as well as all sorts of fear-based negative-oriented drama and fantasized future disaster stories on television and in the movies easily pervade and dominate these media. Negative, fantastic-sounding situations seem to make the news and draw attention, as well as generate sales and profits via advertising. Positive happenings in the news are not as common or popularized and are often perceived by producers and audiences to have low ratings, to be low money makers, or to be boring. Our whole modern culture and society are oriented with a negative slant toward dramas and excitement in the entertainment field, which are often broadcast via violent acts such as murders, crime, and warfare. Positive-sounding briefs and informative educational programs are perceived to be not as exciting, and the 'ratings' easily prove that. The threat and fear that 'bad stuff' occurs or might happen, seem to be the order of the day, e.g., 'If don't you do this certain thing you could be fined, or sued, or arrested, or prosecuted, or sent to jail'.

Our whole educational system and culture, as well as those throughout the world, seem to follow in the same negative excitement, drama, or cataclysmic-sounding format. It is just easier to express something negatively or excitedly with the threat of fear than to suggest it positively, i.e., to threaten or entertain someone with negativity or violence rather than suggesting positive deeds leading to something good and useful that helps people. Perhaps this is because threats to survival are real, and almost anything or issue can be slanted by the culture or media as fear or a threat, leading the way for setting a negative tonality.

Subsection 7(H)- Meditation 1(C)- *Origin and Effect of Negativity in Human Affairs: World Religions*.

Mention should be made on the emphasis of many world religions in promoting negativity instead of a more positive approach. It has been my observation and experience with Catholicism as well as many of the Protestant Faiths for their clear emphasis on mankind's penchant to commit 'sin' or 'evil acts', as opposed to promoting doing more positive or good deeds. These faiths, as well as many others in the world, seem to offer a similar threat mode for an afterlife consisting of a temporary purgation or 'purgatory' cleansing, or worse still the possible damnation fate of an eternal 'hell' for those who lead sinful lives. The fear generated from a lifetime of worry over 'salvation' to a Nirvana or Heaven, versus purgation cleansing or 'damnation' to eternal punishment or hellfire, is sure to cast a negative pall of gloom and doom on the psychologies and lives of so many people, intensifying their negativism.

Many prayers in these faiths seem to overshadow the emphasis on doing good deeds with mention of sin, its constant threat to mankind, and the need to exculpate it. In the same vein, many faiths seem to portray the overall thought that 'we are in this life to suffer', which explains many of the hardships in life that go on in the world that mankind must face, with the emphasis on positiveness, joy, bliss, and fun in life much less prominent from the pulpit. Once again, threat and <u>fear</u> are the prime 'modus operand' to get obedience to church or societal precepts, which perhaps reflect a throwback to man's primitive state and the use of the common threat mechanism to address the long-ago constant-state threats to survival. (Subs.7(H), Medit. 1(A))

What if the emphasis of religious organizations could be guided toward a more <u>positive</u> approach that would strive to promote a church, meditative, or action-oriented focus in carrying out good activities and works to help folks achieve better family and social relationships along with improved living conditions?

Subsection 7(H)- Meditation 1(D)- *Origin and Effect of Negativity &* *Evil in Human Affairs: Evil Comes from Mankind.* (In the text: 'I am' refers to anyone, and is the name of God within each of us as 'Soul')

> 'At the first step in our discussion of evil, let us sensibly get rid of both the devil and hell. Make up your own mind that the intelligence behind the Universe does not destroy itself! The pain-ridden ideas of evil and hellfire as a place for punishment for sin are man's morbid ideas.' note 64

Uell Andersen's thinking is that all thoughts on negativity and evil come from man's imagination and his thinking, as God is not aware of the existence of these negative things. He adds that since people are brought into this world with <u>free</u> will capabilities, they are left to invent their own situations, including the events and happenings of evil and suffering. Neville Goddard would completely agree, as will be shown in the next meditation. The conscious human mind associated with all thinking related to the physical body and its survival generates what Uell calls 'prompters'. These are negative feelings that are then linked in memory from the conscious mind to the subconscious mind, which he defines as the Universal Subconscious Mind or God. These 'prompters' are negative feelings such as lack, limitation, unhappiness, guilt, fear, remorse, doubt, and loneliness, which restrict and prevent us from the proper use of the Infinite.[117]

A person's conscious mind conceives these feelings and projects negative images of these into their subconscious mind, and these come back to revisit the person's conscious mind with negative creations of actuality. The Law of the Universe is that like seeks and renders the like, i.e., negative, or 'prompter' thoughts and feelings will render the same realities in real life. Conversely, positive thoughts projected from the conscious mind to the subconscious, e.g., I am healthy, will render positive realities in life such as good health or feeling good.[118]

Subsection 7(H)- Meditation 1(E)- *Origin and Effect of Negativity & Evil in Human Affairs: The 'Law' of the Universe*. notes 47 to 49 (In the text: 'I' or 'I am' refers to anyone, with the 'I am' also being the name of God within each of us as our Soul)

Neville Goddard divides the mind into conscious and subconscious, the conscious being personal and selective (ego), and the subconscious being impersonal and non-selective. The conscious mind generates ideas, and then through feelings sends them and impresses the idea on the subconscious mind, the origin of all creation affecting humans. The subconscious, being the Universal mind or God, accepts the idea from the conscious mind, and then sets about to bring about the idea's reality into the person's life who originated the idea. An idea goes through feelings (good or bad) to the subconscious Universal mind, and because of this, it must begin to be expressed as a physical reality (the same good or bad) in this life. Neville claims that this is the chief Law of the Universe governing mankind's existence. Feelings are the only medium by which ideas are conveyed to the subconscious mind. Therefore, he suggests we set our feelings on imagining only the positive, good, and joy, and dissuade all negative feelings related to ourselves.

The body is an emotional filter that bears unmistakable marks of prevalent emotions. Emotional disturbances, particularly depressed emotions, cause most sicknesses and diseases. Undesirable feelings, unless overridden by positive feelings, can produce undesirable realities. I am healthy is a much stronger feeling than I hope to be, I want to be, or I will be healthy, which expresses that I am not healthy. What you feel you are is dominant and can easily violate perceptions of any of the 5 senses. Feeling the reality of the state desired and living and acting on that conviction is the way of all miracles.

Subsection 7(H)- Meditation 2(A)- *Origins and Effects of Fear in Human Affairs: Fear from the Primitive to Modern State*.

Fear (an emotion) is the result of human-related instincts, responses, and coping mechanisms in association with threats and dangers to life in both mankind's primal past and more modern times. Fear is often the first emotional response of instinct to threatening danger, which raises the curtain to alert and align the incarnate body and mind of the person being threatened to prepare to deal with an anticipated oncoming crisis. The possible human responses to fear likely represent carry-overs into modern times of buried collective unconscious memories in human minds from mankind's primal past when threats to survival were much greater and more frequent than in more modern times. This primal period has existed for at least the last one million years up to the last few hundred years (modern era).

Much human misery occurring throughout history has inherited roots, via historical mind-memory templates, of a fear-based primitive past when conditions were under a constant state of threat to survival. It is as if 'fire burners' created by fear from mankind's primitive past are 'turned on' during highly stressful modern-life situations to help the victim cope with and survive through a present-day trauma period (e.g., an environmental crisis, a warfare situation, or a child or adult-life abuse situation). Afterward, when that modern stress period has ended or subsided, these 'fire burners' of fear remain barely lit in a ready-alert mode just below the victim's consciously aware mind. This leaves the victim in a low ebbed fear-based mode which could suddenly and unexpectedly elevate in facing more ordinary, less threatening modern-life situations. This means that the person could re-generate into a heightened fear-based mode as if they were still entrained in a modern-life highly stressed situation, or back in the past primal highly stressed time and environment. This would likely create problems in dealing with more ordinary lower-stressed modern-life situations, with a victim overreacting through aggressive thoughts and actions towards others or negative destructive effects upon themselves.

Subsection 7(H)- Meditation 2(B)- *Origins and Effects of Fear in Human Affairs: Rescinding Fear from Childhood*.

Fear is something that very often follows formerly mistreated children throughout their adult lives. From past early-life caretaker threats and negative actions, all formerly mistreated persons can identify with feelings of fear, worry, and humiliation when they were little children. The threat of physical and/or emotional pain that the little body and mind knew was coming, often without justifiable reason, hammered fear and worry into the child's developing mind. These fear and worry feelings/emotions became embedded and repressed into the child's subconscious mind and consciously forgotten, only to re-emerge much later in adulthood. These feelings/emotions re-emerge as needless phobic fears, worries, & angst affecting themselves, or negative acts in dealing with others in ordinary everyday adult-life affairs.

We need to become <u>aware</u> that these past fears, worries, and angst are affecting how we feel and act as adults now, that these represent remnant viral thoughts of love denied when we were young that are re-surfacing now as negative feelings and acts towards ourselves or others. From this awareness, we can re-direct or <u>reprogram</u> our thinking and feelings away from this negative loveless past, which does not affect us now because the past is gone and won't return. Through free will, we can choose to feel, think, and act differently, i.e., to wake up each morning and celebrate 'the new dawn of day' by creating happier thoughts and feelings leading ourselves to a more positive, loving, and prosperous overall future.

Subsection 7(H)- Meditation 2(C)- *Origins and Effects of Fear in Human Affairs: Dealing with the Negativities of Fear*. (In the text: 'I' refers to anyone)

A negative idea continually dwelled upon consciously will create a similar thought form in the subconscious, leading to a negative outcome in one's pathway of life. Florence Shinn claims that what you fear you attract. Rather, act fearlessly because fear can make you a slave, and instead walk up to those who confront and threaten you in your pathway and say: 'The lions in my pathway will be powerless to harm me when I turn to the Universal Power for protection and send goodwill to the lions'.[119] The most negative and envious thought form is the self-pity expression, 'poor me', which if repeatedly stated results in worsening a person's situation, like building a prison. Doubt and fear keep one away from desires hoped for and instead, bring a harvest of misfortune. Rather say: 'Today is the day of amazing prosperity', or 'I see myself bathed in the dazzling bright light of Spirit which dissolves everything not Divinely planned'.[120] Our bodies are composed of spirituality, which is positive, indestructible, timeless, tireless, birthless, and deathless. Ms. Shinn stresses that we should attempt to think positively and wipe out all negative thinking.

The subconscious mind has a plethora of negative remembrances, tidings, and beliefs from all of life's experiences. Instead flood the subconscious with perfect ideas of what Florence Shinn terms as the superconscious mind (via our 'Soul') by excitedly saying: 'The light of Infinite Intelligence streams through my consciousness, dissolving and dissipating all anger and resentment: I am at peace with myself and the whole world'.[121]

Subsection 7(H)- Meditation 2(D)- *Origins and Effects of Fear in Human Affairs- Fear is the Basis of Human Troubles.*

Fear is the basis of practically all misery, intolerance, bigotry, violence, and other troubles between people in this life: fear being the opposite of love, generating hatred that easily leads to evil, producing destructive acts towards others or afflictions upon us. Fear is something that drags down everyone who develops it, particularly those who dwell on it. It is the principal seed underlying almost all abuse of human beings towards others, including children by their caretakers. Fear is also the principal seed for most all violence, murders, mass killings, and other negative and destructive acts within this human life. Folks such as

Anita Moorjani, Eben Alexander, M.D., and Betty Eadie, who each had Near Death Experiences (NDEs) on the Infinite Side, learned that fear in this life was the <u>chief</u> reason causing most all human suffering, violence, and unpleasantness. In addition, it is the principal roadblock preventing us from having full enjoyment in life. Instead, fear creates the need for a constant struggle to have power over others, and amass big status, and/or wealth.

One cannot succeed by being afraid and at the same time carrying out successful true love acts with others. If love acts are accompanied by fear, it likely is a sign of untrue conditional love, but not true unconditional love. Or the fear could be generated from carry-overs of a love-denied or love-loss childhood past. Fear is something that often follows children from difficult early-life situations throughout their adulthood. Physical or emotional difficulties repeatedly endured early on in one's life get hard-wired or inculcated into that child's mind as unconscious memories, which unexpectedly re-emerge during their follow-up adult years as phobic fears, worries, or negative acts towards others or themselves. Likewise, this same negative carry-over effect of fear, worries, or negative acts toward others or themselves can occur in adulthood from love-denied or love-loss situations during this period. With conscious intent, all these negative fears, feelings, and acts can and should be rejected because the past is gone and will not return, and much brighter days and opportunities are currently here.

Subsection 7(H)- Meditation 2(E)- *Origins and Effects of Fear in Human Affairs- A Human Goal of Having Fearlessness.*

Subs. 7(H), Medit. 2(D) above stressed that the origin of most all human misery, intolerance, and violence between people in this life is <u>fear</u> (the opposite of love), which leads to all sorts of negative acts towards others or afflictions upon us. From the NDEs already discussed herein plus others I have reviewed, all the individuals who encountered brief crossover experiences on the Infinite Side brought back one principal message, that having fearlessness within this life is the best way to live, which promotes less stress, more fun, healing, and good health. All these folks had suffered greatly from fear before their NDE experience.

We need to identify and become aware of the origins of worries and fears that are affecting how we currently feel and act in our adult lives. These often represent remnant viral thoughts of love-denied experiences from our past which are resurfacing now as worries and fears that result in negative acts. We should determine that these negative feelings from our past need not affect us now because the past is gone and touches us not, that the present is here, absent of all those fear-based loveless past experiences and people. We can overcome negative influences from our past by choosing through free will to adopt positive and good in all our thinking, feelings, and acts, both in the present-time sense and going forward.

Subsection 7(H)- Meditation 2(F)- *Origins & Effects of Fear in Human Affairs- Dealing with Fear via Spirit of 'Soul'.* (In the text: 'I AM', as the name of God that lies within each of us as our 'Soul'; 'I' or 'my' refers to anyone)

Besides overcoming difficulties from our past by choosing to think and act differently, we need to be consciously aware of our connection with the Infinitely Loving and Peaceful 'Source', 'God', or 'Soul' that lies within each of us. We need to self-generate the healing power of our Source to remove all the present fears and worries we have now from our past negative love-denied or love-loss experiences. Our inner 'Source' or 'Soul' composed of total healing love, perfection, and clarity, is ours to consciously choose by calling on it to relieve present negative worries and fears arising from our past encounters with people.

I AM surrendering to the Infinite, Good, and Perfect Power from within me (via 'Soul') in removing all the hurts that I still feel from the fear carried over from my love-denied or love-loss past. By allowing (via intent and surrender) I have unshakeable faith in the Universal

Wisdom and Power of 'Source' or 'God' to infuse His Infinite Love via my Spiritual part, or 'Soul', which will heal both my body and mind.

I AM allowing His Infinite healing energy to flow from my Infinite 'Soul' throughout my body and mind: first via the top of my head, then internally to all brain/mind parts, then through the eyes, mouth, neck, both shoulders, arms, hands, all fingers, and skin. Then through the heart and circulatory system, lungs and breathing system, aorta to the stomach, through the intestines, liver, gallbladder and spleen, kidneys, and urological system. Then from the upper to lower back, pelvis, legs to knees, down to the feet, and toes. All of these above bring positive healing energy, removing all past negative impacts on my physical body & mind. I AM Infinite Love, Perfection, Clarity, and Healing of my entire body and mind, including the removal of all present fears and disappointments from past love denials and/or love losses.

Subsection 7(H)- Meditation 2(G)- *Origins & Effects of Fear in Human Affairs- Fear of Feeling Alone, Adults/Infants*. (In the text: 'I' refers to the author)

This meditation title is likened to what I well remember back in 1969, watching on TV the Apollo 11 space trip to the moon when Neil Armstrong and Buzz Aldrin landed and walked on the moon's surface. As their spacecraft entered lunar orbit to begin the descent to the lunar surface, I distinctly remember an interpretation of the two astronauts' voices just before they passed on the side of the moon facing away from Earth and lost sight of it and total radio contact with the command center in Houston. The TV commentators indicated that the astronauts seemed fearful at the thought of being completely cut off from sight and radio contact with Home Earth for 15 to 20 minutes. Not having this sight and sound contact, they felt alone in the Universe with a definite loss of faith, despite all the technology that had gotten them to where they were approaching the lunar surface for a landing. Then, when the orbiter with its two astronauts regained sight of Earth on the far side of the moon, and radio contact was regained with the command center in Houston, how greatly elated and relieved they sounded with sighs of relief!

A similar analogy to this is the time when we were very small children and alone, in the hands of parents or caretakers with total dependence on them, and then later as we grew up, we became re-attached to our spiritual side or core (or 'Soul') through maturation and the power of awareness. The astronauts were never actually alone on the blind side of the moon, as they had all the technical backup support from this world that they had trained for and been provided with. And, in our early childhoods, we were never alone because our spiritual cores (or 'Souls') that had always accompanied us were prepared to give us the backup support to help us in body/mind and spiritually later in our childhood and adult lives. This would happen once we grew up and re-awakened spiritually by becoming consciously aware of our Soul's presence along with its potential spiritual power.

Subsection 7(H)- Meditation 3(A)- *Origins and Effects of Ego in Human Affairs- Ego's Definition*.

The ego is principally defined as defending the self (or oneself) along with the physical and rational thought processes that are called on by the individual to best survive, which includes creating and maintaining quality-of-life conditions. Wayne Dyer calls ego (or edging God out) the false sense of self.[122] Ego emerges with us after birth and expands thereafter through parents or caretakers and our culture. Ego trains and nags us throughout childhood to do our best, to compete, i.e., to get the best grades, dress up the best, win in sports, get the highest school honors; and in adult life to earn the most money, have the best job, biggest bank account, fanciest house on the block, and most expensive car. [note. 122] David Simon refers to the ego response as like 'crossing a minefield' of I, mine, or realm of self, in that when our sense of ownership or dominance is threatened, we either lash out in anger to defend it or shut down in resignation.[123] This is the ego's response known as 'the fight or flight syndrome', which means either fighting through anger, protest, and violence or flight by withdrawing into oneself and becoming depressed. ^{note 123}

Ego represents the total opposite of staying in the spirit which we all consisted of before this life. Spirit suggests and reminds us that we all share the same life force with everyone and everything in existence. Human culture and ego do just the opposite: we are each created differently from everyone else, therefore we must compete to defeat others and accumulate what they possess as ours, or else we will feel defeated. In other words, the ego says that we are in this life to defeat everyone else, that we are what we acquire, and if we have or want little then we are of very little value. ^{note 122}

Subsection 7(H)- Meditation 3(B)- *Origins and Effects of Ego in Human Affairs- Suggested Ways to Deal with Ego.* (In the text: 'I' refers to anyone)

Wayne Dyer recommends that the ego must be attacked, destroyed, and silenced. Ego denies our original spiritual perfection, which is what we were before this life, so it must be denied and replaced with the reality (contrary to the 5 senses) that we are Infinitely and eternally made of Love. Ego is not real, but our Infinity and Perfection are. When the ego has convinced us that spirit and/or Infinite Love are absent, we must continually remind ourselves that there is no place in the Universe devoid of spirit and Love and that everything and everyone is of spirit before, during, and after becoming evident in physical form.[124]

Concerning ego, we must choose to let it go, for it is only manifesting our self-interest in maintaining material status, social pecking order, and existence in this world along with our 'elated' physical place in it. This positions worldly power and the ability to control others strictly for our self-interest. Every person needs to say:

> 'I let all this material and social pecking order along with my ego go out the door forever, as these do <u>not</u>

consist of my spiritual or eternal existence, rather they represent an aberration or illusion for only my apparent physical survival within this life, which represents only an infinitesimal part of my eternal existence'. note 124

In place of my ego-ambition drive, I must consciously choose to help and serve others in a more loving and supportive manner during the remainder of my life. I am now allowing any negative aspects I have faced that involve egos of mine and others to pass gently and quietly, without any judgments, out of my body and mind for all eternity.

Subsection 7(I)- Perfection and Wonderment of the Infinite Side

Subsection 7(I)- Meditation 1(A)- *Healing Flow from Book's Title: "Meditation to Healing Freedom thru Infinite Love".*

First, for Meditation to begin, one must quiet the body and particularly the mind in a truly relaxing fashion to 'welcome in' Infinite Spirit to both body and mind. This Infinite Spirit is present within each of us via our 'Soul' and is not an entity apart from us far out in space somewhere. We call on Infinite Spirit via the startup of any meditation technique discussed in Chapter 6 & 7 herein, or from any other meditation source.

Second, for a closeness of Spirit to happen, meditation practice must become part of regular daily activity, with a time and quiet space set aside in one's schedule. Over time a closeness to the Infinite Spirit occurs, with feelings that vary for each person. Human 'feelings' would be a good 'barometer' for identifying the degree of this closeness, which is achieved by a quieting of the mind and placing within this quiet space any reading, sound, or thought that raises positive human feelings, moving one closer to the Infinite Spirit.

Third, once a person's regular meditation practice achieves a closeness to the Infinite Spirit, for healing to begin, the person must specifically identify what healing is needed or desired. Once this is expressed, it is best to assume through feelings as if the healing has <u>already</u> occurred. To continue the healing, this desire and assumption need to be periodically repeated during all future regularly practiced meditation.

Fourth, healing starts to actualize when the sufferer begins to show signs of relief from their existing health affliction(s). Along with this would be a growing sense (or feelings) of 'freedom' triggered by an actual 'release' from the affliction's physical or mental pain. In rare instances, this release creates an especially heightened sense and clarity of freedom evidenced by intense feelings of love, euphoria, and pleasurable bodily joys, indicating a person's closeness with Our 'Source' and Its associated Infinite Love.

In short, the 'path to healing flow':

(1) the person quieting themselves in a truly relaxing fashion, 'welcoming in' Infinite Spirit to both body and mind; *(2)* meditation practice becomes a regular daily activity whereby quietness of mind occurs, and within that quiet space, 'medians' (e.g., sound or reading) move one toward closeness with Infinite Spirit; *(3)* healing starts when a person identifies: *(a)* the healing desired, *(b)* the presumption via intent and feelings that healing has occurred/will continue; *(4)* actual healing occurs, with feelings of release and freedom from pain and in rare instances a heightened sense and clarity of freedom, love, euphoria, and highly pleasurable bodily feelings/joys-- clear signs of Our Infinite 'Source' associated with Its Infinite Love.

Subsection 7(I)- Meditation 1(B)- *Positive Words of God by Watching Your Words*. (In the text: 'I' refers to anyone)

According to authors Uell Andersen, Neville Goddard, and Wayne Dyer, the subconscious mind of man is power without direction, in that whatever is impressed upon it (good or bad) is carried out consciously in life. In a slightly different context, according to Florence Shinn there is a deeper than the subconscious mind, namely a super-conscious mind, (i.e., via one's 'Soul'), which represents the perfection of God or the realm of Intuition. Her idea is that the subconscious mind has a plethora of negative remembrances and beliefs from all of life's experiences. She emphasizes in her work, "The Magic Path of Intuition", that we need to flood the subconscious mind with positive ideas from the perfect super-conscious mind through thoughts such as:

> 'The dazzling white light of love and wisdom flows through my consciousness, eliminating all anger and resentment, thereby my body, mind, and spirit are at peace with the world and its affairs'.[125]

She goes on to say that whatever you think, feel, and say about others comes right back to visit you. If someone sends you injustices and you send those back out to them, they return right back to you. This is the 'Law of Life' in this world. What you visualize in your mind, you sooner or later meet in the outside world.[126] Our early training, by and large, is negative in that children so often hear, 'it's too good to be true', or 'don't expect the good thing to happen again'.[127] These idioms are impressed, through speech, on the subconscious, and quite likely the good happening thing will <u>not</u> happen again. Rather, we should say 'It is good and true, and it can happen again'. A negative idea yields negative thoughts which yield a negative outcome in life. Saying 'poor me' is like building a prison.[note 127] Rather, one should focus on promoting positive ideas and thoughts that lead to good outcomes in life, and these good fortunes will come true.

Subsection 7(I)- Meditation 1(C)- *Forgiveness in Our Worldly State is Unneeded in the Infinite State.*

We here in this life are continuously obsessed with granting and receiving all sorts of forgiveness after the fact: forgiveness at trial, forgiveness for faults or sins, forgiveness as mercy, forgiveness of debts, or forgiveness of what has been said or done. But in the Infinite State, there is no such thing as forgiveness, as within that State we are surrounded and blessed by the ever-loving accepting arms of an Infinite Source or Creator. This Creator has complete compassion, comprehension, understanding, and perfect Love for us despite whatever errors or faults we've committed, or things that were left undone by us during our lives here. What a wonderful feeling and healing assumption it is for us to meditate that this true reality exists within the Heavenly State, including our overwhelming 'welcoming' greeting upon arrival there!

What if we could assume from the ancient, oft-expressed spiritual lore, 'on Earth as it is in Heaven', that individual human acts done here inciting the need for forgiveness had already been absolved from the Infinite (Heaven) State standpoint even <u>before</u> these negative acts were committed here? In other words, Infinite forgiveness would assume an a-priori presumption of 'no-fault finding' as part of the process of granting prior annulment by an Infinitely Loving Creator, without any need to go through a lengthy process of worldly-type forgiveness. This would represent the disguised imprint of an Infinite Love miracle having been generated and transferred from the Heavenly Side to this worldly side. If this is true, it would possibly allow for 'other' imprint miracles to occur here from the Heavenly Side, such as the healing of certain human illnesses, diseases, or difficulties (e.g., love losses). Might any of these miracles represent the cosmic consciousness of humankind reconnecting its spiritual cords to the Source of Divine Compassion?

Subsection 7(I)- Meditation 1(D)- *Infinite Love, One Way of Defining It*.

One way of perceiving Infinite Love is by visualizing a limitless Universe when you are outdoors on a clear night and viewing upward into the vast Universe above your head—seeing the stars, moon, planets, comets, nebulas, and galaxies beyond. Imagine in your view another state of existence other than the physical state you're viewing—an invisible (to the eye) spiritual constellation of stars, planets, and galaxies filled with dimensions of pure and unadulterated Love both surrounding and transcending an Infinite Universe, with the Creator of this good Universe of Love at the center of it all. But instead of this Creator dwelling in an empty void of space, rather existing in a 'home' filled with unparalleled and unending Infinite Love consisting of acceptance, warmth, compassion, understanding, joy, euphoria, and goodness, with the complete and total absence of anything evil, the 'devil' (Satan), or Hell.

Subsection 7(I)- Meditation 1(E)- *Contrasting Examples of 'this Side' with 'the Other Side'.*

In Anita Moorjani's book, 'Dying to Be Me', she describes a particularly impressive account. From her memories of experiences from the Other Side, she compares typical wonders we experience in this life with far more spectacular wonders on the Infinite Side. For instance, she describes a giant warehouse almost limitless in size where you can shine a small pen-like flashlight inside it just to see what is there, and all you can see is part of one aisle both up and down, with a variety of things like in a department store.[128] But this is only a very small part of the entire store. This is exactly like our situation in this life, with time and our sense perceptions so limited. Now suddenly vast flood lights come on showing the contents of a much larger warehouse seemingly limitless in size, where you can see vast aisles with rows upon rows high and low going in every direction with all sorts of magical gadgets in every color, and collections of candies, toys, and other things of every description. note 128 This would be unimaginable in our lives here and is analogous to the Infinite Side she witnessed during her NDE.

She goes on to say that on the Infinite Side, there is nothing to forgive for 'sins', errors, omissions, or lack of accomplishments occurring in worldly life for us to fully experience the joys there.[129] The relief she felt from this responsibility was as magnificent a joy as compared with any other pleasurable feelings she experienced there. From childhood indoctrination, we have all had it hammered into our minds that for us to experience the 'Nirvana' joys and pleasures in the next life, we must 'perform' with good behavior, and have an excellent track record here during this life. This means that we would need to be judged by 'God' at the end of this life as having achieved a highly 'productive', and great behavioral record before entering through those 'golden gates' into the next life. If we have a poor record with a relatively low overall 'score', we will automatically go to a temporary 'purgatory' for a cleansing process, or worse still condemned to eternal 'hellfire'. Anita found out that this was <u>not</u> true from her NDE experience on the Other Side.[130]

Subsection 7(I)- Meditation 1(F)- *I AM Healed via the 'One' (or 'Source'), totally Composed of Goodness.* (In the text: 'I' refers to anyone; 'I AM', as the name of God who lies within each of us as our 'Soul')

I surrender both my body and mind to the 'One', 'Source', or 'God' through my Infinite 'Soul' part, and this transforms into healing throughout my entire physical being. This creates complete peace within me. I AM 'One' through 'Source' with all its power, energy, and knowledge. I AM Universal knowledge, which is completely composed of goodness. I AM repulsed by anything known as evil, badness, negativity, fear, or confusion, for my 'Source' or 'God' does not know of these things because they are all regarded through the Infinite Mind as unreal, and not representing the truth. This is because the actual truth in the Universe is total goodness through His Infinite Love. This Infinite Love is fulfilled within me right now via my mind awareness of its translation throughout my incarnate bodily components (both body and mind) coming from my 'Soul'. Through the process of translation, this love transforms (or actualizes) perfect love, along with perfect knowledge, health, peace, warmth, and happiness throughout my being. This helps me to surrender all the false, materially based impressions and illusions of this physical world, including all evil and human-based ego and power over others. I do not accept anything but the truth, which is always the good of the Infinite Wonder of all the Universe through His Infinite Loving and Unifying 'One' presence.

Subsection 7(I)- Meditation 1(G)- *Incredible Infinite Wonders within the 'Core', the Home of Our Higher Power.*

During Eben Alexander, M.D.'s Near Death Experience (NDE), he witnessed the 'Core' or the ultimate home of our Higher Power, with this 'Core' and its Higher Power identified to him as 'OM'. He described 'OM' as omniscient, omnipotent, and all-loving. This place or home of the Infinite consists of black darkness at the same time incredible light, or as Henry Vaughn, an English writer once said, 'there is, some say in God, a deep and dazzling darkness'.[131] Eben further described this as a place or state where the pleasurable feeling and acceptance of Infinite Unconditional Love was incomparable to anything back in this life. Also, 'OM' possesses qualities of love, acceptance, warmth, compassion, irony, and pathos not only like we humans are capable of but incredibly greater, more genuine, and believable. And 'OM' sympathizes with our human situation in this life much more than we could ever imagine, as this Infinite Power knows how difficult and painful worldly life can really be.[132]

As part of his NDE, Eben was taken on the wings of a giant butterfly as part of a beautiful lady, (which clearly reflects a natal sister of his that he never met in life), who expressed a spiritual message to him (not in language): (1) 'you are loved and cherished dearly forever'; (2) 'you have nothing to fear'; (3) 'you can do no wrong'; (4) in summary, 'you are completely loved and accepted without any reservation'.[133] With this, no selfishness, jealousness, or judgment was possible, but rather only unconditional Infinite Love. No human words or actions can adequately describe this sort of love. This message gave him tremendous relief as if these were the rules and basis of all that he was supposed to have been following in his life but hadn't until then.[134]

AUTHOR'S AFTERWORD

I think I came into this world as an inquisitive and sensitive being, with the persuasion and intent to be extremely curious and explorative in wanting to unconventionally research and discover just 'what makes things tick', or 'why certain things happen', or better still, 'why we are here in this life'. After 79 years in this life, I am simply astounded by the contrasts that can occur between us humans in this world who act individually or collectively through free choice or free will, which can lead to either **(1)** intensely good and focused unconditional love acts which border on or mirror the Infinite <u>Love</u> of God; or **(2)** totally the opposite chaotic and loveless acts of wanton destruction, evil, or (at worst) mass-killings or genocides which destroy so many people's lives. Another factor in this life that astounds me is **(3)** the extraordinary effort that so many folks go through in this life in striving to make perfection out of everything that is so inherently imperfect.

EPILOGUE FINAL NOTES

This book ends with twenty-five final notes that summarize in succinct form, the principal concepts and ideas covered within this work, which form an underlying basis of the Themes in Ch. 2-6 and the 100 Narrative Healing Meditations in Ch. 7. Comprehending principal concepts and ideas in conjunction with these Themes and Meditations provides the reader with an effective connection to the work's prime objective, namely, to institute healing solutions through regular meditation practice for any person's follow-up negative effects from prior life difficulties. Chapter 6, Theme 1 'Preparation to Meditation for All People- Equality' presents the Infinitely based notion of a spiritual 'Soul' or Infinite Existence within each of us, which makes us all equal with one another. Acceptance of this reality best prepares each of us for productive meditation (i.e., our successful 'meshing' with Spirit). Chapter 6, Theme 2 'The Science of Meditation Practice' offers meditation practices, techniques, and related discussion, which foster a person's spiritual growth by going 'with-in' to their Spiritual essence (or 'Soul') and tapping into the <u>healing</u> presence and influence of our 'Source', the 'One', or 'God' with all of Its inherent Infinite Love.

<u>Note 1: 'I Am All that I Am'</u>. What this author has recently come to realize is that all the positive and negative experiences that occur in every individual's life represent 'building blocks' in a truly positive fashion for creating a developed 'architecture' as to where each person is (at a point in time). What this is saying is that each of these building blocks didn't occur randomly or happenstance, but rather occurred as part of a dynamic Divine plan to get each of us to a certain level development-wise at a particular point in time. All our experiences, both positive and negative (including life hardships and tragedies), have contributed <u>positively</u> to building a more highly evolved human being composed of body, mind, and Spirit.

Note 2: 'Self Projection' as a Social Norm. Blame by others that we are to be blamed for having caused certain unfortunate circumstances to happen to them is very often unjustified. Our human minds (via ego) and our world cultures often throw the blame of others for their negative situations and/or actions back onto us as (innocent) individuals. We tend to take these things 'personally' in a negative fashion, when in fact other folks in our lives are often throwing or 'self-projecting' their frustration and guilt over bad circumstances they created back onto us by blaming us for their unfortunate situations. This 'self-projection' of blame onto us cannot be reconciled to make us feel better until it is clearly established in our minds that <u>they</u> are fully at fault for their situations instead of <u>us</u>.

Note 3: The Infinite 'Well' Within. I go within myself into the core or the inner reaches of my conscience to my eternally existing 'Soul' or Spiritual essence near the physical heart area where there is complete peace, tranquility, truth, and harmony. I was not aware of this inner Spiritual core ('Soul') during my early childhood, but now that I am aware of it, I call forth into the recesses of it for total tranquility, peace, and healing of my body and mind. People only encounter my body which is merely a physical manifestation of this life that represents ego. But my true eternal self is Spiritual, an Infinitely Loving, everlasting, and perfect entity. Since this Spirit is perfect, and via my belief that 'I AM Unified as One with God in His All-Loving Universe', this indicates that in my current incarnate state, I can be healed from illnesses/maladies.

Note 4: Equality of all People. Many spiritual leaders have spoken on the concept that all people need to have clear recognition through consciousness and belief in the <u>equality</u> of each person's body, mind, and 'Soul' with everyone else who has ever lived. The rationale behind this is that we are all combined with everything in the Universe under an umbrella of the Unified Infinite, Loving 'One' ('Source' or 'God'). Each of us (body, mind, and 'Soul') has always remained equal with everyone else who has ever existed under the Loving 'One' throughout all our past difficulties and traumas. At the 'tap roots' of all this is each of us possesses a spiritual 'Soul', equal to all other 'Souls' ever created. From this, the equality of all people under the Unity of the Universe's Infinite Loving 'One' represents a golden key to open the door for healing from all our past lifetime difficulties.

Note 5: Invaliding Past Negativity Yields Us Freedom. Our 'Source' or God is strictly composed of the good, with <u>no</u> evil. Therefore, I open my entire being consisting of combined body, mind, and 'Soul' to the total energizing and positive unconditional Love of my Source (God), which heals me from all the effects of negative thinking that may permeate into my mind. This automatically heals my body/mind and protects me from all bad thoughts that may arise from the past. I know that at the center of me (my 'Soul') I AM ageless, limitless, deathless, perfect, warm, happy, and equal, for this Spirit permeates all my bodily and worldly affairs. When I become confused, unhappy, or worried again, I think only of goodness in the present and surrender all bad feelings and thoughts from my past to the Infinite Source, or God. Yes, I AM finally healed and free!

Note 6: Infinite Love Defined. According to Neville Goddard's work, "The Law and the Promise," the greatest thing that exists in the world and Universe is <u>Love</u>, which is the Love of God or Infinite Unconditional Love ('Agape' as St. Paul called it). This is a mere phrase that has tremendous meaning. Nothing ever imagined by man* could ever be compared to this Love. The most intimate relationship in this life is like living in separate cells, as compared with the magnitude of

God's Infinite and vast Love. It is incredible to imagine and meditate on the fact that Infinite Love is better, deeper, clearer, longer-lasting (eternal), perfect, and surpasses all expectations and experiences of the best romantic or unconditional love in this life. This means nothing to buy to satisfy another, nothing to expect from another, nothing to judge or grudge one against another, no egos of one or another to hurt, and no human mind to concoct reasons for giving or non-giving or loving or not loving.

Note 7: Love Gives Meaning to All Life. Uell Andersen's work, "Three Magic Words," stresses that Love governs all and that mankind* in this life is in constant search of it, that through it there is a spiritual unity with all life, and that perfect Infinite Love lies within each of us. This perfect Love within us is complete and absolute, and it cries out from the very depth of our being for expression. But because of the human ego with its pride, competitiveness, and negativity, we often block this Love out. This results in hurting mankind, as Love moves through the entire Universe. In human terms, it is often so difficult to open this channel of Love expression because our egos, self-centeredness, competitiveness, and fear of failure force us to pull away from this Love. But if we allow Love to manifest, it heals the body, comforts the loneliness, lightens darkened paths, redeems evil & fears, and brings prosperity and positive meaning to our lives. [61]

Note 8: Suffering Defines Human Purpose: to Love. Victor Frankl's book, "Man's Search for Meaning", presents a real human eye view of typical life experiences in Nazi concentration death camps where Frankl endured the most horrific conditions for 2½ years during the first part of the 1940s. It seems that his desire to once again experience and love other people on both an individual and collective basis was chief in his mind, which drove him to endure extreme limits to survive to the day when liberation would finally free him from the camps. This says that our main purpose in this life is finding and experiencing true love, no matter how big or small, despite whatever profound negative experiences we must endure here.

Note 9: Infinite Love versus Worldly Love. The Infinite Love State is where we all emerged from before this life, namely an Infinite wonder of totally accepting and encompassing Love, far beyond anything indicated by Dr. David Hawkins or suggested by anyone else within this life. All that Dr. Hawkins mentions as love can be conditional or unconditional, and if conditional is often temporary, i.e., here today and easily 'taken' away or gone tomorrow as happens so often between people in this life. But Infinite Love is not only perfect, omniscient, and comprising everything in the Universe, but it is, always was, always will be, cannot ever be taken away, and is far superior with much greater warmth and euphoric, joyful pleasure as compared to the best romantic relationship in this life.

Note 10: We Grow Toward the Divine. We grow toward awareness of the Infinite Spirit by growing awareness during this life of the essence of true love via the human senses and emotions. We are here to grow toward God through a growing awareness of the Infinite Love that we came from when we were back in the Infinite State. We are here in this life to grow back toward the Divine by growing unconditional true love with others through awareness and experience of carrying out this love by sharing it with another or others, without expectations of the love giver or recipient from past or present circumstances. Any progress towards this in this life is very positive, as Infinite memory of this will only serve to build for us our enhancement of the joys and ecstasy of Infinite Love which we will all experience upon our return to the Infinite State Side.

Note 11: Author's Own Experience with Infinite Love. During meditation by an ocean beach in the summer of 2006, I had the most wonderful 'feeling' completely envelope me with a fantastic, euphoric 'Loving' feeling (energy) that seemed would last forever, which clearly came from within me. This was not like any other typical worldly love or loving feelings I had ever experienced before. Though hard to describe, these love feelings that day were so incredibly great. As intense euphoric feelings developed, an aspect of transparency and clarity came through at the same time. What seemed to envelop me was the clarity of an impenetrable veil of total acceptance, like I had absolutely nothing to feel sorry for nor be disappointed about with <u>anything</u> I had done in my life thus far. Everything had been okay and would be fine going forward. This was truly incredible; I truly felt no possible blame, angst, or negative judgments. I felt the presence of a 'Love' coming through that was so incredibly huge, caring, all-encompassing, and self-assuring in that it could or would never leave me. I was truly under or within a 'veil' of Infinite Love.

Note 12: <u>Strands of Infinite Love Evidenced in Our Worldly Lives</u>. Besides my euphoric experience in 2006, other possible worldly activities that show evidence of effects from (or traces of) Infinite Love include **(a)** the heightened aura of euphoria, excitement, emotional feelings, elation, and joy at the start of many intimate love relationships; **(b)** highly euphoric, joyful, and relaxing feelings when visiting and enjoying beauties of nature, e.g., Grand Canyon, Yosemite Park, or the Rocky Mountains; **(c)** the 'pop' music recording culture in America with its music creations that stir deep emotions, which are likely produced via vestige imprint energies within the music composer's 'Soul' from their Infinite Side past; **(d)** mental focus in the present time-mode while engaged in a pleasurable activity, which amplifies its pleasure; **(e)** infants freely exploring all sorts of things in their brand-new life; **(f)** the thrill of exploration or creations of various sorts, e.g., traveling to new places, creating new ideas or inventions, or writing new books.

Note 13: <u>Hope for a Life-Suffering or Love-Loss Victim</u>. People who have experienced socially related lifetime tragedies or difficulties need to develop contacts and a support structure to form a loving and supportive community of family, friends, and whomever else that is reassuring to the victim. This will provide a mutually supportive social structure that consistently presents positive interactions between people, helping to resurrect and maintain hope and trust for any former suffering individual. Additionally, any person who has undergone past traumatic love-denied or love-loss experiences needs to find new (true) unconditional love with others. The past love-denied or love-loss victim must make the effort to enter whatever amenable social circles that are available to meet new people and develop new unconditional loving ties. This will truly substitute for the many disappointments of love losses in the past.

Note 14: The 'Law' of the Universe. 'The Law' Essay in Neville Goddard's work, "The Law and the Promise," states that every man's conception and opinion of himself is going to be his reward. Mankind's imagination is a Divine activity that creates a world according to what we know and claim to ourselves. If we imagine bad outcomes, we will have bad outcomes. If we imagine good health, wealth, etc., we will manifest those things. Neville claims that the Universe delivers whatever you claim yourself to be. 'Let the weak say, I am strong' (Joel 3:10). By that statement, the fact that 'I am weak' is rearranged to: 'I am strong'. The statement 'I am strong', or 'I am healthy' renders just that; on the other hand, 'I am sick', 'I am weak', or 'I am tired' will render the reality of those things in this life. Unfortunately, in the same instance, 'I wish to be healthy', or 'I will be healthy', will continue the reality of unhealthiness or negativity.

Note 15: Ultimate Healing Strategy via 'I AM'. Uell Andersen's only major lifetime book, "Three Magic Words", relates the magic words near the end of this book as 'You Are God', i.e., that we are each composed of God within us as our Spiritual essence or 'Soul'. Two additional magic words 'I AM' (or 'I am') coming from Moses and Jesus long ago represent the formal self-definition or name of God within us (via our 'Soul'). Note that 'I AM' (or 'I am') and 'You are God' are similar and can therefore be combined as 'I AM'. Three other attendant magic words are: 'Infinite Love and Power'; two other magic words are: 'Infinite Warmth'; three other magic words are: 'Infinite Perfection and Clarity'; two other magic words are: 'Infinite Peace'; and three other magic words are: 'throughout my Being'. Combining all the magic words into one phrase: 'I AM Infinite Love, Power, Warmth, Perfection, Clarity, and Peace throughout my Being', gives us a powerful tool for asking what we want from Infinite Source, e.g., 'healing from body/

mind illnesses', or 'finding new true love', or 'finding a new job', or for 'any other good thing'.

Note 16: The Infinite (Love) State and Forgiveness. A significant part of the wisdom and dimension of Infinite Love is the reality that forgiveness for prior errors, sins, or wrongs committed, or things left undone during this life is completely unnecessary and absent in the Infinite State, including our entry into that State. Along with this, Anita Moorjani's Near-Death Experience related that despite an emphasis here on a traditionally taught judgment day facing each of us upon entry into the next life, this is false. Anita found more relief from these two realities than anything else on the Infinite Side. Instead, our entry there will consist of an opening of 'arms of love and acceptance' by an Infinitely Loving Creator, with nothing to judge nor forgive, that all faults with associated guilt and blame experienced here are completely meaningless and absent there.

Note 17: NDEs Enhance a Person's Faith/Belief. The Near-Death Experiences (NDEs) reviewed herein have strengthened my faith in the existence of a Higher Power. From reviewing numerous NDE encounters over many years, it is very clear to me that a huge loving force lies quite close at hand which is an integral part within each of us, and not outside in a distant location as many organized religions teach. From these NDEs, the clear fact is that each of us within our physical existence and presence here has a much more magnificent and powerful part than just our physical bodies. This consists of a Spiritual essence or 'Soul' which is eternally existing and Infinitely Loving. These NDEs reveal something very special for each of us to look forward to in the next life, namely that we will experience the joys of our spiritual 'Soul' as part of and Unified with the 'One' ('Source' or 'God') under an umbrella of Universal Infinite Love.

Note 18: The Origin of Evil- from Mankind. 'At the first discussion of evil, let us sensibly get rid of both the devil and hell. Make up your own mind that the intelligence behind the Universe does not destroy itself! The pain-ridden ideas of evil and hellfire as a place of punishment for sin are man's morbid ideas'. ^note 64 Uell Andersen's thinking is that all thoughts on negativity and evil come through man's* (or humankind's) imagination and his thinking, as God is not aware of the existence of these negative things. He adds that since people are brought into this world with <u>free</u> will capability, they are left to invent their own situations, including the events and happenings of evil and suffering instead of good outcomes. This means we can either create a 'Heaven' or a 'Hell' in this life, and this is our clear choice. Neville Goddard, Wayne Dyer, Anita Moorjani, and Florence Shinn discussed herein would also wholeheartedly agree.

Note 19: Fear from Man's Primal Past. Fear (an emotion) is the result of human-related instincts, responses, and coping mechanisms in association with threats and dangers to life from mankind's (or humankind's) distant primal past, as well as from more modern-life conditions. Fear is often the first emotional response of instinct about a threatening danger, which raises the curtain to alert and align the incarnate body and mind of the person being threatened to prepare to deal with an anticipated oncoming crisis. The threat of death brings on the greatest elevation of fear in response to this threat. Possible explanations for fear with its responses likely include (1) carry-overs in modern human minds of buried unconscious memories from mankind's (or humankind's) primal past of constant-state threats to survival; (2) conscious effects of threats of danger to a person in more recent human-time contexts.

Note 20: Childhood Fear Carryovers. Fear is something that often follows formerly mistreated children throughout their adult lives. The reflex 'fight or flight' response to fear from physical and emotional traumas suffered early in life becomes inculcated or 'hard-wired' into a developing child's mind as negative memory imprints. These often re-emerge in their adult life as imagined fears that can negatively impact thoughts and actions in their ordinary current life situations. Once we become aware that the origins of these worries and fears currently affecting us represent remnant viral thoughts of love that were somehow denied to us when we were little, then we can determine that these are irrelevant now because the past is gone and will not return. Via our intent and free will, we can instead shift our attention and situation away from all the past worry and fear, and instead embrace thinking, feeling, and acting that reflects on 'the dawn of a new day' which is inherently ours producing more rewarding and positive times.

Note 21: Mental Imprisonment by Past Trauma- Adult or Child. Any past severe trauma period can immobilize a person by having residual memories of the trauma 'locked within' their unconscious mind, preventing them consciously from doing anything to 'free themselves' from the mental prison they find themselves in. In other words, the victim cannot see the 'forest for the trees' until conscious awareness hits them that they have been unconsciously imprisoning themselves from doing anything to free themselves from their past negativities. From the oft-quoted phrase, 'God helps those who help themselves', past victims must recognize that it is high time to 'move on' with their lives by reminding themselves to relinquish and surrender all their past negativities. Through conscious <u>awareness</u> and intent of mind, each victim can empower themselves to divest away from these past negativities and come out now into the 'rising light of sunshine' of positive thinking, feeling, love, and participating in enjoyable activities with others.

Note 22: Reprogramming Our Past into a Changed Future. To this author, the oft-quoted phrase, 'God helps those who help themselves', represents a set of 'magic words' that come from the Scriptures and other Western world spiritual sources. Paramahansa Yogananda (from India) during the early 1900s stated very similarly: 'God has endowed everyone with potential faith, free will, conscious reason, and common sense to help themselves from all suffering'. From this, a person can apply a native Brazilian Matis chieftain's story/metaphor: 'that a snake's bite doesn't kill, but what could is the lethal venom, unless the bite victim learns to release/extricate it from their system or assimilate/change it from being toxic into a medicine'. For any victim to survive a lethal snakebite would require tremendous willpower to live. A direct analogy to this story/ metaphor is the primitive, yet highly evolved notion that 'we can look at the most damaging and painful sufferings in our lives and <u>turn</u> these into our greatest teachers or gifts to heal ourselves'. The lesson from this is that reversing a lifetime of remorse over damaging/painful suffering or hatred/regret doesn't simply occur like 'a bolt out of the blue' but instead requires great personal effort and intent to reverse a person's past negative lifetime state into a truly transformed, positive paradigm.

Note 23: Recreating a Happy Child Within. Another important avenue for enhancing a love of self is to re-make any unhappy child currently within a grown adult into a happy child. Besides poor treatment by caretakers, people can endure other lifetime tragedies or difficulties during their earliest years such as the death of parents or siblings, illness or disease, poverty, large families, wars, and climatic disasters; or in later-on adult years such as a divorce or an end to a long-term love relationship. Any of these can certainly create an unhappy 'tonality' that can persist for the remaining lifetime of any victim who has endured these sufferings. This could very well involve a victim's child within. Often an adult person's unhappy child awaits to spring forth as a happy child by re-doing some of the fun things remembered from long ago which made that child happy then, or even doing fun things learned more recently. These fun things can be done now with the total absence of any worry over the prior 'watchdog' presence of any caretakers or other folks.

Note 24: Reinterpreting the Meaning of 'Sin'. The Scribes, Pharisees, and other religious leaders that surrounded Jesus both during and following his lifetime would often preach about the 'sins' of this life such as sex philandering, lying, cheating, gambling, stealing, and violence, etc., and the need to prevent these. Instead, both Jesus and Brother Andre as well as other more modern writers such as Uell Andersen, Neville Goddard, Wayne Dyer, Florence Shinn, as well as myself have interpreted 'sin' in a somewhat different context. Both Jesus and Brother Andre as well as the writers above were asking the people whom they were trying to help to <u>forget</u> about their past inner sorrows, weaknesses, afflictions, and mistakes (in the past often referred to as 'sins'). Instead, they were asked to focus on the inner sanctum of perfection & goodness (or 'Soul') that existed within each of them. By forgetting (forgiving) their past negativities and focusing on their Spiritual perfection or 'Soul' within, the victims facilitated their healing.

Note 25: The Lord's Promise. His 'Promise' is part of a narrative from Neville Goddard's work, "The Law and the Promise", which begins with: 'all the world's a stage and all the men and women merely players'. 'The purpose of God's play, or Christ Jesus's time in this life, was to transform man*(the created) into God the creator. God loved man, his creation, and became man in faith and body so that through this act of self-commission, man the created would be transformed into God the Creator. The play begins with the crucifixion of God (via Jesus) as man, and ends with the resurrection of man as God, with God ending up spiritually in man (via 'Soul'). God became as we are so that we might become as He is. God became man so that man might become first a living being and then a living spirit of God. His 'Promise' is that through death on the cross, He (Jesus) has returned to each of us via our 'Soul' and is available for each of us now'.

Both Neville Goddard and Uell Andersen have stated that the chief message of all Jesus's teachings is: 'the good news I bring you is that the Kingdom of Heaven is within each of us (i.e., via our 'Soul')'.

*The words 'man', 'man's, and 'mankind' in the Epilogue Final Notes above and other parts of this work, often represent an older, literary term that now implies 'all of mankind', or 'humankind', i.e., including both men & women.

FINAL THOUGHT

Any thought, reflection, or meditation on <u>Infinite Love's</u> magnificence, its eternal 'goodness', and its coalescence with the 'One' (or God), begins a person's path toward healing any maladies and/or pain within this worldly state. This will be experienced as feelings of a clarity of freedom, relief, and bliss, bringing to the person mental and spiritual peace.

FOOTNOTES/
REFERENCES

1   Neville Goddard. The Power of Awareness. Pacific Publishing. pp 1-2.
2   Uell S. Andersen. Three Magic Words. Paperback Edition, Wilshire Book Co.,
    Chatsworth CA. pp 5-12.
3   Neville Goddard. Feeling is The Secret, Pacific Publishing Studio, pp 1-3.
4   Bruce Perry, MD, Ph.D. The Boy Who Was Raised as a Dog. Basic Books
    Publishing. pp 231-4.
5   Neville Goddard. The Neville Reader, Chapter entitled: The Law and the
    Promise, Devorss & Co. Publishing.
6   Eben Alexander, MD. Proof of Heaven, a Neurosurgeon's Journey into the
    Afterlife. Simon and Schuster Paperbacks Publishing. pp 46-8; 85-6.
7   Ibid.
8   Uell S. Andersen. Three Magic Words, Paperback Edition. pp 75-6.
9   Ibid., pp 105-9; 205-6.
10 Brother Andre Book: Official Canonization Album of Brother Andre. Archives
    Department of Quebec and Canada, Publishers. pp 1-25.
11 Anita Moorjani. Dying to be Me, My Journey from Cancer from Near Death
    to True Healing. Hay House Publishers. pp 42-64.
12 Ibid., pp 65-6.
13 Ibid., pp 132-5.
14 Ibid., p 76.
15 Ibid., pp 69-70; p 171.
16 Ibid., p 139.
17 Ibid., pp 145-6.
18 Ibid., p 148.
19 Ibid., pp 136-7.

20 Ibid., pp 143-5.

21 Betty Eadie. Embraced by The Light. Bantam Books Publishers. pp 40-41.

22 Ibid., pp 59-61.

23 Ibid., pp 51; 60-6.

24 Ibid., pp 50-1; 84.

25 Ibid., pp 45-6.

26 Eben Alexander, MD. Proof of Heaven, a Neurosurgeon's Journey into the Afterlife. pp 30-5; 80-1.

27 Ibid., pp 45-9.

28 Ibid., pp 71-3; 84-6.

29 Ibid., pp 48-9; 83.

30 Ibid., p 40; pp 168-9.

31 Ibid., p 40.

32 Neville Goddard. The Neville Reader, from the section of 'Law and the Promise'. p 122.

33 Alexander, MD. Proof of Heaven, a Neurosurgeon's Journey into the Afterlife. p 41.

34 Ibid.

35 Ibid., pp 46-8; 85-6.

36 Ibid.

37 Todd Burpo, with Lynn Vincent. Heaven is for Real. W. Publishing Group, 2010; 2014 by HIFR Ministries. Brief accounts from pp 7-150, summarizing highlights of Colton's experiences in the 'Beyond'.

38 Ibid.

39 Neville Goddard. The Power of Awareness. Pacific Publishing. pp 1-2.

40 Wayne Dyer, Ph.D. Wishes Fulfilled, Mastering the Art of Manifesting. Hay House Publishing. pp 110, 122.

41 Ibid., pp 110-111.

42 Dr. Wayne Dyer and Esther Hicks. Co-Creating at its Best, a Conversation Between Master Teachers. Hay House Publishing. pp 5-9, 19-21, p 84.

43 Ibid., pp 135-6.

44 Uell S. Andersen. Three Magic Words, Paperback Edition. Wilshire Book Co., Chatsworth CA. pp 5-12.

45 Ibid., pp 5-20.

46 Ibid., pp 205-6; 105-9.

47 Neville Goddard. The Power of Awareness. Pacific Publishing. pp 1-2.

48 Ibid., Neville Goddard pp 1-3; also Ascended Master, Sainte Germaine. The 'I AM Discourses', Volume 3. Saint Germaine (Foundation) Press.

49 Ibid., Neville Goddard pp 5-7; also Ascended Master, Sainte Germaine. The 'I AM Discourses', Volume 3.

50 Ibid., Neville Goddard pp 4; 6-7.

51 Wayne Dyer, Ph.D. Wishes Fulfilled, Mastering the Art of Manifesting. Hay House Publishing. pp 56- 63; also Ascended Master, Sainte Germaine. The 'I AM Discourses', Volume 3.

52 Ibid., Wayne Dyer, Ph.D. pp 87-91; also Ascended Master, Sainte Germaine. The 'I AM Discourses', Vol. 3.

53 Ibid., Wayne Dyer, Ph.D. pp 126; also Ascended Master, Sainte Germaine. The 'I AM Discourses', Volume 3.

54 Florence Scovel Shinn. The Magic Path of Intuition. Hay House Publishers. pp 3-4.

55 Ibid., p 4.

56 Ibid., pp 22-26.

57 Ibid., pp 28-9.

58 Ibid., pp 24-5; 39-40.

59 Ibid., pp 49-51.

60 Ibid., pp 55-60.

61 Uell S. Andersen. Three Magic Words, Paperback Edition. pp 166-72.

62 Ibid., pp 175-7.

63 Florence Scovel Shinn. The Magic Path of Intuition. Hay House Publishers.

64 Uell S. Andersen. Three Magic Words, Paperback Edition. pp 25.

65 Ibid., pp 8-24.

66 Ibid., pp 8-24; pp 202-3.

67 Ibid., pp 202-3.

68 Wayne Dyer, Ph.D. Inspiration, Your Ultimate Calling. Hay House Publishing. pp 28-33. also, Wayne Dyer, Ph.D. The Shift, Taking Your Life from Ambition to Meaning. Hay House Publishing.

69 Ibid., Inspiration, etc. p 33.

70 Ibid., Inspiration, etc. p 34.

71 Bruce Perry, MD, Ph.D. "Traumatized Children: How Childhood Trauma Influences Brain Development". Journal of the California Alliance for the Mentally Ill, 11:1 pp 48-51, 2000.

72 davidji. Secrets of Meditation, a Practical Guide to Inner Peace and Transformation. Hay House Publishers. Preface p xiv.

73 Ibid., pp 24-26.

74 Ibid., p 188.

75 Ibid., pp 61-168.

76 Ibid., pp 191-204.

77 Matthew Sockolov. 75 Essential Meditations to Reduce Stress, Improve Mental Health, and Find Peace in the Everyday. Althea Press, Emeryville CA. (the year 2018).

78 Benjamin W. Decker. Practical Meditation for Beginners, 10 Days to a Happier, Calmer You. Althea Press, Emeryville CA. (the year 2018).

79   Worthy Stokes. The Daily Meditation Book of Healing, 365 Reflections for Positivity, Peace, and Prosperity. Rockridge Press, Emeryville CA. (the year 2020).

80   Official Transcendental Meditation Website for finding more Information: https://www.tm.org.

81   Wayne Dyer, Ph.D. Soundtrack, "I AM Wishes Fulfilled Meditation". Hay House Publishers.

82   Wayne Dyer, Ph.D. Soundtrack, "Getting in the Gap Meditation". Hay House Publishers.

83   Wayne Dyer, Ph.D. The Book and Soundtrack, "Getting in the Gap Meditation". Hay House Publishers. In the Book, pp 71-86.

84   Official Website of davidij for finding more Information: https://davidji.com.

85   Official Website of Eben Alexander, M.D. for finding more Information: www.ebenalexander.com.

86   Alice Miller, Ph.D. Free from Lies, Discovering Your Own True Needs. WW Norton & Company Publishers, New York. pp 94-5.

87   Victor E. Frankl. Man's Search for Meaning. Beacon Press, Boston MA, 1959. pp 37.

88   Ibid., pp 37-8.

89   David Hawkins, MD, Ph.D. The brief narrative: Let Go and Love. From the Wayne Dyer Hay House Website, Feb. 2015

90   Anita Moorjani. Dying to be Me, My Journey from Cancer from Near Death to True Healing. Hay House Publishing. pp 171-2.

91   Prince of Peace' painting by Akiane Kramarik, a noted Midwest poet & artist. Info: www.Art-SoulWorks.com

92   Neville Goddard. The Neville Reader, Chapter entitled: The Law and the Promise, pp 122-4.

93   Ibid, pp 122-3; the Biblical Quote taken from the English Bible Standard Version.

94   Ibid, pp 123-4.

95   Alexander, MD. Proof of Heaven, a Neurosurgeon's Journey into the Afterlife. p 41.

96   Neville Goddard. The Law and Other Essays on Manifestation. Wilder Publications. pp 2-10.

97   Uell S. Andersen. Three Magic Words. Paperback Edition. Ideas learned from the 12 meditations in this work.

98   Anita Moorjani. Dying to be Me, My Journey from Cancer from Near Death to True Healing. pp 113-5.

99   Ibid, p 137.

100 Ibid, pp 141-153.

101 Wayne Dyer, Ph.D. Sound Disc, "I AM Wishes Fulfilled Meditation" CD, or "Getting in the Gap Meditation" CD Hay House Publishing. These are available as an 'e-file'.

102 Theolyn Cortens. Your Guardian Angel Needs You! Piakus Publishing (Great Britain), 2011. pp 9-11.

103 Ibid, p 8.

104 Theolyn Cortens. Working with Archangels, a Path to Transformation and Power. Piatkus Publishing (Great Britain). Archangel Information Sandalphon 104a pp 55-8; Auriel 104b pp 63-7; Raphael 104d pp 90-4; Zaphkiel 104f pp 109-114; Zadkiel104h pp 140-4.

105 Eric Von Daniken. Miracles of the Gods: a hard look at the supernatural. Random House Publishing Group.

106 Paramahansa Yogananda, 'God helps those who help themselves, Triumph of the Spirit'. Google author/title.

107 Alice Miller, Ph.D. Alice Miller's Website: The Roots of Violence, Alice Miller's New Flyer 2008. Alice Miller Ph.D. Thou Shalt Not be Aware: Society's Betrayal of the Child. Meridan Printing, NY.

108 Uell S. Andersen. Three Magic Words, Paperback Edition. pp 5-12.

109 Ibid, pp 75-6.

110 Brother Andre Book: Official Canonization Album of Brother Andre. Archives Department of Quebec and Canada, Publishers. p 56.

111 Ibid., pp 1-26.

112 Dr. Wayne Dyer/Esther Hicks. Co-Creating at its Best, a Conversation Between Master Teachers. Hay House Publishing. pp 19-21,84.

113 Ibid.

114 Ibid., pp 135-6.

115 Neville Goddard. The Neville Reader, Chapter entitled: The Law and the Promise. pp 9-14.

116 bid, pp 13-14.

117 Uell S. Andersen. Three Magic Words, Paperback Edition. pp 8-12.

118 Ibid., pp 12-16.

119 Florence Scovel Shinn. The Magic Path of Intuition. Hay House Publishers. pp 60.

120 Ibid., pp 24-5; 39-40.

121 Ibid., p 72.

122 Wayne Dyer, Ph.D. Inspiration, Your Ultimate Calling. Hay House Publishing. pp 28-33.

123 davidji. Secrets of Meditation, a Practical Guide to Inner Peace and Transformation. Hay House Publishers. p 47.

124 Wayne Dyer, Ph.D. Inspiration, Your Ultimate Calling. Hay House Publishing. p 33. Wayne Dyer, Ph.D. The Shift, Taking Your Life from Ambition to Meaning. Hay House Publishing.

125 Florence Scovel Shinn. The Magic Path of Intuition. Hay House Publishers. pp 72; 80.

126 Ibid., pp 22-26.

127 Ibid., pp 28-9.

128 Anita Moorjani. Dying to be Me, My Journey from Cancer from Near Death to True Healing. pp 71-2.

129 Ibid., pp 171-2.

130 Ibid., pp 142; 171.

131 Alexander, MD. Proof of Heaven, a Neurosurgeon's Journey into the Afterlife. pp 46-8; 85-6.

132 Ibid

133 Ibid., p 71

134 Ibid

OTHER WORKS CITED
OR REVIEWED IN TEXT

Dr. Wayne Dyer, Ph.D., and Lynn Lauber. My Greatest Teacher. pp 1- 94. Hay House Publishers. Carlsbad, CA. February 2012.